Integrating the US Military

# INTEGRATING THE US MILITARY

*Race, Gender, and Sexual Orientation since World War II*

EDITED BY

Douglas Walter Bristol, Jr.,
and Heather Marie Stur

Johns Hopkins University Press
*Baltimore*

Johns Hopkins University Press
2715 North Charles Street
Baltimore, Maryland 21218-4363
www.press.jhu.edu

Library of Congress Cataloging-in-Publication Data

Names: Bristol, Douglas Walter, 1965– editor of compilation. | Stur, Heather
    Marie, 1975– editor of compilation.
Title: Integrating the US military : race, gender, and sexual orientation
    since World War II / edited by Douglas Walter Bristol, Jr., and
    Heather Marie Stur.
Description: Baltimore : Johns Hopkins University Press, [2017] | Includes
    bibliographical references and index.
Identifiers: LCCN 2016034885| ISBN 9781421422473 (pbk. : alk. paper) |
    ISBN 9781421422480 (electronic) | ISBN 1421422476 (pbk. : alk. paper) |
    ISBN 1421422484 (electronic)
Subjects: LCSH: United States—Armed Forces—Minorities—History. |
    United States—Armed Forces—African Americans—History. | United
    States—Armed Forces—Women—History. | Gay military personnel—
    United States—History. | Sociology, Military—United States.
Classification: LCC UB417 .I58 2017 | DDC 355.008/0973—dc23
    LC record available at https://lccn.loc.gov/2016034885

A catalog record for this book is available from the British Library.

*Special discounts are available for bulk purchases of this book.*
*For more information, please contact Special Sales at 410-516-6936*
*or specialsales@press.jhu.edu.*

# Contents

Integrating the US Military

# Introduction

BETH BAILEY

In the long run-up to the 2008 presidential election, Democrats and Republicans took sharply different positions on Don't Ask, Don't Tell (DADT), the 1992 policy that denied gay men and lesbians the right to serve openly in the US military. Hillary Clinton called the policy (which was enacted during her husband's presidency) "transitional" and borrowed a pithy quote from a previous presidential candidate, Republican Barry Goldwater, to make her point. "You don't have to be straight to shoot straight," she told the audience in the hall at New Hampshire's Saint Anselm College and those watching television at home. Two days later, in the same room, Mitt Romney offered his take: "This is not the time to put in place a major change, a social experiment, in the middle of a war going on."[1]

Neither Romney's claim nor his language was new. The initial debates that yielded the policy of DADT in the early 1990s relied heavily on claims that the military was not the proper place for "social experimentation" and "social engineering." So did arguments against military racial integration in the 1940s and 1950s and against gender integration from the 1970s forward.[2] Many who opposed one or more of these changes were social conservatives, intent on preserving what they believed to be the proper ordering of society; some members of that group were undoubtedly racist or sexist or homophobic. But some also made such claims in good faith, concerned about military efficacy rather than about social order. It says a great deal about the limits of American values that the United States fought the Nazis with a racially segregated military. However, it's also possible to make a reasonable case that the right time to end racial segregation in the military—in a nation where white racism was so powerful that the Red Cross segregated "Negro" blood—was not in the midst of world war.[3] If the purpose of the military is to defend the nation and guarantee national security, it is reasonable for Americans—military leaders, elected officials, and citizens alike—to ask how changes in personnel policy will affect military readiness and to pay attention to the answers. Such questions have been used to great effect by opponents of social change. But opponents of DADT also embraced that logic, and the arguments that helped end DADT in 2011 depended on evidence that the policy harmed US military readiness and efficiency.

Military leaders from all ranks have, over the past three-quarters of a century, argued (though not always publicly) that the military cannot be a site of social experimentation. Those positions matter; they reveal military concerns and shape public conversations and the political strategies of those who seek or oppose such change. But no matter how steadfastly some members of the military and their political allies condemn what they label "experimentation," a more significant fact remains. The changes they worried about were necessary, and the military carried them out in ways that were necessarily experimental. And, in a claim that may surprise some of the readers of this book, the various services often dealt with change in ways that were serious, committed, imaginative, and well in advance of civilian institutions in the same historical moment.

Change, of course, rarely came by choice. The military is subject to civilian control, and key changes in the status of racial minorities, women, and gays and lesbians were usually mandated from outside. Sometimes change was ordered by the commander in chief, as in 1948 when President Harry S. Truman used an executive order to desegregate the armed forces. Sometimes change was forced by circumstance: Congress's decision to end the draft in 1973 left an awful lot of boots to fill (the army estimated it needed twenty to thirty thousand new volunteers each month) and gave rise to the recruiting ad "Some of our best men are women." And sometimes change was directly due to acts of Congress, as when it ordered military academies to begin accepting women in 1976 and ended Don't Ask, Don't Tell in 2012.

All these decisions, of course, were prompted by broader movements for social change, both within the military and without. The African American movement for civil rights and social justice helped produce Truman's executive order; Congress voted to admit women to military academies on the heels of its overwhelming bipartisan support for the Equal Rights Amendment and in response to women's claims of equal rights; the repeal of DADT was the result of a broader movement for equal rights that also encompassed marriage equality and other protections of civil rights and social standing. Changes in military policy were also the result of battles fought within the army, navy, air force, and marines. America's struggles over race, over gender, and over sexuality spilled over the line between civilian society and the military. Men and women in uniform worked for equal rights, equal opportunity, and equal treatment, often confronting circumstances that had no parallel in civilian life.

Americans have traditionally used military service to justify claims to the full rights of citizenship. They have also treated the military as a critical institution in their campaigns for full equality and have insisted that personnel policies and military regulations do matter. And while change was often hard-fought within the armed forces as well as outside them, men and women of all ranks claimed rights and worked to create models of equality in keeping with the stated mission of the armed forces: to defend the nation, to fight and win the nation's wars.

That mission, along with the tenets of military readiness and effectiveness, has often been the reason offered by military leaders and other interested parties for resisting integration of various sorts: [fill in the blank] is not fully capable and will hinder combat effectiveness; [fill in the blank] will disrupt unit cohesion and so diminish military effectiveness; allowing [fill in the blank] to serve will undermine training, make it impossible to recruit successfully, and disrupt military order. At the same time, that focus on mission and readiness was, for military leaders, a powerful incentive to solve the problem at hand. If the mission of the military was threatened by racial conflict, racial conflict became a problem of the first order, one that must be managed, if not solved. If the move to an all-volunteer force left the army relying more heavily on women than in the past, it would—of necessity—steer female recruits to "nontraditional" fields.

Historians—including those in this volume—have written about struggles over race, gender, and sexuality in the US military. But in most broader stories of social movements—the African American civil rights movement, the women's movement, the campaigns for GLBTQ rights—the military rates a mention at best. This volume, as it portrays the experiences of those who serve, now and in the past, is meant to contribute to our understanding of the role the military has played in the civil rights struggles of our age. It is also meant to change the stories we tell about movements for African American, women's, and gay and lesbian civil rights and equality.

I argue here, as I have elsewhere, that it is not possible to fully understand the rights movements of the last half of the twentieth century without taking the US military into account. That is, first of all, because of its reach and range. In the mid-1950s, 65 percent of American men were veterans. Sixteen million Americans served during World War II; 6.8 million were on active duty during the Korean War (with close to one million serving in both). Almost 9.1 million Americans saw active duty during the Vietnam era (August 1964 to May 1975), and the active-duty military was roughly the same size in 1990 as it was in 1975. Millions of Americans spent time in the military and were subject to its regulations, to its policies, and to its training. They carried their military experiences and the understandings born of them back to all corners of the nation.

Second, even as military service ceased to be an obligation of (male) citizenship when the United States moved to an all-volunteer force, it was and remains closely linked to our definitions of citizenship. In pursuing the right to serve on equal terms in the US armed forces, African Americans, women, and gay and lesbian Americans emphasized the tie—even if symbolic—between military service and the full rights of citizenship. And third, military policies are fundamentally important to broader struggles for civil rights because of the public nature of discussion about them and the transparent and official nature of policies adopted. Congressional hearings and debates—whether over regulations barring women from combat or men from the nurse corps, over policies of affirmative action or over the impact of integration on unit cohesion—identify civilian and military experts who frame the topic for the members of Congress and present arguments that both reflect and shape contemporary opinion.

The military is, of course, an exceptional institution, not easily compared to civilian bodies (assuming ones of similar size and scale existed) even in the limited sphere of personnel policy and relations. As an article in the *American Bar Association Journal* noted in October 1993, the US Supreme Court has accorded the military legally exceptional status, defining the US armed forces as "a separate and distinct society within the larger society," governed by "military necessity," which was almost by necessity at odds with the "uniform body of law" based in an "equal opportunity model."[4] According to the courts, the fundamental mission of the military takes precedence over some individual rights of its members; claims of "military necessity" are not easily dismissed. The military services also regulate the behavior of their members in ways that extend well beyond the "workplace": the Uniform Code of Military Justice prohibits conduct that brings discredit on the armed forces as well as conduct that is prejudicial to good order and discipline. And, finally, the authority of a civilian boss doesn't compare to that of a commanding officer. The armed forces have different tools for managing difference than do institutions in civilian society and are given greater legal latitude in doing so. But while military practices and policies are not truly comparable to civilian ones, they matter, both in and of themselves and because their influence reaches well beyond the boundaries of military service and the military as an institution.

*Integrating the US Military* focuses on the military experiences of African Americans, Japanese Americans, women (sometimes in relation to men), and gay men and lesbians, beginning with African American resistance during World War II and concluding with the fight for gay military service in America's very recent past. The experiences of each of these groups, as well as military efforts to deal with their particular differences, obviously vary. So does the nature of their respective struggles and military responses to each group over time. But by tracing how the US military dealt with different groups over a period of seventy years, this volume helps us understand commonalities and differences; it illuminates (in the words of the volume editors) the ways that challenges launched against the racial, gender, and sexual status quo in the years after World War II transformed overarching ideas about power, citizenship, and America's role in the world.

A very brief overview of key turning points in US military policy on race, gender, and sexuality may be useful context for the remainder of this volume. The book begins in World War II. While the nation's military confronted issues related to race, gender, and sexuality through its entire history, World War II was a significant turning point for military policies on race, gender, and sexuality and is thus an obvious starting point. The United States fought World War II with racially segregated armed forces; both African Americans and Japanese Americans served in racially defined units (though members of other racial and ethnic minorities did not). When President Truman ended the racial segregation of the armed forces by executive order in 1948 the military resisted initially, but integration was largely accomplished by the end of the Korean War in 1953. While racism and discrimination against African Americans did not disappear, when it came to race relations and equal opportunity the military services were far in advance of most of American civilian society during the 1950s and early 1960s. However, racial conflict—tied to both military policies and to the shifting nature of the African American movements for social justice—became a significant military problem during the divisive war in Vietnam.

Women's expanded roles in the US military reach back to the founding of the Women's Auxiliary Army Corps (WAAC) in May 1942, soon thereafter followed by the WAVES (Navy), SPARS (Coast Guard), and Marines. (The WAAC was converted to regular status as the Women's Army Corps in 1943, though all branches defined women's service as a short-term response to the wartime emergency.) In 1948, concerned about the extent of US military commitments, the US Congress passed legislation allowing women to serve as permanent, regular members of the armed forces. Significant restrictions existed: women could make up no more than 2 percent of total military strength. They could not hold a permanent rank above the equivalent of lieutenant colonel or hold positions of authority over men. Nonetheless, female service members found greater opportunity in the military than in most civilian occupations. In 1967, Congress lifted the 2-percent ceiling and made women eligible for promotion to the highest ranks.

The mandated move from a conscription-based system to an all-volunteer force in 1973 significantly changed the race and gender composition of the armed forces. The army, most particularly, expanded both the number of its women members and their role. Congress decreed that women must be admitted to the nation's military academies beginning in 1976; separate women's corps were gone by the end of that decade. In an overlapping shift, African Americans (male and female) joined the military in much higher numbers. In general terms, black Americans fared less well in the civilian job market, and in the difficult economic situation of the 1970s the military offered opportunity.

While it is possible to trace women's and African American activism from World War II forward, high-profile struggles for gay rights in the military did not emerge until significantly later. World War II marked a significant change for gay men and lesbians, as military policy shifted from punishing specific sexual acts to attempts to identify and purge all who were homosexual. The military did not uniformly ban homosexuality until1949, when the newly created Department of Defense mandated "prompt separation" of "known homosexuals" from the military. The following year, Congress defined "unnatural carnal copulation" as a crime in the new Uniform Code of Military Justice. During the 1970s, several key legal cases challenged the exclusion of homosexuals from the military, though without significant result. Following a complicated struggle between President Bill Clinton and members of Congress, including those in his own party, Don't Ask, Don't Tell became official military policy governing the service of gay men and lesbians in 1994. Congress repealed DADT in December 2010; enforcement of the policy ended in September 2011.

The essays that follow are arranged in roughly chronological order. Four of the chapters focus primarily on race or ethnicity (three on African Americans and one on Japanese Americans) and four on women or gender. The final essay analyzes the struggle over gay military service. Most authors treat the military as a single institution, aware of the significant differences among the services but focusing on broader, cross-service policies and debates.

In the first essay, "Terror, Anger, and Patriotism: Understanding the Resistance of Black Soldiers during World War II," Douglas Walter Bristol, Jr., lays the groundwork for the volume. Portraying pervasive racial discrimination and the not infrequent terrorization of African American servicemen, he shows black GIs risking their lives not only in defense of their nation but in struggles against Jim Crow and racism. Their resistance, Bristol claims, strengthened the resolve of African American civil rights leaders and civilians in the years following the war and played a significant role in ending racial segregation in the military soon after war's end.

James M. McCaffrey, in "Nisei versus Nazi: Japanese American Soldiers in World War II," traces the creation, training, deployment, and combat performance of the Japanese American soldiers of the 442nd Regimental Combat Team and, most particularly, the 100th Battalion that was made up of Hawaii-born Nisei. Fighting in segregated units and regarded by many with animosity and suspicion—as well as confusion about how they fit into an assumed white/black racial divide—these soldiers, McCaffrey demonstrates, performed with valor in combat on the European front.

Charissa Threat's chapter, "Does the Sex of the Practitioner Matter? Nursing, Civil Rights, and Discrimination in the Army Nurse Corps, 1947–1955," analyzes army gender restrictions—but, in a surprising move, by focusing on discrimination against men rather than against women. Concentrating on the postwar era of the 1940s and 1950s, she traces official debates over personnel policies that relied on assumptions about the proper roles of men and women—and that also reveal servicewomen's attempts to maintain separate spheres of control and leadership in a heavily male-dominated institution.

In "'An Attractive Career for Women': Opportunities, Limitations, and Women's Integration in the Cold War Military," Tanya L. Roth also examines assumptions about gender roles in the Cold War military. Focusing on the Women's Armed Services Integration Act of 1948, she demonstrates that military needs opened possibilities, however limited, for women. Tracing the opportunities and limits of this "attractive career" through the following decades, Roth emphasizes servicewomen's movements for equality as she argues that military reliance on gender difference to structure military service has worked against the most effective use of female personnel.

James E. Westheider offers an overview of military racial policies and civil rights struggles from World War II forward as context for his study of "African Americans, Civil Rights, and the Armed Forces during the Vietnam War." Closely linking what he calls two of the seminal events of the mid-twentieth century—the war in Vietnam and the civil rights movement—he shows the connections between military and domestic protest and resistance, the growing frustration and discontent of black troops in the face of continued institutional racism, and the resulting pressures that led military leaders to seek solutions to the ongoing discrimination and racial conflicts in the late-Vietnam-era military.

In another take on military approaches to racial conflict during the Vietnam War and beyond, Isaac Hampton II traces the origins and development of the Defense Race Relations Institute (DRRI), which was created in 1970 to confront the racial crisis that threatened military cohesion and efficiency, in "Reform in the Ranks: The History of the Defense Race Relations Institute, 1971–2014." Using interviews with former DRRI personnel, Hampton traces the ways DRRI leaders managed resistance to the institute's mission—and its very existence—and developed an innovative curriculum. In 1979 the DRRI was renamed the Defense Equal Opportunity Management Institute and broadened its focus to include gender conflict and discrimination.

Gender is the focus of Heather Marie Stur's chapter on the post–Vietnam war all-volunteer force, "Men's and Women's Liberation: Challenging Military Culture after the Vietnam War." Stur describes the ways that gender ideologies shaped the perceived meaning of military service in the early Cold War United States, showing the powerful persistence of such understandings and the conflicts they engendered even in the face of changed military policies and the challenges to those ideologies brought by the cultural movements for men's and women's liberation in the late 1960s and 1970s.

In "Mobilizing Marriage and Motherhood: Military Families and Family Planning since World War II," Kara Dixon Vuic shows how the military dealt with difference—in this case, women's biological, sexual, reproductive, and familial roles that differed from those of men—in the decades following World War II. She argues that changes in prevailing civilian sexual and gender norms and a series of political struggles and legal decisions helped shape military policies on family planning, including on pregnancy and motherhood, birth control, and abortion.

Finally, in "The Dream That Dare Not Speak Its Name: Legacies of the Civil Rights Movement and the Fight for Gay Military Service," Steve Estes analyzes activists' failed attempts to use parallels between African American and gay struggles to end the ban on gay men and lesbians serving openly in the US military. His is a cautionary voice as he demonstrates the continuing divisions of difference. In this case, as is frequently true, change in US military policies did not stem from the combined efforts and shared agendas of minority groups but instead from arguments about military needs and efficiency.

The essays that follow offer new arguments about social change within the United States military and the relationship of that change to civilian society and culture. They also show what an excellent lens the US military offers to those who wish to understand the social and cultural changes of a critical era in US history.

NOTES

1. Robin Toner, "For 'Don't Ask, Don't Tell,' Split on Party Lines," *New York Times*, June 8, 2007, A1, A24.

2. For examples of "social experimentation" language describing racial desegregation, see Byron Porterfield, "4 Bias-Free Years Hailed at Air Base: Men at Mitchel Can Scarcely Recall Segregation Era—Dance Music Only Snag," *New York Times*, March 8, 1953, 48. On women, see House Military Personnel Subcommittee Hearings, *Women in the Military*, 96th Cong., 1st and 2nd sess., November 13–16, 1979, and February 11, 1980. On gay men and lesbians, see Rep. Packard (CA), "Against Lifting the Ban on Homosexuals in the Military," *Congressional Record Daily Edition* (January 27, 1993), E209.

3. Of course, as the military learned during the Korean War (race) and the first Gulf War (gender), integration is more likely to succeed when pressure is on and performance matters more than identity.

4. Joseph E. Broadus, "Yes: Don't Second-Guess the Military," in "At Issue: Don't Ask, Don't Tell," *American Bar Association Journal* (October 1993): 54. The case is Chappell v. Wallace, 462 U.S. 296 (1983).

# 1

## Terror, Anger, and Patriotism

### Understanding the Resistance of Black Soldiers during World War II

DOUGLAS WALTER BRISTOL, JR.

While Americans celebrate the "Greatest Generation" for its willingness to serve their nation during World War II, this chapter points out that most Americans know little of the sacrifices made by black soldiers and black members of the Women's Army Corps and the reasons why they made them. African Americans suffered from pervasive racial discrimination in a segregated military and were frequently attacked by civilians who lived near southern military bases. Despite this hostility, African Americans continued to fight for the opportunity to go into combat. Black soldiers not only were willing to risk their lives for their country but also risked their lives to demand equal treatment. In turn, the resistance of black soldiers gave black leaders more leverage when they sought to integrate the military. As seen in other chapters, the personnel needs of the military created new opportunities for legally marginalized groups. During World War II, African Americans served their nation in order to claim equal citizenship.

African Americans have served in the United States military with distinction since the American Revolution, and the courageous actions of Dorie Miller showed that the tradition was alive and well during World War II. On December 7, 1941, the Japanese Empire attacked Pearl Harbor. Dorie Miller was a young black messman on the battleship *West Virginia*, which was hit by two bombs and two torpedoes. As the *West Virginia* was on fire and sinking, Miller helped drag his wounded captain to safety. Then, he manned a .50-caliber machine gun. Despite never having been trained to fire the weapon, Miller shot down one of the attacking planes before he ran out of ammunition. Miller was awarded the Navy Cross for his bravery. He showed that, from the very first day of the war, African Americans helped defend their country.[1]

Although these facts about one of the first heroes of World War II are well known, the rest of Dorie Miller's story is not. On January 1, 1942, the navy released a list of commendations for actions on December 7. One of them was for an unnamed African American. Black newspapers had to badger the navy for twelve weeks before the service released Dorie Miller's name. Even after he received the Navy Cross, the first ever given to an African American, Navy regulations only allowed him to serve as a messman. He still worked in the same position when, nearly two years later, he died in the sinking of the escort carrier *Liscome Bay*. This more complete version of Dorie Miller's story reveals as much about the discrimination that he faced as it does about the patriotism that he displayed. But there is more to the history of black sailors like Dorie Miller. By the end of the war, the navy had begun integrating ships and opening new positions to African Americans.[2] In this chapter, I argue that discrimination, patriotism, and integration were connected in the stories of ordinary African Americans who served in the military during World War II.

Military necessity was the driving force in the stories of these young black men and women. Because the United States adopted the strategy of fighting a war on two fronts, the number of people mobilized dwarfed earlier preparations for war in American history. Sixteen million Americans wore uniforms between December 1941 and December 1945, which included one-sixth of the American male population. Since African Americans formed 10 percent of the population, the United States could not meet its manpower needs without them, and by 1945, one million African Americans had joined the military. Such widespread mobilization created a paradox for black men and women in uniform. Though the military trained African Americans to perform the same duties as their white counterparts, military leaders were unwilling, for most of the war, to assign African Americans to the positions for which they had been trained. Military necessity also dictated locating military bases in the South, where the climate allowed year-round training.[3] Because white Southerners thought black men and women in uniform represented a threat to the racial order, the communities around military bases were flash points for racial conflict.

Black men and women in uniform grew angry over their treatment, and their resistance ultimately forced the government to experiment with integration. After examining the paradox of mobilization and the failure of the Roosevelt administration to give African Americans equal opportunities as it had promised, this chapter looks at how the resistance of African Americans in the military inspired a mass movement organized around protecting black soldiers. This mass movement, in turn, strengthened the position of black government officials, who convinced Secretary of War Henry Stimson to experiment with integrated military units. The patriotic black soldiers who volunteered for combat fought valiantly. Their performance shattered the myth that African Americans were not equal to white soldiers and undermined the argument that military necessity dictated relegating African Americans to a second-class status.

By focusing on the wartime experience of ordinary African Americans like Dorie Miller, this chapter draws on the latest scholarship to better understand what kinds of discrimination they faced, how they resisted it, and why their actions had an impact on the eventual integration of the US armed forces. Many books have been written about African Americans in the US military during World War II, but until recently, most scholars have only looked at them in the abstract. The first wave of studies assessed the performance of black men and women in uniform, the evolution of military polices on African Americans, and the causes of troubled race relations during the war. A second wave looked at how black civil rights leaders and journalists, along with a handful of government officials and politicians of both races, sought equal rights for African Americans in the military and in the larger society during the war.[4] It was only in the last twenty years, however, that scholars have turned their attention to the military experience of ordinary African Americans during World War II.

Introducing the perspectives of ordinary African Americans complicates the story of World War II in fruitful ways. Scholars have shown that African Americans did not have uniform views about the war. A significant minority of African Americans, including Malcolm X and the noted historian John Hope Franklin, opposed serving in a segregated military to fight what they viewed as a white man's war. This chapter, however, looks at those who served, so the most relevant scholarship is about black men and women in uniform. These studies find that African Americans in the military did not always agree with the agendas of black leaders and that they persuaded their families to champion their views on the home front. Although scholars note that the fear of violence was the primary concern of black soldiers and their families, they have been reluctant to explore the mistreatment that caused African Americans in the military to disagree with their leaders. This chapter aims to fill that gap by examining the reign of terror inflicted on black soldiers in southern military camps and the anger they felt as a result. It will draw on the small number of works that examine how black soldiers transformed strategies of resistance from their civilian lives to the military experience.[5] Finally, it will extend studies of collective resistance within the military by arguing that the opposition of African Americans in uniform to discrimination gave black leaders the leverage to gain concessions from military officials.

## Fighting for Equal Rights in the Military

African Americans expected better treatment in return for serving their country, and they had good reasons to be hopeful. American traditions supported their claim. Since the American Revolution, the defense of the nation has been associated with citizenship. The United States, for most of its history, had gone to war with volunteer soldiers. American men volunteered because they thought that military service was an obligation of citizenship. African Americans sought to fight in combat during World War II in order to link their military service to their claims for equal citizenship.

There was a historical precedent for this strategy. During the Civil War, 186,000 African Americans served in the Union forces, and their military service was cited after the war by supporters of the Fifteenth Amendment, which gave black men the right to vote. World War I, by contrast, disappointed African Americans. Even though black man had fought in France to make the world safe for democracy, after the war there were race riots in Chicago, St. Louis, and other cities. Because military service in World War I had led to few gains for civil rights, African Americans from different walks of life were skeptical when Winston Churchill, Franklin Roosevelt, and others warned of the Axis threat. However, statements of principle such as Roosevelt's Four Freedoms, which summarized the values of democracy to provide a rationale for the war, encouraged black leaders and, in particular, the worried families of black soldiers stationed in the South to call for equal treatment and equal rights. A more practical source of African American leverage against the Roosevelt administration was the fact that, by 1943, racial conflict had become one of the largest barriers to mobilizing the nation for war. Believing that change was at hand, many African Americans struck a militant tone during World War II. The black author Chester Himes captured this tone when he wrote: "Now is the Time! Here is the Place!"[6]

A. Phillip Randolph grasped the opportunities that the war provided black civil rights activists when he organized the March on Washington Movement in January 1941. As a key leader of the Brotherhood of Sleeping Car Porters, one of the few black unions, Randolph appreciated the value of organizing people. He proposed getting 100,000 African Americans to march in Washington, DC. Randolph's goal was to embarrass Roosevelt with the spectacle of American citizens demanding an end to racial discrimination while the United States was supporting Britain in a war against the racist Third Reich. More specifically, the March on Washington Movement demanded that Roosevelt open jobs in war factories to black workers and abolish segregation in the military. Roosevelt kept the march from happening by signing Executive Order 8802 banning racial discrimination in employment at defense industries. However, instead of ordering the desegregation of the military, Roosevelt established the office of the civilian aide to the secretary of war. It was understood that a civil rights leader would be appointed, and his mandate would be to ensure there was no discrimination against black troops.[7]

The first civilian aide to the secretary of war, Judge William Hastie, found out early on how difficult it would be to get the Roosevelt administration to make antidiscrimination efforts a high priority. Hastie had distinguished legal and civil rights credentials. A graduate of Harvard Law School, Hastie had served as a federal judge in the Virgin Islands before taking over as dean of the Howard University Law School, where he helped lead the National Association for the Advancement of Colored People's (NAACP) legal campaign against racial discrimination. Although Hastie's job at the War Department was to look out for the interests of African Americans in uniform, he had his hands full just trying to look out for himself. He had to fight for an office in the Munitions Building where the War Department was located. Shortly after he had settled into his new office, Hastie found that he was routinely excluded from meetings and that his reports were generally ignored by War Department officials.[8] Hastie nevertheless fought to hold the War Department accountable for ensuring that African Americans were treated equally.

Hastie was willing to fight a losing battle because he was very aware of the problems that African Americans faced in a segregated army. Due to his prominence as a civil rights leader, African Americans looked to him for help, sending hundreds of letters about the mistreatment of their sons, husbands, and brothers to the civilian aide and his hand-picked assistant, Truman K. Gibson. In addition, black newspaper editors and civil rights leaders passed along hundreds of letters from their readers and members of their organizations. The correspondence from black soldiers, their families, their friends, and their advocates directly recorded what concerns ordinary African Americans had about the military. Out of these letters, three themes stand out: demands for protection from racial terror, anger over the bad faith of the military, and an often frustrated patriotism.

## Terror, Anger, and Black Soldiers on Southern Military Bases

African Americans began to experience terror as soon as mobilization started. On June 16, 1941, a little less than six months before Pearl Harbor, Thomas Brewer, a black physician from Columbus, Georgia, sent Hastie a letter about the shooting of Private Albert King. Brewer informed Hastie that the official account of the young black private being shot dead at nearby Fort Benning by white military policemen was false. Military police had defended the shooting by claiming it was made in self-defense. According to Brewer, King "was shot while running and shot in the back." He also let Hastie know that "we, the [black] citizens here in this community feel that an investigation should be made of the killing." Brewer explained, "there were eyewitnesses and all of their reports are contra to that issued by Fort Benning."[9] The black physician insisted that the federal government protect black soldiers. He also made it clear that he was expressing the demands of the entire African American community in Columbus. Six months before the war started, the plight of black soldiers had already inspired collective grassroots protest.

In response to Brewer's letter, Hastie opened an investigation on Private King. He learned to his chagrin that the white military policeman had been exonerated in a court-martial. Then he got the transcripts of the court martial and found the proceedings had been highly irregular. Hastie contacted the adjunct general of the army, and he pulled no punches in his letter. The trial, wrote Judge Hastie, had relied on "utterly specious and wholly unbelievable testimony." In his closing note, he was even more frank, saying that "I am increasingly concerned lest Negro soldiers, despairing of official action in cases such as this, resort to self-help and violent reprisal." Tragically, Hastie possessed great foresight. In 1943, race riots broke out throughout the nation on military bases and in major American cities. But at the beginning of the World War II, racial conflict was focused in the South, as Private King's sad story illustrates.[10]

Truman Gibson, Hastie's successor as civilian aide, wrote in his memoirs of a paradox related to mobilizing black troops. On the one hand, they were being trained as proud combat soldiers, while on the other hand, "they are generally told to 'remain in their places' in the South," where most of them received their training. Gibson said African Americans disliked the South with good reason. "It means," he explained, "not walking on sidewalks, not being able to board buses if there are any white people to ride, [and] not possessing any rights to freedom from physical violence." In Gibson's opinion, the army made unreasonable demands on black troops when it assigned them to southern military bases. This was especially true for the many black conscripts from the northern states who had never been to the South before and who quickly developed a visceral hatred of Jim Crow. As one member of the Twenty-Seventh Aviation Squadron explained in a letter to Carl Murphy, the president of the *Afro-American* newspaper chain, "If they [black soldiers] had their choice they would rather serve 5 years in an Eastern prison, than serve 6 months in this southern camp. Even the non-coms all hate it here. It is really a cracker's paradise."[11] The young black man's dislike of white Southerners found a quick response in the contempt that white Southerners exhibited toward black GIs.

Many white Southerners were unhappy about black GIs in their midst. So many rumors of impending race war swirled around that Howard Odum, a distinguished sociologist at the University of North Carolina at Chapel Hill, commissioned a study of rumors connected to race. The study devoted an entire chapter to rumors about "Eleanor Clubs," named after First Lady Eleanor Roosevelt. There was some logic to associating the first lady, who was disliked intensely in the white South because of her advocacy for civil rights, with the demands of black women for better wages. The Eleanor Club slogan was alleged to be: "A white woman in every kitchen by 1943" since black women hoped to have better jobs by then. Since Odum found no proof that Eleanor Clubs existed, what the rumors about black women organizing actually reveal is the intensity of white fear that the racial status quo was under attack.[12]

In addition to being worried about preserving Jim Crow, many white Southerners feared that African Americans would repay past insults from whites by siding with the enemy. A white attorney named James Mayfield grew so worried about what he called "perversive [sic] propaganda" that he contacted military intelligence. Mayfield claimed that African Americans in Tuscaloosa, Alabama, were "being subjected to alien propaganda" that encouraged them to side with the Axis powers. This "perversive" propaganda, according to Mayfield, told African Americans that "the Japs are 'colored people'" and that black soldiers were "being sent to fight 'their own kind.'" It also claimed that African Americans were "foolish not to want Hitler to win" because he would grant more rights to them. Military intelligence responded to Mayfield's letter by assigning an agent, John Nedza, to conduct an investigation in Tuscaloosa. In his report, Agent Nedza confirmed "that perversive [sic] propaganda is being directed at the Negroes of Tuscaloosa, and the situation is sufficiently grave to warrant close attention."[13] Whether or not a mysterious white man talked sedition to members of the African American community in Tuscaloosa, as Agent Nedza claimed, his sense of alarm was certainly genuine and illustrated a larger trend.

Rumors and the presence of armed black men prompted some local white officials from southern towns next to military bases to unleash a campaign of terror. As seen earlier from Private Albert King's story, black soldiers in the South were in danger of being murdered even before Pearl Harbor. In fact, three months before King was shot in the back, at the very same military base, Fort Benning, another black soldier was murdered. Private Felix Hall was found hung by the neck from a tree. The civilian aide, Hastie, frustrated that no finding had been made about whether Hall's death was murder or suicide, sent his assistant, Truman Gibson, to Georgia to conduct his own investigation. Gibson concluded the evidence "indicates that Hall was murdered." A black soldier had been lynched on an American military base. Moreover, because the subsequent investigation by the military was inconclusive, no one was ever charged with Private Hall's murder.[14]

Large numbers of African Americans were affected by violent clashes in southern towns near military bases. In several well-noted instances, such as in Alexandria, Louisiana, southern police escalated tense situations into race riots. Alexandria was surrounded by three large military bases, which brought thousands of black and white soldiers downtown to mingle with the local residents every Saturday night. On January 10, 1942, it was a typical Saturday night until a black soldier responded to a white woman driver honking at him while he crossed Lee Street. He asked the white woman, "Would you hit a veteran?" She responded by calling over a city policeman, who arrested the soldier for "using vile and unnecessary language." A group of black soldiers thought the arrest was excessive, and they crowded around the policeman and his prisoner. In very short order, white military police officers, state troopers, and national guardsmen from nearby Camp Beauregard reinforced the Alexandria police. Instead of restoring order, however, the armed white men began a police riot on Lee Street, firing volley after volley of shots into businesses patronized by African Americans. White men even drove black soldiers from barbershops, where they had been waiting for a haircut, into a hail of gunfire on Lee Street. According to one observer, "For five blocks along Lee Street, from fifth to twelfth street, [the street became] a replica of a miniature aerial bombardment." Several sources claimed that ten African Americans had been killed.[15]

The president of the NAACP branch in Alexandria, S. Bradley, wrote Hastie to urge him to do something about what he described as a "reign of terror." His explanation was blunt: "Negro civilians were brutally beaten and intimidated . . . Negro soldiers were huddled together like cattle and subjected to all kinds of atrocities." The branch president ended his description by using the same phrase that he had started it: "The whole Negro population was terrorized for over five hours." Bradley went so far as to say, "There was a striking parallel between the Gestapo of Nazi Germany and the white military and civilian police of Alexandria." Georgia Johnson, another member of the Alexandria NAACP, wrote to Hastie that she feared white authorities would intercept her letter. She wrote Hastie that "You may think it is a joke really, [but] my writing these facts to you may cause me some harm." Johnson's letter exposed the risks of protest during a reign of terror. It also shows that, regardless of their views, African Americans who lived near military bases with large numbers of black troops were affected by the often violent response of white Southerners to the perceived threat of black men in uniform.[16] Because racial violence toward black soldiers was widespread, the controversy over black soldiers directly touched the lives of thousands of black civilians.

Racial violence involving black soldiers followed a number of revealing patterns that help explain how resistance to mistreatment evolved over the course of the war. One scholar constructed a database of 209 such incidents and found they were most likely to occur in places with large numbers of black troops. Given the concentration of black troops on southern military bases, it is unsurprising that two-thirds of the violent incidents involving black soldiers happened in southern states. These conflicts in the South were ultimately caused by the paradox of mobilization. By maintaining segregation, the military and, by extension, the Roosevelt administration accepted the status quo in the Jim Crow South, where most of the military bases were located. At the same time, proud black men and women in uniform quickly grew frustrated with segregation in the military. Consequently, they were less deferential to whites than southern custom required them to be, which enraged local white civilians. Rather than protect black soldiers, the military emboldened southern law enforcement officials by allowing them to police race relations near military bases, leading to clashes such as the Alexandria riot. Violent conflicts broke out on or near northern bases too, with the common denominator being large concentrations of black soldiers. For instance, after a fight broke out at a United Service Organizations dance at Fort Dix, New Jersey, one soldier died, two more were wounded, and one white military policeman was beaten.[17]

Region also appeared to influence who was drawn into violent incidents. For example, the black soldiers of the Ninety-Fourth Engineer Battalion were from the Chicago-Detroit area, and they were stationed at a base near Gurdon, Arkansas, in 1941. When members of the Ninety-Fourth went to a nightclub in Little Rock, they got in a fracas with city police. Afterwards, the men of the Ninety-Fourth discussed that the police had left a group of southern-born black soldiers alone in the club while harassing them, prompting thoughts that they were singled out for being from the North. On August 11, 1941, a false rumor spread that white military police had arrested and beaten a member of the Ninety-Fourth. Members of the engineering battalion armed themselves with clubs and stones before marching on the town of Gurdon, where military authorities ordered the Ninety-Fourth to leave town and march to a distant bivouac. The next night, members of the Arkansas state police ordered the marching unit off of the road and into a water-filled ditch surrounded by state police. When one of the white officers of the Ninety-Fourth protested their treatment, a state policeman called him a "Yankee nigger lover" and punched him in the face. Only at that point did white military policemen, who had been passive bystanders up to then, intervene to save the northern black soldiers and their white officers.[18] In addition to showing that northern soldiers were often singled out for confrontations in the South, the decision of some members of the Ninety-Fourth to arm themselves and advance as a group also illustrates how the resistance of black soldiers changed over time.

Over the course of the war, the pattern that emerges from the database of 209 violent incidents is a trend from individual resistance to collective action by black soldiers. Early on, from 1940 to 1941, conflicts tended to involve individual black soldiers who were trying to fend off violence. The Lee Street riot was a good example of that type of incident, and so was another major attack on black soldiers in 1941 at Fort Jackson, South Carolina. During the spring and summer of 1941, there were also violent incidents in Fayetteville, North Carolina; Murfreesboro, Tennessee; and in Louisiana, at Camp Claiborne and Camp Livingston. In 1942 and 1943, the number of race riots increased, and there were major incidents at Camp San Luis Obispo, California; Camp Phillips, Kansas; Camp Shenango, Pennsylvania; Camp Stewart, Georgia; Camp Breckinridge, Kentucky; Lake Charles, Louisiana; and Camp Van Dorn, Mississippi.[19]

The Mississippi incident is an example of group defense becoming the norm in major incidents during 1943 and 1944. It also fits the trend of violent conflicts moving from towns to military bases. After black soldiers of the 364th Infantry

Regiment got in a big fight in Phoenix, Arizona, where they were stationed, the 364th was transferred to Camp Van Dorn in May of 1943. Some of the men believed they had been transferred to Mississippi as punishment for getting in trouble, so they had a chip on their shoulder. Men from the first group of the 364th to arrive at Camp Van Dorn said they were going to "take over the camp, the [nearby] town of Centreville, and, if necessary, the state of Mississippi." When the sheriff shot a member of the 364th, several companies attempted to break into the supply rooms where weapons were kept. At least one was successful. The armed soldiers joined a crowd of several hundred other black soldiers by the regimental exchange. When the military police arrived, the crowd tried to rush them, but they were repelled by a volley of gunfire from the policemen that left one soldier wounded. Finally, the regimental commander and the chaplain arrived. They persuaded the men to return the weapons and to go back to their barracks.[20] Such collective protest against discriminatory treatment was the backdrop against which military leaders agreed to send black troops into combat in late 1943, as will be discussed later in this chapter.

One scholar argues that military reforms changed the nature of violent conflict in 1944 and 1945. On the one hand, reforms such as better intelligence and more black military policemen helped military officials prevent conflicts from escalating. On the other hand, reforms such as integrating the recreational facilities on military bases gave black soldiers a legal basis for collectively expressing their grievances with discrimination. They took advantage of these reforms. The percentage of incidents caused by organized protests grew from 3.4 percent in 1942 to 19.4 percent in 1944. To give an example, a black company of the Ninety-Second Infantry stationed at Camp Gordon Johnston, Florida, appointed a committee to present their grievances over camp conditions to the commandant.[21] In sum, the ways that black soldiers resisted mistreatment from 1940 to 1945 were becoming increasingly collective and formal.

However, throughout the war, segregation on public transportation caused violence between white civilians and black military personnel in the South. Segregation had always been difficult to manage on buses because the black and the white seating areas changed every time passengers got on and off. As millions of people travelled around the country during the war, the buses and trains became more crowded than ever before, which made it more difficult for bus drivers to maintain segregation. One scholar described wartime buses as "small war zones." To better understand wartime conflicts on buses, it is important to know that southern bus drivers were sworn in as deputy sheriffs and issued a gun.

White bus drivers routinely abused black military personnel and not infrequently shot black soldiers.[22]

While military uniforms sometimes made African Americans into targets for abuse, they also empowered young black men and women by letting them feel they represented a higher authority. If they resisted white discrimination, they were acting upon the principles for which they were fighting. At the same time, one scholar has said it is possible to exaggerate the role of black soldiers in causing incidents because zoot suiters, members of hipster culture who avoided military service, made a sport of harassing bus drivers. Moreover, a study of bus incidents in Birmingham during the war found that twice as many black women than black men were arrested for bus incidents. The women were more likely to need to use the bus to get to work than the men, so they spent much more time riding on them.[23] So, people from all walks of life in the African American community increased their resistance to segregation during the war, but black soldiers had the most harrowing experiences.

Even when black soldiers did what bus drivers told them to do, they could still be treated unfairly. At 7:45 p.m. on Christmas Eve, 1945, Sergeant Joseph Haley got on a bus in Hattiesburg, Mississippi. There were no white passengers on the bus at that time. Since there were no more seats available behind the sign that separated the black and white seating areas, another black soldier moved the sign forward one seat and sat down behind it with Haley. H. F. Williams, the bus driver, hollered at the men to leave the sign alone but then left them in peace. When more white passengers boarded at Johnson's Crossing, a mile outside the city limits of Hattiesburg, Williams told the black soldier to straighten the sign he had moved. The soldier refused. Haley, wanting to avoid trouble, straightened the sign. This made Williams focus on him. The bus driver then called Haley a "son-of-a-bitch" and shot him in the abdomen. Afterwards, white as well as black witnesses said Haley had done nothing to provoke the confrontation. The black soldier was guilty of nothing more than being on the wrong bus at the wrong time, for which he suffered a life-threatening injury. For his part, Williams had few worries about being prosecuted. He had shot another black soldier on March 19, 1944, and he had been released on bond. The military report on the incident held out no hopes that Williams would be prosecuted.[24] Such random acts of violence illustrated the dangers African Americans faced in the South and justified the use of the word "terrorism" by black leaders.

Black GIs also had to be fearful of random white civilians. In 1944, Private Riley B. King, later known as bluesman B. B. King, was riding on a bus in Mississippi from Indianola to Camp Shelby, just south of Hattiesburg. Along the way, the bus passed a group of workers, and one of the black soldiers said hello to a couple of the white women who were sitting beside the road. When the bus arrived in Jackson, an enraged white man, armed with a rifle, got on the bus. King recalled the white man saying, "Which one of you [blacks] was screaming at the girls?" No one on the bus said a word. King said the white man then said, "I'll just start shooting you coons one by one, till you give up the man." According to King, "No one budged." The showdown between the armed white man and the silent black soldiers ended as quickly as it began. Embarrassed that his tirade had failed to yield results, the white man stomped off the bus. White officials on the bus had also remained silent during the whole incident. As these stories illustrate, black GIs had legitimate fears for their physical safety. Truman Gibson, who as civilian aide had unrestricted access to War Department reports during the war, wrote in his memoir that "it might only be a slight exaggeration to say more black Americans were murdered by white Americans during the course of World War II than were killed by the Germans."[25]

Although black GIs had many causes for complaint, they were angered more by the government's failure to protect them and to send them into combat than by the issue of segregation. In fact, most black soldiers appeared to have resigned themselves to a segregated military. According to a 1943 survey of black troops by the War Department, only 20 percent "thought the Army unfair." That resignation did not translate into accepting the status quo. The same War Department survey asked black soldiers what subject they would raise with President Roosevelt if they had a chance to speak with him, and half answered they would talk about racial discrimination. The survey illustrates how World War II was a turning point in the lives of these black GIs. They expected more, spoke out, and fought back. For example, when black soldiers were asked whether they thought they would have more rights and privileges after the war, 43 percent said yes.[26]

The determination to be treated with respect was the origin of black GI resistance. Placed in insufferable conditions, black men and women in the military occasionally snapped. Take the story of Jackie Robinson's run-in with a bus driver headed toward Camp Hood, Texas. After winning national fame for his two years playing football at UCLA, Robinson, with the help of Truman Gibson, was admitted into Officer Candidate School and became a lieutenant in the army. He served as a morale officer for black GIs at Camp Hood. The bus driver spoke to the black lieutenant as he stood in the aisle talking to a female friend, "Nigger, get to the back of the bus," to which Robinson replied, "I'm getting to the back of the bus. Take it easy." Angered, the bus driver said, "You can't talk to me like that." Robinson stood his ground, saying, "I can talk to anybody any way I want." The driver got his dispatcher to summon the military police, who arrested Robinson. Back at the guard room, Robinson grew enraged when a white private, Ben Mucklerath, called him a nigger. The military police initially dealt with the incident by claiming that a drunken black lieutenant had tried to incite a riot. Due to Robinson's fame as an athlete, both US senators from his home state of California wrote the Secretary of War about the charges brought against him. Robinson was acquitted of all charges at his court-martial. He later recalled saying during his trial that the incident was "simply a situation in which a few individuals sought to vent their bigotry on a Negro they considered 'uppity' because he had the audacity to exercise his rights that belonged to him as an American and as a soldier."[27] Confrontations like this one show how combustible black pride and white prejudice were when mixed together and help explain why they posed a threat to the efficient operation of the military.

Less well-connected black GIs paid dearly for challenging Jim Crow, but some still did it. Truman Gibson reported that "Thousands of black soldiers faced court martial for insubordination and mutiny." Since he blamed most of the racial problems in the military on inadequate training and poor leadership, he viewed most of the convicted black soldiers as victims of institutional racism, who "got unfairly branded as troublemakers and unfit for serious duty." His final judgment of the military justice system was harsh: "it was a criminal squandering of manpower and talent in a time of war." Several scholars have confirmed Gibson's judgment that African Americans were disproportionately punished, making it remarkable that so many black soldiers defied military authorities in the face of harsh military discipline.[28]

Black women in the military also defied segregation, and in the process, they revealed a new mindset in the African American community. That was true in the case of two black members of the Women's Army Corps (WACs) travelling on a nearly full civilian bus from Attalia, Alabama, to Gadsden on December 23, 1944. When two white women got on the bus, the driver told the two WACs, who were seated in the last row before the back seat, to move to the back seat. They changed seats then, but after a few passengers had exited the bus, they moved back to their former seat. After a while, the driver noticed that the women had moved and asked them to go back to the rear seat. The two WACs told the driver there was not enough room, and they refused to give up their seat. The driver said the black women had to move back, leave the bus, or be arrested. The WACS chose the last option. They refused to get up for the four Gadsden police officers sent to arrest them. One of the WACs had to be forcibly removed from the bus. Once outside, she punched one of the policemen in the mouth.[29]

Another WAC, Private Beatrice Jackson, went a step further than her sister WACs in Alabama, refusing to comply with segregation at all. On November 22, 1944, she not only "refused to sit in the colored section of the bus" in Chattanooga, Tennessee, but she also cursed the white bus driver and the white passengers. She also foretold of "a coming revolution which would completely change the situation for the colored race."[30] World War II had changed Jackson's expectations. When confronted with Jim Crow, she lashed out because she could no longer tolerate racial discrimination. Black WACs at Camp Breckinridge, Kentucky, and at Camp Devens, Massachusetts, went on strike and faced courts-martial because they refused assignments to cook and clean. Their commanders thought such work was appropriate for black women. This resistance of black soldiers and WACs put pressure on military leaders. For example, military authorities intervened with local officials to get the charges dropped against the three WACs in Alabama. Black GI resistance, when combined with protests from black civilians, brought about reform in policies on black troops, especially committing black troops to combat.

### Patriotism and the Fight to Enter Combat

As hard as it may be to believe in the twenty-first century, African Americans had to fight to get into combat during World War II. The number of black soldiers in the Army peaked at 701,678 in September 1944. At that point and for the rest of the war, African Americans made up almost 10 percent of the enlisted personnel in the army, which equaled the proportion of Americans who were black. To state it another way, from the middle of the war onward, black civilians were just as likely to end up serving in the military as white civilians. Segregation, however, made their military experience very different from that of white soldiers, limiting the positions that African Americans could hold. Black soldiers were diverted from combat assignments. At the end of 1943, just 20 percent of black troops served in combat units—of which only a handful of had been deployed—compared to nearly 40 percent of white soldiers.[31]

Most black GIs worked in service units, and many of those units had distinguished records. Black engineering squadrons helped build strategic highways in Alaska and China. In Europe, African Americans made up 75 percent of the drivers, mechanics, and administrative clerks in motor transport units. One of them, the Red Ball Express, became legendary for speeding ammunition and gas to the front lines in France. The Triple Nickels, the first all-black paratrooper squadron, put out wildfires set by Japanese balloons carrying incendiary bombs.[32] And although these men were not in combat units, they often saw combat. More importantly, they made significant contributions to the war effort.

In spite of the contributions of black service units, military officials had generally refused to send black troops into combat during the first two years of World War II. Yet until January of 1944, no high-ranking military official had exposed the racial stereotypes that were keeping black soldiers out of combat. Then Secretary of War Henry Stimson ignited a controversy with his response to a letter from Representative Hamilton Fish, a congressman from New York. Fish, a white man who had commanded black troops in World War I, wanted to know why the Army had failed to send black troops into battle during the current war. In reply, Stimson explained that the low educational scores of black conscripts meant black units "have been unable to master efficiently the techniques of modern weapons." Representative Fish had Stimson's letter read into the *Congressional Record*, and a firestorm of controversy erupted. Black newspapers used headlines such as "Too Dumb to Fight" to explain Stimson's letter to their readers. Black Congressman William Dawson wrote a letter of protest to Undersecretary of War John McCloy that made his thoughts on the matter abundantly clear. "The letter of the Secretary of War," Dawson wrote, "is widely regarded as a direct insult to every Negro in the country and a gratuitous slap in the face of many thousand Negro soldiers in the Army." As a veteran of World War I, Dawson was familiar with racism in the army. He wrote that Stimson's letter "represents the attitude with which I . . . am all too familiar."[33]

Stimson had inadvertently mobilized the African American community to demand reform of the military. Congressman Dawson expressed feelings that were repeated in the hundreds of letters sent by African Americans to the War Department. At the same time, black organizations circulated a petition addressed to President Roosevelt that asked him to fire Stimson. Thousands of African Americans signed the petition because they were determined that black GIs would serve the armed forces in a capacity higher than as a cook or a laborer. They were also not going to sit by quietly when the secretary of war insulted the intelligence of black soldiers.[34]

In turn, black protests against the military strengthened the influence of Civilian Aide Truman Gibson inside of the War Department. Gibson used the controversy over Stimson's remarks as an opportunity to win the secretary's confidence. First, he wrote a memo that was passed along to Stimson critiquing his response to Congressman Fish. Gibson stated the letter was "most unfortunate" because it "will, in my opinion, accentuate the greatly increasing criticism and resulting resentments which have already reached alarming proportions." To put it less diplomatically, Stimson's remarks had poured salt onto the wounds of the African American community. Gibson also extended an olive branch to Stimson. According to Gibson, Stimson would have been spared the bad press if the inquiry had "been sent to those of us who had some knowledge of the facts." Gibson was implying that if the Secretary of War would rely on his civilian aide to deal with racial matters, he could expect a change in the tone of black public opinion. At the same time, Gibson bluntly stated that "no problem was ever solved by temporizing" to make it clear he expected significant changes in military policies on race. Stimson let Gibson draft his reply to Congressman Dawson's letter and to all subsequent letters from black leaders.[35]

Gibson moved quickly to use his influence with Stimson to get black troops sent into combat during the spring of 1944. He had himself appointed to the Advisory Committee on Negro Troop Policies, from which his predecessor, Judge Hastie, had been excluded. Shortly thereafter, the committee recommended to Stimson that black troops be sent into combat "as soon as possible." Stimson agreed, and the tide had turned in the struggle for black civil rights in the military.[36]

Black soldiers won the most acclaim in smaller combat units. The number of black squadrons in the Tuskegee Airmen never surpassed eight, organized into two groups, the 332nd Fighter and the 477th Bombardment. Only the 332nd fought overseas. Out of this group came the memorable airmen of the 99th Fighter Squadron, who were the stars of the 2012 film *Red Tails*. The 99th was awarded Distinguished Unit citations for the invasion of Sicily and for fighting in Italy. By war's end in 1945, the 99th was added to the 332nd Fighter Group, which escorted bombers into Germany. Black ground units also won awards. The very first to receive a Distinguished Unit citation in World War II was a platoon from Company C, 614th Tank Destroyer Battalion. Even though the platoon suffered a 50 percent casualty rate, its surviving members drove off a German force that had stalled the advance of the 411th Infantry. Similarly, the 761st Tank Battalion blazed its way from a landing at Omaha Beach in France into Germany. A few months after their arrival, the 761st received the honor of being addressed by General George Patton, who said he had high expectations for the black soldiers. "I would never have asked for you if you weren't good," said Patton. He continued: "I have nothing but the best in my Army. I don't care what color you are, so long as you go up there and kill these Kraut sonabitches. Everyone has their eyes on you and is expecting great things from you." In 1978, President Jimmy Carter awarded the 761st a Presidential Unit citation.[37] These examples show that black marines, sailors, and soldiers helped defeat the enemy in spite of limited opportunities for combat. In fact, it was the success of experiments such as the Tuskegee Airmen that cleared the way for the grandson of General Robert E. Lee to break the color barrier on the West European front.

After suffering 125,000 casualties in the first month of combat after D-day, Lieutenant General John C. H. Lee, commander of the Communications Zone of the European Theater and descendant of the Confederate war hero, convinced General Eisenhower to let black service troops volunteer as infantry replacements. The Battle of the Bulge had created a manpower crisis in December of 1944. American forces were losing men faster than they could be replaced. In response, General Lee proposed letting African Americans from service units under his command volunteer to be trained for combat against the Germans. The official call for volunteers went out the day after Christmas, 1944. Within two months, 4,500 black men had stepped forward. The army sent 2,800 black volunteers to combat training, formed them into black rifle platoons, and assigned them to various white units invading Germany in 1945. In this manner, integration came to American forces in the European theater.[38]

### Social Science Research and Military Necessity

These black troops fought well, which had lasting consequences. Their performance shattered myths about black cowardice and low intelligence, or at least it should have. Although black GIs had won medals for their military exploits in France during World War I, military leaders justified segregation at the beginning of World War II by saying that African Americans were cowardly and unintelligent. Based on that unfair assumption, military leaders such as General George Marshall contended that adding black GIs to white units would hurt morale.[39] The major civil rights breakthrough of World War II was to gather indisputable evidence that the exact opposite was true.

To understand how this achievement came about requires looking at the strategy of civil rights activists and the new research of social scientists. Civil rights activists had assumed that if black and white GIs served together, white GIs would change their opinion of African Americans for the better. Through the Office of the Civilian Aide, Truman Gibson worked with black newspapers and civil rights organizations to lobby for experiments with integrated military units, and they were successful. Their strategy paid off: most white GIs who fought side by side with black GIs in Germany came to favor integration.

This fact became known when, for the first time, social scientists began conducting surveys of GIs. During World War II, the army established a Research Branch and staffed it with social scientists from the faculties of Washington-area universities. Their findings undermined the last prop of legitimacy for segregation, the argument that integration would be bad for unit cohesion. Instead, the Research Branch showed that the experience of fighting with black GIs in Germany changed the attitudes of white GIs. Before the experiment with integration, only 33 percent of the white soldiers had a positive opinion about having black soldiers in their companies. After the experiment, 77 percent of the white soldiers said their opinion of serving with African Americans had become more favorable. Part of the reason white soldiers changed their minds was they were impressed with black soldiers. When surveyed, 84 percent of white officers and 81 percent of white enlisted men said black troops performed "very well" in combat. This positive evaluation translated into openness to desegregation: 55 percent of the white officers and 72 percent of the white enlisted men agreed that it would be a "good idea" to use black soldiers in the infantry.[40] If race did not hurt the efficiency of a unit, then segregation was inefficient because it required duplicate facilities and caused racial tensions. The logic of military necessity, therefore, had changed in ways that favored the equal treatment of African American soldiers.

The Army Research Branch was also interested in understanding black GIs, but it encountered difficulties because the white staff members did not understand their subjects. The Research Branch staff asked 234 black soldiers why they volunteered for combat. The majority, 60 percent, indicated they were unhappy with their current situation in the military; a sizable minority, 19 percent, had volunteered to help break down prejudice against African Americans. Surprisingly, only 14 percent gave patriotism as their reason for volunteering. Men risked their lives when they volunteered to fight, so they would not have made their decision lightly. But did the survey answers mean these men were not patriotic? A note in the survey clarified that patriotic reasons for volunteering had no "explicit reference to racial problems."[41] Consequently, the survey failed to record an important belief of black soldiers: that racial pride was inseparable from love of country. The military and the Roosevelt administration had promised equal treatment to black men and women. These promises of equality made them determined to end Jim Crow. In addition, the military gave black soldiers a sense of accomplishment and of confidence that would make them natural leaders in the civil rights movement of the 1950s and 1960s.

Patriotism, then, along with terror, anger, and resistance, defined the military experience of ordinary African Americans during World War II. The paradox of mobilization explains why war brought terror to African Americans. Just as black men upgraded their status by becoming soldiers, the military refused to send them into combat and instead assigned the overwhelming majority of them to southern bases. Fearful white Southerners exchanged rumors about Eleanor Clubs, but commanding officers remained silent, which empowered white communities to fight for Jim Crow. Southern law enforcement officers repeatedly turned minor incidents into full-fledged riots in which black people died. Southern bus drivers shot black passengers. African Americans cried out that they were being subjected to a reign of terror. They resisted by using their leverage as soldiers, voters, and workers to demand federal protection from violent attacks. Although the response of the Roosevelt administration was mixed, reforms such as experiments with integrated combat units set important precedents for the future.

During the war, however, the failure of the federal government to protect black men and women in the military was a leading cause of black anger. Racial confrontations on buses and trains exemplified the changing race relations of World War II America. As young black men and women traveled far away from home and pursued new opportunities, they were transformed. They had less patience, and the prospect of dying overseas made confronting other threats, such as segregated buses and prejudiced secretaries of war, appear less daunting. As military and police records show clearly, resistance spread quickly and widely in the ranks of the army. Resistance grew more organized and focused directly on civil rights issues. Black military personnel demanded to be treated with the respect to which they were entitled for wearing their nation's uniform.

If anger was a cause of growing resistance by African Americans in the military, it was also a spur to greater patriotism. Resistance was connected to patriotism because angry young men wanted to prove they could fight. They did, and their contributions to victory overturned stereotypes about African Americans. In the last year of the war, black soldiers also broke through the color barrier. The number of black volunteers accepted for combat training was relatively small, but they had a lasting impact on the military. By proving that white attitudes could be changed without a loss of military efficiency, this experiment laid the foundation for ending segregation in the military during the Korean War.

The black military experience during World War II also offers insights into the struggles of other groups for integration in the military. The foremost is that resistance in many different forms can undermine discriminatory policies. During World War II, wide-scale protests by black civilians as well as the resistance and the valor of black soldiers forced the military to change its policies for African Americans. Before the war started, the March on Washington Movement failed to abolish Jim Crow in the military, but it did get a black official in the War Department, the civilian aide. Meanwhile, more and more black soldiers and WACs resisted mistreatment and segregation. They and their families began letter-writing campaigns to the civilian aide, to civil rights leaders, and to the editors of black newspapers, laying the groundwork for a full-blown crisis. Secretary of War Henry Stinson trigged that crisis by airing his views on the capabilities of black soldiers. In turn, the resulting controversy gave Truman Gibson more leverage, which he used to get black troops sent into combat. Huge casualties from the invasion of Europe prompted the military to experiment with integrating black and white troops. Motivated by the desire to prove their equality, black volunteers fought well. In the process, they convinced young white men to re-think their opinions about race and undermined the argument that African Americans were detrimental to military efficiency.

The other insight concerns the problem of stereotypes and the meaning of military service. During World War II, military officials justified segregation by claiming black soldiers were not brave enough or smart enough to participate in combat. Similarly, the military has cited stereotypes to keep women and gays out of combat. Women were allegedly too fragile, and gays were too disruptive.[42] The common thread running through the military experience of each group is the battle against negative stereotypes. The black military experience during World War II suggests that the best way to overcome stereotypes is to prove them wrong. Yet before that can happen, legally marginalized groups have to earn the right to serve in the military and to fight in combat, which is the story told in the following chapters.

NOTES

1. Barnard C. Nalty, *Strength for the Fight: A History of Black Americans in the Military* (New York: The Free Press, 1986), 186.

2. Nalty, *Strength for the Fight*, 186; Lee Finkle, *Forum for Protest: The Black Press during World War II* (Cranbury, NJ: Associated Universities Press, 1975), 94–95; Sherie

Mershon and Steve Schlossman, *Foxholes and Color Lines: Desegregating the U.S. Armed Forces* (Baltimore: Johns Hopkins University Press, 1998), 127–134.

3. Daniel Kryder, *Divided Arsenal: Race and the American State during World War II* (New York: Cambridge University Press, 2000), 2–3. Army Chief of Staff George Marshall wrote that the consideration of stationing black troops in areas where they would be more welcome "must be second to military requirements." Quoted in Robert F. Jefferson, *Fighting for Hope: African American Troops of the 93rd Infantry Division in World War II and Postwar America* (Baltimore: John Hopkins University Press, 2008), 127.

4. The first wave includes Bell I. Wiley, *The Training of Negro Troops* (Washington, DC: Army Ground Forces Historical Section, 1946); Samuel Stouffer et al., *The American Soldier: Adjustment during Army Life*, vol. 1 (Princeton, NJ: Princeton University Press, 1949); Jean Byers, *A Study of the Negro in Military Service* (Washington, DC: US Department of Defense, 1950); Mattie E. Treadwell, *The Women's Army Corps* (Washington, DC: Office of the Chief of Military History, 1954); Ulysses Lee, *The Employment of Negro Troops* (Washington, DC: Office of the Chief of Military History, 1966); Alan M. Osur, *Blacks in the Army Air Forces during World War II: The Problem of Race Relations* (Washington, DC: Office of Air Force History, 1977); Morris J. MacGregor, *The Integration of the Armed Forces, 1940–1965* (Washington, DC: Center of Military History, 1981); Mershon and Schlossman, *Foxholes and Color Lines*; Martha S. Putney, *When the Nation Was in Need: Blacks in the Women's Army Corps during World War II* (Metuchen, NJ: Scarecrow Press, 1992); Brenda L. Moore, *To Serve My Country, To Serve My Race: The Story of the Only African American WACs Stationed Overseas During World War II* (New York: New York University Press, 1996); Kryder, *Divided Arsenal*; Daniel K. Gibran, *The 92nd Infantry Division and the Italian Campaign in World War II* (Jefferson, NC: McFarland & Co., 2001); Melton A. McLaurin, *The Marines of Montford Point: America's First Black Marines* (Chapel Hill: University of North Carolina Press, 2009). The second wave includes Richard M. Dalfiume, *Desegregation of the US Armed Forces: Fighting on Two Fronts, 1939–1953* (Columbia: University of Missouri Press, 1969); Neil A. Wynn, *The Afro-American and the Second World War* (New York: Holmes & Meier, 1973); Lee Finkle, *Forum for Protest: The Black Press during World War II* (Cranbury, NJ: Associated University Presses, 1975); Patrick Scott Washburn, *A Question of Sedition: The Federal Government's Investigation of the Black Press during World War II* (New York: Oxford University Press, 1986); Graham Smith, *When Jim Crow Met John Bull: Black American Soldiers in World War II Britain* (New York: St. Martin's Press, 1988); Phillip McGuire, *He, Too, Spoke for Democracy: Judge Hastie, World War II, and the Black Soldier* (New York: Greenwood Press, 1988); Harvard Sitkoff, "African American Militancy in the World War II South: Another Perspective," in *Remaking Dixie: The Impact of World War II on the American South*, edited by Neil R. McMillen (Jackson: University Press of Mississippi, 1997); Barbara Diane Savage, *Broadcasting Freedom: Radio, War, and the Politics of Race, 1938–1948* (Chapel Hill: University of North Carolina Press, 1999); Kevin Kruse and Stephen Tuck, eds., *Fog of War: The Second World War and the Civil Rights Movement* (New York: Oxford University Press, 2012).

5. For an overview of African American opposition to unequal treatment in the military and to America's wars, see Kimberly Phillips, *War! What Is It Good For? Black*

*Freedom Struggles and the US Military from World War II to Iraq* (Chapel Hill: University of North Carolina Press, 2012). See also Ernest Allen, Jr., "When Japan Was 'Champion of the Darker Races': Satokata Takahashi and the Flowering of Black Messianic Nationalism," *Black Scholar* 23 (Winter 1994): 23–46; Reginald Kearney, *African American Views of the Japanese: Solidarity or Sedition?* (Albany: State University of New York Press, 1998); George Lipsitz, "'Frantic to Join . . . the Japanese Army': Black Soldiers and Civilians Confront the Asia-Pacific War," in *Perilous Memories: The Asia-Pacific War(s),* edited by Takashi Fujitani, Geoffrey M. White, and Lisa Yoneyama (Durham, NC: Duke University Press, 2001). For two exceptions to the general avoidance of examining violence against black soldiers, see James A. Burran, "Urban Racial Violence in the South during World War II," in *From the Old South to the New: Essays on the Transitional South,* edited by Walter J. Fraser and Winfred B. Moore (Westport, CT: Greenwood Press, 1981) and Andrew H. Myers, *Black, White, & Olive Drab: Racial Integration at Fort Jackson, South Carolina, and the Civil Rights Movement* (Charlottesville: University of Virginia Press, 2006). For groundbreaking studies of ordinary African Americans in the military, see Leisa D. Meyer, *Creating GI Jane: Sexuality and Power in the Women's Army Corps during World War II* (New York: Columbia University Press, 1996) and Jefferson, *Fighting for Hope.* My discussion of resistance is informed by Robin D. G. Kelley, *Race Rebels: Culture, Politics, and the Black Working Class* (New York: Free Press, 1994).

6.  Beth Bailey, "Individual Freedom and the Obligations of Citizenship," in her *America's Army: Making the All-Volunteer Force* (Cambridge, MA: The Belknap Press of Harvard University Press, 2009); Ira Berlin, Joseph Reidy, and Leslie Rowland, *Freedom's Soldiers: The Black Military Experience in the Civil War* (New York: Cambridge University Press, 1998); Adriane Lentz-Smith, *Freedom Struggles: African Americans and World War I* (Cambridge, MA: Harvard University Press, 2009); Chad Louis Williams, *Torchbearers of Democracy: African American Soldiers in the World War I Era* (Chapel Hill: University of North Carolina Press, 2010); Neil A. Wynn, *The Afro-American and the Second World War,* rev. ed. (New York: Holmes and Meier, 1993), 1–20; Kryder, *Divided Arsenal,* 2, 228–233; Chester Himes, "Now Is the Time! Here Is the Place!" *Opportunity,* vol. 20 (September 1942).

7.  Herbert Garfinkel, *When Negroes March: The March on Washington Movement in the Organization Politics for FEPC* (Glencoe, IL: The Free Press, 1959), 1–36; Truman K. Gibson, Jr., with Steve Huntley, *Knocking Down Barriers: My Fight for Black America, a Memoir* (Evanston, IL: Northwestern University Press, 2005), 77–82.

8.  Phillip McGuire, *He, Too, Spoke for Democracy: Judge Hastie, World War II, and the Black Soldier* (New York: Greenwood Press, 1988); Gibson, *Knocking Down Barriers,* 77–82.

9.  Thomas H. Brewer, MD, to Judge William Hastie, Civilian Aide to the Secretary of War, July 16, 1941, Office of the Civilian Aide to the Secretary, Subject File, 1940–1947, Violence Against Negro Military Personnel to Veteran's Readjustments, Record Group 107 (Secretary of War), Box 255, National Archives Records Administration (hereafter NARA), College Park, MD. Hereafter Office of the Civilian Aide, Box Number.

10.  William Hastie, Civilian Aide, to the Secretary of War to the Adjutant General, January 23, 1942, Office of the Civilian Aide, Box 255. For an in-depth study of the biggest riot of 1943, see Dominic J. Capeci, Jr., and Martha Wilkerson, *Layered Violence: The Detroit Rioters of 1943* (Jackson: University Press of Mississippi, 1991). For an

account of how the Roosevelt administration responded to urban rioting in 1943, see Kryder, *Divided Arsenal*, 229–233.

11. Gibson, *Knocking Down Barriers*, 17. Gibson said: "I am becoming convinced that the only way out of the dilemma in which Negro soldiers find themselves in the South is to take them out of the South." Truman Gibson to Carl Murphy, President of *The Afro-American*, November 11, 1943, Office of the Civilian Aide, Box 236.

12. Howard W. Odum, *Race and Rumors of Race: The American South in the Early 1940s* (Chapel Hill: University of North Carolina Press, 1943), 165–166. Jason Morgan Ward argues that mass resistance to desegregation actually began during the Great Depression and became a potent force during World War II. He surveys the views of ordinary white Southerners as well as of white political officials. See his *Defending White Democracy: The Making of a Segregationist Movement and the Remaking of Racial Politics, 1936–1965* (Chapel Hill: University of North Carolina Press, 2011).

13. James J. Mayfield to Military Intelligence Officer in Charge, Fourth Corps Area Headquarters, Atlanta, Georgia, March 16, 1942 and Memorandum for the Officer in Charge from John J. Nedza, Agent, CIC, March 27, 1942, Army Intelligence, Decimal File, 1941–1948, Record Group 319, Box 381, NARA II, College Park, MD. Although the Japanese aimed propaganda at African American troops in the Pacific, military police records contain little proof of subversion on the home front. While George Lipsitz shows that admiration for Japan was widespread in the African American community because it was a powerful, non-white nation, he also documents that the "overwhelming majority of African Americans who were eligible for the draft accepted induction and served effectively.' Lipsitz, "Frantic to Join . . . the Japanese Army," 348. T. Fujitani shows War Department officials were concerned that Japan would appeal to non-white Americans successfully. He argues that contributed to the decision to exclude Japanese Americans from the army. See his *Race for Empire: Koreans as Japanese and Japanese as Americans during World War II* (Berkeley: University of California Press, 2011), 94–95.

14. Judge William Hastie, Civilian Aide to the Secretary of War, to the Director of Bureau of Public Relations, May 14, 1941, "Killing of Private Felix Hall at Fort Benning, Ga.," Office of the Civilian Aide, Entry 91, Box 182; Lee, *The Employment of Negro Troops*, 349.

15. James B. LaFourche, President, Public Relations Counsel, NAACP, Southern Regional Branches, to Walter White, Secretary, NAACP, January 19, 1942, Office of the Civilian Aide, Entry 91, Box 179, Folder: Alexandria Riot. See also William M. Simpson, "A Tale Untold? The Alexandria, Louisiana, Lee Street Riot (January 10, 1942)," *Louisiana History* 53 (Spring 1994): 133–149 and Adam Fairclough, *Race and Democracy: The Civil Rights Struggle in Louisiana, 1915–1972* (Athens: University of Georgia Press, 1995), 74–75.

16. S. Bradley, President, National Association of Colored People, Alexandria Branch, no date; Georgia M. Johnson to the Honorable William Hastie, Civilian Aide to the Secretary of War, January 24, 1942; Georgia M. Johnson to the Honorable William Hastie, Civilian Aide to the Secretary of War, January 17, 1942; all in Office of the Civilian Aide, Entry 91, Box 179, Folder: Alexandria Riot. Robert Jefferson made a very significant contribution by noting the importance of lobbying and protest by the family members of black service personnel. Robin Kelley and Adam Fairclough add the observation that living near bases drew black residents into protests, although Fairclough

says "they did not add up to collective resistance." See Jefferson, *Fighting for Hope*, 4–6, 113–115, 117–119; Kelley, *Race Rebels*, 64–65; Fairclough, *Race and Democracy*, 83.

17. According to Daniel Kryder, the percentage of such incidents occurring in the South were 68% in 1942, 68% in 1943, 68% in 1944, and 55% in 1945. See Kryder, *Divided Arsenal*, 141–142; Lee, *Employment of Negro Troops*, 375.

18. Lee, *Employment of Negro Troops*, 352–353.

19. Kryder, *Divided Arsenal*, 141–142; Lee, *Employment of Negro Troops*, 366, 375.

20. Lee, *Employment of Negro Troops*, 366–369, quotation on 368.

21. Kryder, *Divided Arsenal*, 157.

22. Gibson, *Knocking Down Barriers*, 12; Lee, *Employment of Negro Troops*, 315–324. For a pioneering analysis of resistance aboard buses in Birmingham during World War II, see Robin D. G. Kelley, "Contested Terrain: Resistance on Public Transportation," in his *Race Rebels*, quotation on 62.

23. Ibid.

24. Report, "Negro Soldier Shot Without Provocation by White Bus Driver, Hattiesburg, Mississippi," Headquarters Fourth Service Command, Atlanta, Georgia, January 9, 1945, Army Intelligence Decimal File, 1941–48, Record Group 319, Box 381C, NARA II, College Park, MD.

25. B. B. King with David Ritz, *Blues All Around Me: The Autobiography of B. B. King* (New York: Avon Books, 1966), 88–89; Gibson, *Knocking Down Barriers*, 11.

26. Wynn, *Afro-American and the Second World War*, 28; Samuel A. Stouffer et. al., *The American Soldier: Adjustment during Army Life*, vol. 1 (Princeton, NJ: Princeton University Press, 1949), 504, 514.

27. Quotes from Gibson, *Knocking Down Barriers*, 13; Arnold Rampersad, *Jackie Robinson: A Biography* (New York: Knopf, 1997), 92–93, 102–109. Rampersad dismisses Gibson's version of the incident, which ends with Robinson knocking out the bus driver's front teeth.

28. Ibid., 13. For studies of black soldiers being disproportionately punished by the military justice system, see Walter A. Luszki, *A Rape of Justice: MacArthur and the New Guinea Hangings* (Lanham, MD: Madison Books, 1991); J. Robert Lilly, "Dirty Details: Executing U.S. Soldiers during World War II," *Crime and Delinquency* 42 (October 1996): 491–516; J. Robert Lilly and J. Michael Thompson, "Executing US Soldiers in England, World War II: Command Influence and Sexual Racism," *British Journal of Criminology* 37 (Spring 1997): 262–287; Colonel Glen Felder, "A Long Way since Houston: The Treatment of Blacks in the Military Justice System," *Army Lawyer* (October 1987): 8–11.

29. Report, "Two Negro WACs Create a Disturbance on Civilian Bus," Headquarters Fourth Service Command, Atlanta, Georgia, January 9, 1945, Army Intelligence Decimal File, 1941–48, Record Group 319, Box 381C, NARA II, College Park, MD. For other examples of black WACs resisting discrimination, see Meyer, *Creating GI Jane*, 95–98.

30. Report, "Racial Incident—Pvt. Beatrice Jackson, WAC (Negro)," prepared by Special Agent Jackson Lee for the SIC Field Area No. Seven, Army Intelligence Decimal File, 1941–48, Record Group 319, Box 381C, NARA II, College Park, Md. After both of the incidents involving black WACs, the military secured their release from civilian authorities and took no disciplinary action.

31. Lee, *The Employment of Negro*, 406, 415.

32. Nalty, *Strength for the Fight*, 179.

33. Stimson letter to Hamilton Fish quoted in Dalfiume, *Desegregation of the US Armed Forces*, 94; Finkle, *Forum for Protest*, 183; Representative William Dawson to Assistant Secretary of War John McCloy, February 28, 1944, Office of the Assistant Secretary of War, General Correspondence of John J. McCloy, 1941–45, 291.2 (Race), Record Group 107, Box 39, NARA II, College Park, MD.

34. Robert D. Morgan to Mr. Henry Stimson, Secretary of War, March 1, 1944, General Correspondence of John J. McCloy, 1941–45, 291.2 (Race), Record Group 107, Box 39, NARA II, College Park, MD; Dalfiume, *Desegregation of the US Armed Forces*, 94–95.

35. Truman Gibson, Civilian Aide, to John McCloy, Assistant Secretary of War, February 23, 1944, and Gibson to Lt. Col. Harrison Gerhardt, Assistant to the Assistant Secretary of War, March 3, 1944; John McCloy, General Correspondence, Decimal File 291.2 (Race/Negroes), Record Group 107, Box 39, NAII, College Park, MD. For Gibson's recollections of events, see Gibson, *Knocking Down Barriers*, 132–140.

36. Gibson, *Knocking Down Barriers*, 132–140.

37. Nalty, *Strength for the Fight*, 150–153, 160, 175–176; Lee, *The Employment of Negro*, 660–667.

38. Dalfiume, *Desegregation of the US Armed Forces*, 98–101; Gibson, *Knocking Down Barriers*, 190–193; Nalty, *Strength for the Fight*, 176–178.

39. Marshall argued that dealing with a complex social problem would "jeopardize discipline and morale." George Marshall, Chief of Staff, to the Secretary of War, December 1, 1941, Office of the Chief of Staff, Record Group 165, Box 299, NAII, College Park, MD. Ulysses Lee argues that, although desegregation did not become the policy of the army until after the war, these experiments with integration were the "genesis for the change." Lee, *The Employment of Negro*, 704.

40. Dalfiume, *Desegregation*, 100; Gibson, *Knocking Down Barriers*, 190–193; "Table 26: Evaluation of Negro Infantrymen by White Officers and Enlisted Men Serving in the Same Companies with Them" and "Table 27: Attitudes of White Officers and Enlisted Men Serving in Same Companies with Negro Platoons Towards the Utilization of Negro Infantrymen" in Stouffer, *American Solider*, 588, 591. The Research Branch was led by Samuel Stouffer, a Harvard graduate and sociology professor at George Washington University. For the background of the Army Research Branch, see Office of the Assistant Secretary of Defense (Manpower, Personnel, and Reserve), Research Division Historical File, 1941-June 1955, Record Group 330, Entry 89, Box 969, NARA II, College Park, MD.

41. "Table 15: Reasons Given by Former Members of the Second Cavalry Division Who Wished to Volunteer for Combat, Mediterranean Theater, September 1944" in Stouffer, *American Solider*, 533.

42. For overviews, see Randy Shilts, *Conduct Unbecoming: Gays and Lesbians in the US Military* (New York: St. Martin's Press, 1993); Meyer, *Creating GI Jane*.

# 2

## Nisei versus Nazi

Japanese American Soldiers in World War II

JAMES M. MCCAFFREY

The Japanese attack on Pearl Harbor dramatically changed the lives of
Americans of Japanese ancestry. In his lively overview, James M. McCaffrey
traces how the racist backlash from Pearl Harbor led to the forcible relocation
of more than 100,000 Japanese-Americans to internment camps and to the
widespread mistrust of Japanese-American troops. He then follows Japanese-
American combat units—the 100th Infantry Battalion and the 442nd Infantry
Regiment—from their training at Camp Shelby, Mississippi, where they
sometimes resisted mistreatment on segregated buses. The rest of the chapter
tells the story of the 100th and 442nd in combat in Italy, France, and Germany.
McCaffrey shows the valor of the soldiers by examining several actions that
led Japanese American soldiers to win military honors. He argues that, like
African American soldiers, Japanese American soldiers fought for the United
States to disprove racial stereotypes and to claim equal citizenship.[1]

P eople living in and around Honolulu watched in horror as Japanese planes
strafed and bombed military targets in the area. The coming of war at last
probably did not surprise anyone, as Japanese-American relations had become
more and more strained over the previous several months. But it is unlikely that
anyone on the ground that day expected the war to start there. Nelson Akagi, for
example, an American of Japanese descent, thought that the attack was some
kind of giant hoax, like Orson Welles's "War of the Worlds" that had been on the
radio in 1938. Or maybe, as Irving Akahoshi speculated, it was an early-morning
session of anti-aircraft artillery practice.[2]

The Japanese attack on Hawaii in December 1941 did more than plunge the
United States into war. It also resulted in near-hysterical bigotry aimed at all
things Japanese. Sadly, this included tens of thousands of native-born American

citizens of Japanese ancestry, or Nisei. Authorities on Oahu mandated that no language other than English was to be used in written communications—even private communications—or on the telephone. And five Nisei politicians who had won primary elections in the spring of 1942 were pressured into taking themselves off the ballot before the general elections. "How I hated the Japs for bringing this upon us!" remembered Samuel Sasai.[3]

Soon after the last Japanese plane had left the area, residents began to hear rumors that Japanese infantry would soon be landing on the island. The regular army and navy troops already had their hands full, so the tasks of mounting guards at electric power plants, water treatment plants, telephone exchanges, and other strategic locations fell to the three thousand men of the recently federalized 298th and 299th Regiments of the Hawaii National Guard and the University of Hawaii students enrolled in the Reserve Officer Training Corps (ROTC). About a third of Hawaii's population was of Japanese descent, and about half of the guards-men were of Japanese ancestry, as were many of the ROTC cadets. This caused a great deal of uneasiness among some of the other citizens. If the Japanese really did have a landing force on the way, they worried, how trustworthy were these men with Japanese faces but wearing American uniforms? Would they do their sworn duty? Or would they instead welcome the invaders ashore?

### Anti-Japanese Sentiment Following Pearl Harbor

Little effort was made to hide these concerns, and on January 21, all of the Japanese American ROTC cadets were disarmed and dismissed. These men had conscientiously performed every duty assigned them and considered themselves 100 percent American. "All of a sudden they kick you in the ass," one man bitterly recalled. Another felt as if "they had dropped a bomb in our midst," and that it "was far worse than Pearl Harbor." A few months later the Nisei members of the two Hawaiian National Guard regiments were culled out and formed into a Hawaiian Provisional Battalion, a unit which some of its members feared was destined to become nothing more than a labor battalion. Continuing a pattern of racial prejudice that had long been in place with regard to black troops in the army, only Caucasian officers were appointed.[4]

Much of the Japanese population was of the laboring class in Hawaii—along with Filipinos, Portuguese, and Puerto Ricans. The various groups seemed to get along well with one another until the attack. After that, they self-segregated. Many began referring to their former co-workers as "Japs," which is like addressing an African-American with the word "nigger." "During lunch," Kiyoshi Shimizu remembered, "we all sat down on our side of the fields, and while we were eating our food the Filipinos would bring out their long knives that they had made from the steel of old automobile springs. While we ate, they'd be out there practicing fighting with their long sword-like knives." On the Big Island a Filipino supervisor even requested permission to start shooting the Japanese![5]

The anti-Japanese feelings were not restricted to Hawaii but also permeated much of the mainland and were particularly bitter in the Pacific states of California, Oregon, and Washington, each of which had significant populations of Japanese Americans. Anti-Asian feeling first worked its way into immigration law with the passage of the Chinese Exclusion Act in 1882. Thousands of Chinese had immigrated to furnish labor in the mines and to build the railroads of the western United States, but this law halted all further immigration of Chinese laborers. Other Asians, Koreans, and Japanese began to arrive on America's shores in increasing numbers by the turn of the century although, like the Chinese before them, they were banned by the Naturalization Act of 1790 from ever becoming naturalized American citizens. Then, in 1924, another law closed off all further immigration from Asia. Although the first-generation Japanese, known as *Issei* in their native language, were barred from citizenship, their children who were born in the United States, Nisei, achieved citizenship by right of birth. Rumors circulated widely up and down the West Coast that local Japanese, both Issei and Nisei, were actively assisting Japan's war effort. They were said to be in regular radio contact with enemy naval force off the California coast, providing them with valuable information on likely targets for attack. In fact, the stories continued, Japanese naval forces had attacked every American ship that left one of the West Coast ports in January 1942, and twenty thousand Japanese Americans in San Francisco were eagerly awaiting a signal to rise up in revolt.[6]

The editors of the popular illustrated magazine *Life* ran what they must have considered a public service article in the December 22, 1941, issue. Titled "How to Tell Japs From the Chinese," it used carefully selected representations and stereotypical descriptions to assist readers in discerning the difference between the friendly, industrious, hard-working Chinese and the sly, evil, cunning Japanese. Indeed the descriptions of the Chinese could almost have served to describe mainstream Americans of European descent. Chinese men, the article claimed, were generally tall and slender, with rather pale complexions and scant facial hair. The Japanese, on the other hand, were characterized as "short and squat" with an "earthy yellow complexion" and heavy beards.[7]

Even the government's own *Pocket Guide to China*, printed to help servicemen to accustom themselves to life in that allied country, carried an eleven-page insert by popular cartoonist Milton Caniff entitled "How to Spot a Jap." It was full of stereotypes. The Chinese man, according to Caniff, was physically a lot like the common American, but the Japanese was short and stocky with almost no discernible waistline and "looks as if his legs are joined directly to his chest."[8]

Nisei soldiers already serving in the US Army often found themselves sent home or assigned menial tasks at army bases far from the Pacific Coast. An agent of the Federal Bureau of Investigation, questioning Corporal Akiji Yoshimura about his loyalty, lost his composure when the soldier calmly replied that he, as an American soldier, would of course fight against Japan if ordered to do so. "You sonovabitch," the agent yelled, "I expect you to say that you will shoot down the Emperor and tear down the Jap flag and stomp it into the ground!" This soldier soon was dismissed from active service and sent home. At Jefferson Barracks, near St. Louis, Nobo Ikuta and a dozen other soldiers of Japanese ancestry were locked in jail. Each time they left for meals or for regular periods of exercise, one of their guards counted them and then announced: "Thirteen Jap prisoners!" This was particularly insulting because these men were American soldiers, not "Jap" prisoners. A final blow against Japanese American participation in their nation's war came in March 1942, when the Selective Service System declared all men of Japanese heritage—even those who were American citizens—to be enemy aliens and, therefore, unfit to serve.[9]

Reports soon surfaced in the press of suspicious Japanese activity in the United States. Respected columnist Damon Runyon reported—falsely, as it turned out—that agents had discovered a powerful radio transmitter in a Japanese boarding house, the type of transmitter that could easily be used to communicate with Japanese submarines off the coast. Another reporter, Westbrook Pegler, demanded the arrest of all Japanese in California "and to hell with *habeas corpus* until the danger is over."[10]

There were twice as many residents of German descent in Los Angeles than there were of Japanese descent, but there was no similar outcry leveled against them. In fact, the governor of California, Culbert Olson, rather disingenuously claimed: "When I look out at a group of Americans of German or Italian descent, I can tell whether they are loyal or not. I can tell how they think . . . but it is impossible for me to do this with the inscrutable Orientals, and particularly the Japanese." And he probably believed that. "Once a Jap always a Jap," declared segregationist Mississippi Congressman John Rankin. "You cannot regenerate a Jap, convert him, change him, and make him the same as a white man any more than you can reverse the laws of nature. Damn them! Let us get rid of them now!" On February 14, 1942, Lieutenant General John L. DeWitt, commanding the Western Defense Command, publicly proclaimed: "The Japanese race is an enemy race." It did not matter much to him whether they lived in Tokyo or California.[11]

There had been some anti-Japanese sentiment in California even before the attack on Pearl Harbor, but it was not universal. In a Labor Day speech three months earlier, popular Mexican American movie actor Leo Carrillo empathized with the plight of Japanese Americans. Even though his family had been in California for several generations, he still faced the occasional racial slur and promised to work to dispel such discrimination aimed at the Nisei. After the attack on Pearl Harbor, his message changed drastically. In early January 1942 he sent a telegram to his congressman. "I travel every week through a hundred miles of Japanese shacks on the way to my ranch," he wrote, "and it seems that every farmhouse is located on some strategic elevated point. Let's get them off the coast into the interior. You know and I know the Japanese situation in California. The eastern people are not conscious of this menace. May I urge you in behalf of the safety of the people of California to start action at once."[12]

Giving in to this racist hysteria, President Franklin Roosevelt signed Executive Order 9066, authorizing the army to remove individuals from areas it determined to be militarily sensitive. General DeWitt quickly prescribed that all of western California, Oregon, and Washington—and even southwestern Arizona—were sensitive areas and ordered the removal of all Japanese and Japanese Americans therein. Well over one hundred thousand men, women, and children were forced out of their homes and businesses and into internment camps where they lived in shabby barracks, surrounded by barbed wire and armed guards.[13]

### Japanese Americans in the Army

While this process of relocation got underway, authorities in Hawaii dispatched the Hawaiian Provisional Battalion to the mainland for additional combat training. The men in this unit, which had been renamed the 100th Infantry Battalion (Separate), arrived at Camp McCoy, Wisconsin, in the spring of 1942. Most residents found them to be more a curiosity than anything sinister, but there were a few occasions of overt racism. A couple of the men were hitchhiking on a weekend pass when a local farmer, seeing them in uniform and cognizant of their Hawaiian nativity, offered them a lift. During the course of their friendly conversation, the farmer proclaimed that if he ever got a chance at some Japanese Americans, he would kill them with his bare hands. The GIs took this pronouncement in stride; only when they were exiting his vehicle did they laughingly inform him that they were Japanese Americans. He must not have read *Life* magazine's guidelines.[14]

Military officials saw how eagerly the men of the 100th Battalion took to their training and reconsidered the ban on allowing other Japanese American men to serve in the army. Here, after all, was a large pool of young men that was not being utilized. So in early 1943, army ranks were opened up to Nisei volunteers and draftees. Opening the ranks met with great enthusiasm in Hawaii; young Japanese American men rushed to the recruiting offices. And just like soldiers of every other race, they came with a variety of reasons besides patriotism. "Loyalty was secondary," remembered Takao Ito. "I volunteered to get the hell out of the pineapple field and to go to the Mainland." "I got an F in English 100," Charles Shigeru Ota ruefully admitted, "and joined the Army to save face."

Recruitment on the mainland, on the other hand, was much slower. It seemed to many of the residents of the relocation camps to be the height of hypocrisy for the same government that had imprisoned them to now come looking for military volunteers. "That government had incarcerated me against my will," recalled Minoru Kiyota, "taken away my freedom, prevented me from getting an education, subjected me to the intolerable humiliation of an interrogation by the FBI, caused me to despair of ever leaving the camps, and now—on top of all this—it was trying to coerce me into pledging my unconditional loyalty to it. I did not want to yield to that kind of oppressive force." Victor Izui's reaction was more visceral. "Up your ass, Uncle Sam!" And although he later served, his first reaction was that he "certainly had no incentive to serve, much less die for this FDR brand of democracy."[15]

The decision to enroll Japanese Americans into the army led to some probably unforeseen supply problems. A lot of these men were smaller in stature than the average Caucasian American, many of them barely reaching five feet in height. One young soldier, whose feet were size two and half, had to make do with size eight boots by cramming the toes with padding. Outfitting them in properly fitting uniforms was very difficult, to put it mildly. Shirts with thirteen-and-a-half-inch necks and twenty-seven-inch sleeves, for example, were not readily available. Nor were trousers with twenty-six-inch waists and twenty-five-inch inseams. In fact, the army sometimes sent them clothing that had originally been meant for female soldiers. One such shipment, in the bitter winter of 1944, contained women's raincoats, which were very welcome. But when the underwear accompanying this shipment turned out to be women's panties, the men decided to make do with what they had or do without.[16]

The issue arose of whether to simply integrate these men into existing units, as had been the case before the war, or place them, like the black troops, in completely segregated units with white officers. The Japanese American community favored a segregated unit. It was confident that Nisei soldiers not only were up to the task of fighting for their country but would do so in gallant style. Then when the newspapers reported on their heroism they would be identified as members of an all-Nisei combat command, thereby reflecting some of the praise onto the unit itself. Army authorities thus established the 442nd Infantry Regiment and assigned it to Camp Shelby, Mississippi, for training. Shortly thereafter, military authorities decided to expand the regiment into a regimental combat team (RCT). Thus, in addition to the three infantry battalions that were common to a regiment, they added a field artillery battalion, a combat engineer company, an anti-tank company, and a cannon company along with a medical unit.

### Training in Mississippi

Most of these new soldiers had experienced a certain amount of antipathy because of their race, but prior to the attack on Pearl Harbor it had not been particularly virulent. When they arrived at Camp Shelby, where the 100th Battalion had also been transferred, they saw, most of them for the first time racial, real, deep-seated, hateful prejudice. It was not directed toward them but toward African Americans, and it had been going on for a long, long time. In the town of Hattiesburg, near the post, they learned that when they went to a movie they were not to sit upstairs because balcony seating was referred to as "nigger heaven."[17]

They witnessed segregated bus seating that required blacks to sit in the back of the buses and whites (and, apparently, Japanese Americans) to sit in the front. On more than one occasion this infuriated the Nisei soldiers to the point of violence. George Goto remembered getting on a bus with a number of other soldiers headed for a weekend in New Orleans. When a black soldier got on the bus, the driver ordered him to the back. The other soldiers tried to intercede with the driver on behalf of their fellow soldier. "This bus doesn't move until that nigger gets in the back of the bus," the driver insisted. Goto remembered thinking "that was the worst thing that I had ever seen down South. He [the black soldier] looked as though somebody had smashed his world. It was sickening, the worse [*sic*] case of discrimination I had ever seen up to that point." In another instance, when a driver physically kicked a black soldier off his bus, a Nisei rose up and proceeded to administer a severe beating to the driver. In New Orleans, soldiers waited for a bus to take them back to camp. When an elderly black woman tried to board the bus before the white riders got on, the driver got off the bus and pushed her to the ground. Seeing this, a half-dozen Nisei soldiers, in the words of one of them, "kicked the hell out of him for knocking that poor black woman down."[18]

It was in Mississippi that the Japanese soldiers encountered separate public restrooms and drinking fountains labeled "white" and "colored." At first this presented a dilemma. They certainly did not consider themselves white, nor did they think of themselves as colored. They decided to use the ones marked "white." As one man later recalled, "We weren't white, but we thought, 'We'll show them, we'll use the white one. If they say anything, we'll have a fight, you know.'"[19]

Of course, the men with Asian faces came in for their share of bigotry from white Southerners as well. When one of the men met, fell in love with, and married a local girl, the Ku Klux Klan burned a cross at the home of her parents. Some of the married soldiers had brought their wives and children to live in Hattiesburg while they trained at nearby Camp Shelby. The city of Hattiesburg would not allow their children to attend white schools. The Nisei, perhaps engaging in a little prejudice themselves, refused to send their children to the black schools, forcing the city to pay for a small one-room school for the Japanese American children. Black Hattiesburg drew some smug satisfaction from the dilemma that the city faced due to the arrival of this third segment of society. One of Hattiesburg's long-suffering blacks stated: "My community especially enjoyed the reports of conflicts between men of the 442nd Regiment and white bus drivers and policemen."[20]

### Into Combat in Italy

While the men of the 442nd Regiment continued their training, the 100th Battalion reached the end of its preparations and departed, arriving in Algeria on September 2, 1943. In spite of their outstanding training accomplishments, there were still some doubts about how well they would perform in actual combat. The fighting in North Africa had ended by this time, and one of the biggest concerns was theft by local tribesmen from the trains traveling between Casablanca and the port city of Oran. One suggestion emanating from local headquarters was to assign the newcomers to guard that railway. But the battalion commander, Hawaiian-born Farrant Turner, strenuously objected. His men had come to fight, not to become railroad policemen. So instead of patrolling the railroad, the 100th Battalion was added to the 133rd Infantry Regiment of the 34th Infantry Division, preparing to deploy to Italy. Their new regimental commander quickly moved to head off any problems related to race or national origin when he informed the officers in his other battalions: "They are not Japanese but Americans born in Hawaii . . . . And tell your men not to call them Japs, or there'll be trouble."[21]

Within three weeks, the men of the 100th Battalion were ashore in Italy as part of the push to liberate Rome. One week later, on September 29, Sergeant Shigeo "Joe" Takata became the battalion's first combat fatality. There were to be many, many more.

The presence in Italy of the Japanese Americans led to considerable confusion as to their ethnicity. The local people "knew" they could not be Japanese because Japan was allied with Germany. Therefore they must be Chinese, and grateful Italian villagers welcomed them as such. Nor did all of their fellow soldiers know about them. Later in the campaign, after Naples had been secured, a couple of inebriated Caucasian GIs turned a corner and almost collided with some sightseeing Nisei soldiers. "My god," one of them sadly observed, "all is lost. The Japs have captured Naples."[22]

The Niseis' ethnicity also came into play later when the enemy captured a handful of them. The German officer could not understand why these "Japanese" men should be fighting for the United States when Japan was fighting against it. One of them tried to explain to him that they were not Japanese; they were Americans of Japanese ancestry who owed their allegiance to the United States, the land of their birth, not Japan, the land of their ancestors. He seemed unable to comprehend. "Did you know," he asked one of the prisoners, "that a cat born in the fish market isn't a fish?" The prisoner accepted that view but reminded him that such a cat still belonged to the fish market. Once, when the shoe was on the other foot and some men of the 442nd had captured some Germans, they told their prisoners that they, in fact, were members of the Japanese army and that Japan, like Italy, had switched sides and was now fighting against Germany.[23]

Back at Camp Shelby, training continued for the 442nd Regimental Combat Team. By that time the War Department had seen the wisdom of recruiting soldiers who were proficient in both written and spoken Japanese for service in the Pacific. They would be able to interrogate captured Japanese soldiers and translate captured documents. Officers from the Military Intelligence Service Language School at Camp Savage, Minnesota, sought volunteers for further language training. Most of the trainees had at least a smattering of conversational Japanese, but fewer than 3 percent possessed a sufficient level of knowledge to advance to further training. Some, like Frank Fukuzawa, were woefully deficient, such that the language school recruiter told him: "Soldier, by the time we train you the war will be over." Those who were chosen, however, performed valiantly and were of vital importance to the war effort in the Pacific.[24]

While the men of the 442nd RCT completed their preparations at Camp Shelby, the Hawaii-born Nisei of the 100th Battalion fought their way slowly up the Italian peninsula with the 34th Division, taking part in such costly battles as those of Monte Cassino and Anzio. They soon established an outstanding reputation as combat soldiers. This came at a price, however, and that price was measured in killed and wounded. The 442nd, back in Mississippi, sent more than five hundred replacement officers and men from its First Battalion to fill these voids, and one result was that when the time came for the 442nd to ship out only the Second and Third Battalions were up to required manpower levels. The first battalion thus remained at Camp Shelby as a training cadre for Japanese American draftees who would follow.[25]

The Second and Third Battalions boarded trains for the East Coast on April 22, 1944. Then, after completing final paperwork in Virginia, they boarded Liberty ships on May 2 and headed toward Europe. Authorities had not officially told the men where they were headed, but it was not difficult to figure out that they would be joining the 100th Battalion in Italy.

For most of these men, except those from Hawaii, this was their first experience on the ocean, and their accommodations were far from luxurious. Their sleeping places were crowded, with hammocks sometimes stacked six high and allowing barely enough room to turn over without bumping into the man in the bunk directly above. Their food was unimaginative to say the least, often consisting of boiled eggs, toast, and coffee for breakfast; soup and crackers for lunch; and potatoes, rice, and Spam for the evening meal. Teenaged Daniel Inouye remembered "an endless river of chipped beef and beans [and] great bottomless jars of apple jelly." They sometimes seemed to be spending all of their waking hours either eating one meal or standing in line for the next one. Seasickness ruined many appetites, but most of the sufferers seemed to have gained their sea legs after a few days and were no longer bothered by it. One unfortunate officer, however, had an extreme case. He started to feel unsteady the moment he stepped foot upon the deck of the ship—when it was still securely moored to the dock—and remained sick for the entire four-week voyage to Italy.[26]

By the time the two untested battalions caught up with the 100th Battalion in Italy, Rome had fallen. As the senior battalion pushed up Highway 7 on the way to the Eternal City, the men saw widespread carnage. Going through one village motivated one soldier of the Thirty-Fourth Division to later recall that "the stench of dead humans permeated the air so profusely that even a gas mask was not a deterrent to the odor. For all the cleanliness efforts of the human being there is nothing more obnoxious than the smell of a human body during decay and here the awful odor of hundreds of them wafted in the air." By the afternoon of June 4, 1944, the Nisei soldiers were within six miles of Rome, and there appeared to be no significant German resistance between them and their goal. And then they received orders to halt so that the First Armored Division could assume the role of the city's liberators. The decision to send this unit ahead may have been based upon the possibility that its heavier firepower would be needed, but the Japanese American soldiers believed that they had been denied their due spot in the history books because of their ethnicity. In spite of this disappointment, they soldiered on.[27]

The two battalions of the 442nd RCT finally caught up with the 100th Battalion about a week later. The men of the more experienced 100th Battalion were justifiably proud of the reputation they had earned thus far and resented being assigned as the First Battalion of the 442nd. They became more accepting of the new arrangement, however, when army officials allowed them to retain their distinctive unit designation. Instead of being the First Battalion of the 442nd Regimental Combat Team, they would continue to be known as the 100th Battalion, although they were now a part of the 442nd.

Three months later the entire combat team was reassigned to the 36th Infantry Division for the coming invasion of Southern France. Planners had decided that it was essential to get anti-tank guns ashore as soon as possible to deal with the threat of German panzers and planned to send them in by gliders. They chose the 442nd's Anti-Tank Company for this assignment.

The gliders, designated CG-4A, were lightweight aircraft that were designed to be towed behind a powered airplane until shortly before they reached their destinations. The pilots then disengaged the tow lines, allowing the gliders to drift silently forward. The lack of engine noise made it more difficult for enemy gunners to effectively take them under fire. Each glider could carry up to twelve combat soldiers with all of their personal weapons and gear, or it could carry a

Jeep or an anti-tank gun and half as many soldiers. The Nisei anti-tankers spent the last two weeks of July undergoing glider familiarization training. Each gun team required four gliders. One carried the gun, two carried Jeeps, and the fourth one carried the ammunition trailer.

The 442nd's Anti-Tank Company took part in the initial assault on August 15 and found that getting airborne in a glider was a lot easier than landing in hostile territory. German engineers had erected stout poles every fifteen to forty feet in fields that offered likely landing areas for gliders. A glider landing atop one of these poles would have been wrecked. Captain Geoffrey M. T. Jones of the Office of Strategic Services rather indelicately put it, "The barbs ripping through the flimsy floors of the gliders would have torn the balls off of an awful lot of Americans." Luckily, paratroopers who had already landed cleared most of these obstacles away. This is not to say that the landings were smooth, however. A soldier already on the ground observed: "I watched one glider come whistling in at about 100 mph, hook a wing, and go cartwheeling down the field like a cheerleader at a football game." Six Nisei were among the hundred or so glider troops injured in the landings.[28]

Combat in the forests of France brought with it a new, and unwelcome, aspect. German mortar crews often fused their shells to detonate on contact. In relatively open surroundings, soldiers could simply dig foxholes down below the level of the ground to avoid most damage. None of the shrapnel from a shell that exploded on the ground ten feet away could hurt them. In the forests, however, these rounds often detonated upon hitting tree limbs, thus showering lethal shards of metal downward. The soldiers quickly learned to protect themselves from these "tree bursts" by adding log-and-dirt roofs to their foxholes. Even with overhead protection, these mortar or artillery barrages were terrifying, and many men found solace in prayer. "I'm not ashamed to say that I have never prayed so hard in all my life," remembered Mich Takada. "I prayed in English, I prayed in Japanese, I recited Christian prayers and I recited Buddhist meditations. Had I known other prayers I would have recited them too."[29]

On the afternoon of October 24, most of one battalion from the Thirty-Sixth Division advanced so far from its own lines that the Germans cut it off and surrounded it. Efforts to rescue this lost battalion were unavailing for three days, so the division commander called upon the Nisei troops to effect the rescue. While the Second Battalion provided flank security, the other two battalions began working their way toward the imperiled GIs from two different directions. Progress was slow and costly, but on the afternoon of October 30, Matsuji "Mutt"

Sakumoto of Company I became the first man to reach the "lost battalion," and Company B also soon made contact.

Losses were significant, and when it was over some of the men complained about being used as cannon fodder when there were other—Caucasian—troops available from the trapped battalion's own regiment who should have been used for the rescue. Some others, however, looked at the assignment as a backhanded compliment. The army could not allow this battalion to be swallowed up by the Germans, so it called upon its best available troops—the Japanese American men of the 442nd Regimental Combat Team—to accomplish the task. A "man who is being shot at daily, has a hard time recognizing it as a compliment," wrote a former battalion commander, "but it is a compliment, nevertheless."[30]

The fact remained that by mid-November the combat effectiveness of the 442nd had reached dangerously low levels. In addition to the men who had been killed or wounded in the fierce fighting, hundreds more were sick in hospitals, including a large number suffering from trench foot. This latter ailment was common among soldiers, who spent days—or weeks—at a time in the cold and rain without much opportunity to change into warm, dry socks. Sufferers saw their feet swell up and turn a bluish-white color. Sometimes this was accompanied by a burning sensation and pain so acute that even the weight of a hospital bed sheet became almost unbearable. Left untreated, trench foot could lead to gangrene and the ultimate amputation of toes or even an entire foot. At this stage of the war there were some forty-five thousand GIs—the equivalent of three entire divisions—in European hospitals with trench foot.[31]

By this time the men of the 442nd RCT had made quite a name for themselves—sometimes too much of a name. The *Honolulu Star-Bulletin* had carried an article about an earlier rescue carried out by the brave Nisei soldiers. Almost two dozen men from another unit had been cut off by the enemy when a patrol from the 442nd saved them from annihilation. Unfortunately for the sake of the headlines, however, the trapped men had already fought their way free by the time the patrol arrived. "I don't mind being written up for things I did," one of the would-be rescuers wrote to the newspaper, "but neither do I want to be glorified for things I didn't do."[32]

In spite of the outstanding record being forged by Japanese Americans, there was still a considerable amount of racial prejudice aimed at them. The American Legion post at Hood River, Oregon, had, like similar organizations in other towns and cities across the nation, erected a monument to the local men serving in the armed forces. Included were the names of seventeen men of Japanese ancestry—until, that is, Legion members removed those names. Such an outcry followed, including critical messages from almost every other American Legion post in the country, that the names were finally restored.[33]

Even well-meaning accounts sometimes continued to use the offensive term "Jap" when referring to Nisei soldiers. William Tsuchida commented in a letter home to his brother about a recent article in the army's own *Stars and Stripes* newspaper. "As usual," he complained, "their captions still call us Japs or Jap-Americans. Gee it sure will be the day when they quit hyphenating and leave off the first part."[34]

In mid-December, the Japanese American combat team was pulled out of the line and sent to a quieter zone in the Maritime Alps of southern France to regain its strength and keep an eye on the French-Italian border. Many of the wounded returned from hospitals, replacement troops arrived from Camp Shelby, passes to towns along the French Riviera were issued, and the pace of combat was drastically reduced. About a week before Christmas, Privates Yoshio Hikichi and Donald Nakamura from the Anti-Tank Company spotted something suspicious in the water about fifty yards from the shore. Grabbing automatic rifles, they and four other men waded out to discover a German one-man submarine hung up on a sandbar and unable to move. They captured the disoriented pilot and turned his craft over to the navy. Not to be outdone, some men from Cannon Company captured two Italian marines in a small torpedo boat about six weeks later.[35]

After three months of this milder duty it was time to return to more active campaigning, but this time the team was broken up. The artillery battalion, the 522nd Field Artillery, moved back into northeastern France for the push into Germany as part of the Seventh Army. The rest of the combat team returned to northern Italy, where it was assigned to the all-black 92nd Infantry Division, and where General Clark welcomed it back to his command.

Armed resistance in Germany crumbled before the Allied onslaught. Late in April 1945, Captain Billy Taylor and Sergeant Shozo Kajioka from the 522nd, ranging ahead of the main body to reconnoiter, suddenly came upon a large cluster of barracks buildings surrounded by barbed wire. The residents were not soldiers but gaunt, emaciated men and women wearing what looked like striped pajamas. This was one of the subcamps at Dachau. There were no German soldiers to be seen, so Sergeant Kajioka shot the lock off of the main gate with his carbine, allowing the inmates to slowly shuffle their way out into freedom. Tadashi Tojo and Robert Sugai, also from the 522nd, were temporarily attached to an armored battalion when it discovered a similar camp and simply knocked down the gates with one of their vehicles.[36]

The Americans were horror-stricken at what they saw. "It was a sight that burned in our minds," recalled Corporal Katsugo Miho. "Skin and bones that once were men. I wondered if they could ever recover." An army doctor from another unit observed that nothing "in all the lexicon of medical horrors could have so shriveled the flesh from around the bones and from under the skin, leaving those varnished skeletons, those incredible painful bird's eyes, those unearthly nasal screams."[37]

There was an added bit of bitter irony for some of the Nisei observers. Joseph Ichiuji, who had been interned with his family at one of the relocation camps early in the war, remembered: "When I saw the temporary barracks and barbed wire fences it reminded me of the Poston [relocation] camp from which I volunteered. It is ironic," he continued, "that many of us who came from the relocation camps in the US would come to Germany to help release the Jewish victims. While the scope and purpose of the Japanese Americans and the Jews were different, the reason for incarceration was the same: racial discrimination."[38]

With the German surrender in May, the men of the 442nd RCT, as well as all other American soldiers in Europe, had time to slowly work themselves back into almost a civilian frame of mind. They still had duties to perform, such as guarding prisoners of war, but gone were the fatiguing road marches up and down the steep Italian mountains. Gone was the fear, except in a few lingering cases, of a nighttime bombardment by the big German guns. Even the weather began to get better as the men waited their turns to be rotated home.

President Harry Truman welcomed home the final contingent of troops from the 442nd RCT on a rainy July day in 1946. "You fought not only the enemy," he told them, "but you fought prejudice—and you have won. Keep up that fight, and we will continue to win—to make this great Republic stand for just what the Constitution says it stands for: the welfare of all the people all the time."[39]

### After the War

The welcomes home extended to the Nisei soldiers, in spite of their outstanding performances on the European battlefields, were not always positive. Lieutenant Daniel Inouye's is a case in point. He had received a battlefield commission in recognition of his bravery and leadership skills and returned to the United States having lost his right arm to a German grenade in Italy late in the war. On his way home to Hawaii, he stopped at a barbershop in California wearing his officer's uniform with its empty sleeve. Before he could even enter the shop, an employee met him at the door and told him: "You're a Jap and we don't cut Jap hair." Spark

Matsunaga, still on crutches recovering from wounds, had an almost identical experience in another barber shop. When Mitsuo Usui, another recently returned Nisei veteran still in uniform, boarded a bus in his hometown of Los Angeles, a woman passenger commented loudly, "Damn Jap!" At that, the Caucasian bus driver, himself a recently returned veteran, stopped his vehicle and demanded that she "apologize to this American soldier." When she refused, he kicked her off his bus.[40]

The 442nd RCT lost a lot of men, and the survivors were justifiably proud of their valiant service. Many historians have dubbed the 442nd as the most decorated unit of its size and length of service in all of World War II. And although that claim is nearly impossible to verify, it is true that over fifty of the Nisei soldiers received the Distinguished Service Cross, the nation's second-highest award for valor, hundreds of others received Silver Star Medals, and the number of Bronze Star Medals and Purple Hearts ranges into the thousands. But no Medals of Honor were awarded. Even the heroism of Sadao Munemori, who sacrificed his life by throwing himself upon a German hand grenade to protect two other soldiers, received no such recognition. Not until the intervention of Democratic Senator Albert Thomas of Utah was Munemori's Distinguished Service Cross upgraded to a Medal of Honor in 2010.

Some questioned whether the valor of other Nisei soldiers was overlooked for the nation's highest military honor because of their race. And by the 1980s, others observed that no African-Americans had earned Medals of Honor in either of the two world wars. After much detailed investigation, both of these oversights were corrected. President George H. W. Bush presented a Medal of Honor in April 1991 to the elderly sister of an African American soldier who had earned it posthumously by his heroism in World War I, and almost six years later President William Clinton presented Medals of Honor to seven black soldiers from World War II. Finally, on June 21, 2000, President Clinton presented Medals of Honor to twenty of Sadao Munemori's fellow Nisei heroes.

With the coming of peace, the men of the 442nd Regimental Combat Team sought to return to civilian life. Many of them made use of the Servicemen's Readjustment Act of 1944—or GI Bill—to obtain college degrees that helped them succeed in a wide variety of fields. Some learned trades instead of earning formal degrees. Some became successful lawyers, engineers, or physicians while others entered business or politics. Yeeichi Kuwayama, for example, already held a Princeton bachelor's degree in politics, economics, and history before the war and afterward earned a Harvard MBA and went to work for the Securities and

Exchange Commission. Victor Izui went to dental school; Wallace Kagawa became an architect; Virgil Westdale, who had legally changed his surname from
Nishimura, became a chemical engineer; Susumu Ito earned a PhD in biology
and then did postdoctoral work in cytogenetics at a German university before
joining the faculty at Harvard; and Daniel Inouye wound up spending almost a
half century as a US congressman and senator from Hawaii.[41]

NOTES

1. For a more complete coverage of this topic, see James M. McCaffrey, *Going for
Broke: Japanese American Soldiers in the War with Nazi Germany* (Norman: University of
Oklahoma Press, 2013).

2. Interview with Nelson Akagi, August 15, 2002, The Go for Broke Educational
Foundation, Tape 2. All of the interviews by the Go For Broke Educational Foundation
cited in this chapter may be found at www.goforbroke.org/oral_histories/oral_histories
_hanashi.asp. Interview with Irving Akahoshi, November 18, 2000, The Go for Broke
Educational Foundation, Tape 1.

3. Tomi Kaizawa Knaefler, *Our House Divided: Seven Japanese American Families in
World War II* (Honolulu: University of Hawaii Press, 1991), 9; Hawaii Nikkei History
Editorial Board, comp., *Japanese Eyes American Heart: Personal Reflections of Hawaii's World
War II Nisei Soldiers* (Honolulu: Tendai Educational Foundation, 1998), quotation on 86.

4. J. Franklin Odo, *No Sword to Bury: Japanese Americans in Hawai'i during World
War II* (Philadelphia: Temple University Press, 2004), first quotation on 127; John
Tsukano, *Bridge of Love* (Honolulu: Hawaii Hosts, 1985), second quotation on 54.

5. Kiyoshi Harry Shimizu, *Proving Our Loyalty: The World War II Story of a Young
Nisei Infantryman Fighting for His Country in the Hundredth Battalion* (n.p.: ca. 1995), 2.

6. Greg Robinson, *By Order of the President: FDR and the Internment of Japanese
Americans* (Cambridge, MA: Harvard University Press, 2001), 84–87.

7. "How to Tell Japs from the Chinese," *Life*, December 22, 1941, 81–82.

8. Milton Caniff, "How to Spot a Jap," *Pocket Guide to China* (Washington, DC: War
and Navy Departments, 1942), 66. www.ep.tc/howtospotajap/howto04.html.

9. Bill Hosokawa, *Nisei: The Quiet Americans* (Boulder: University Press of Colorado,
2002), first quotation on 230; Nobo Ikuta, "My Many Steps from Childhood to
Adulthood," in *And Then There Were Eight: The Men of I Company 442nd Regimental
Combat Team* (Honolulu: 442nd Veterans Club, 2003), second quotation on 157.

10. Mike Masaoka and Bill Hosokawa, *They Call Me Moses Masaoka: An American
Saga* (New York: William Morrow, 1987), 78.

11. Betty E. Mitson, "Looking Back in Anguish: Oral History and Japanese-American
Evacuation," *The Oral History Review* 2 (1974): first quotation on 40; Congressman
Rankin of Mississippi, *Congressional Record*—House, 77th Congress, 2nd Sess. Vol. 88,
pt. 1, second quotation on p. 1419, Feb. 18, 1942; Arvarh E. Strickland, "Remembering
Hattiesburg: Growing Up Black in Wartime Mississippi," in Neil R. McMillen, ed.,
*Remaking Dixie: The Impact of World War II on the American South* (Jackson: University

Press of Mississippi, 1997), third quotation on 91; Eric L. Muller, *Free to Die for Their Country: The Story of the Japanese American Draft Resisters in World War II* (Chicago: University of Chicago Press, 2001), fourth quotation on 23.

12. Masaoka and Hosokawa, *They Call Me Moses Masaoka*, 60.

13. Muller, *Free to Die for Their Country*, 23.

14. Hawaii Nikkei History Editorial Board, *Japanese Eyes American Heart*, 57–58.

15. Dorothy Matsuo, *Boyhood to War: History and Anecdotes of the 442nd RCT* (Honolulu: Mutual Publishing, 1982), first quotation on 53; Charles Shigeru Ota, "A Tale of One Soldier and His Best Friend," in *And Then There Were Eight*, second quotation on 274; Hosokawa, *Nisei*, 364–365; Minoru Kiyota, "From Beyond Loyalty," in *Only What We Could Carry: The Japanese American Internment Experience*, edited by Lawson Fusao Inada (Berkeley, CA: Heyday Books, 2000), third quotation on 306–307; Interview with Victor Izui, April 29, 2000, The Go For Broke Educational Foundation, fourth quotation on Tape 2.

16. Lyn Crost, *Honor by Fire: Japanese Americans at War in Europe and the Pacific* (Novato, CA: Presidio Press, 1994), 152; Chester Tanaka, *Go for Broke: A Pictorial History of the Japanese American 100th Infantry Battalion and the 442nd Regimental Combat Team* (Richmond, CA: Go For Broke, 1982), 2, 79.

17. Hawaii Nikkei History Editorial Board, *Japanese Eyes American Heart*, 373.

18. Thelma Chang, *"I Can Never Forget": Men of the 100th/442nd* (Honolulu: Sigi Productions, 1991), first quotation on 121; Chang, *"I Can Never Forget,"* second quotation on 124; Hawaii Nikkei History Editorial Board, comp., *Japanese Eyes American Heart*, third quotation on 373.

19. Chang, *"I Can Never Forget,"* 121.

20. *JAVA* [Japanese American Veterans' Association] *Newsletter* 13, no. 2 (April–June 2005); Strickland, "Remembering Hattiesburg," 156.

21. This was Col. Ray C. Fountain. Thomas D. Murphy, *Ambassadors in Arms: The Story of Hawaii's 100th Battalion* (Honolulu: University of Hawaii Press, 1954), 121.

22. Murphy, *Ambassadors in Arms*, 131–132; Audie Murphy, *To Hell and Back* (New York: Henry Holt and Company, 2002[1949]), quotation on 79.

23. Quotation from oral history of Stanley Masaharu Akita, Center for Oral History, University of Hawaii, http://nisei.hawaii.edu/object/io_1158866319689.html; John H. Hougen, *The Story of the Famous 34th Infantry Division* (Nashville, TN: Battery Press, 1989[1949]), 79; Murphy, *Ambassadors in Arms*, 137.

24. Takashi Matsui, "Teaching at the Military Intelligence Service Language School," in *American Patriots: MIS in the War Against Japan*, edited by Stanley L. Falk and Warren M. Tsuneishi (Washington, DC: Japanese American Veterans Association of Washington, DC, 1995), 4; Interview with Frank Fukuzawa, February 24, 2001, The Go For Broke Educational Foundation, quotation on Tape 3.

25. Orville C. Shirey, *Americans: The Story of the 442nd Combat Team* (Washington, DC: Infantry Journal, 1946, 1947), 26–28.

26. Daniel K. Inouye and Lawrence Elliot, *Journey to Washington* (Englewood Cliffs, NJ: Prentice-Hall, 1967), quotation on 102; Asaya Naguwa, "Monte's Life," in *And Then There Were Eight*, 242; Tooru Joe Kanazawa, *Close Support: A History of The Cannon Company of the 442nd Regimental Combat Team* (Self-published, 1993), 12–13.

27. Homer R. Ankrum, *Dogfaces Who Smiled through Tears: The 34th Red Bull Infantry Division and Attached 100th (Hawaiian) Battalion and 442nd "Go For Broke" Regimental Combat Team in World War II: A Chronicle of Heartbreaks, Hardships, Heroics, and Humor of the North African and Italian Campaigns* (Lake Mills, IA: Graphic Publishing Company, 1987), quotation on 526.

28. Robert H. Adleman and George Walton, *The Champagne Campaign* (Boston: Little, Brown, 1969), first quotation on 43; Gerard M. Devlin, *Silent Wings* (New York: St. Martin's Press, 1985), second quotation on 89–91.

29. Ronald Oba, *The Men of Company F, 442nd Regimental Combat Team*, 2nd ed. (Honolulu: 1993), 58.

30. Colonel Sherwood Dixon saw the use of the 442nd as rescue troops as a compliment. Tsukano, *Bridge of Love*, 270.

31. Roland Shaw Pruette, *Memories of an Infantryman from World War II* (n.p., 1994), 19–20; Albert E. Cowdrey, *Fighting for Life: American Military Medicine in World War II* (New York: The Free Press, 1994), 267.

32. *Honolulu Star-Bulletin*, January 5, 1944, as quoted in Murphy, *Ambassadors in Arms*, 197.

33. Masayo Umezawa Duus, *Unlikely Liberators: The Men of the 100th and 442nd*, translated by Peter Duus (Honolulu: University of Hawaii Press, 1987), 233–234.

34. William Shinji Tsuchidal, *Wear It Proudly: Letters* (Berkeley: University of California Press, 1947), 17.

35. Shirey, *Americans*, 76; Murphy, *Ambassadors in Arms*, 247; James M. Hanley, *A Matter of Honor: A Memoire* (New York: Vantage Press, 1995), 81–82.

36. Ted Tsukiyama, "The 522d Field Artillery Battalion," in *Fire For Effect: A Unit History of the 522 Field Artillery Battalion*, by The Historical Album Committee of the 522 Field Artillery Battalion of the 442 Regimental Combat Team (Honolulu: 522d Field Artillery Battalion Historical Album Committee, 1998), 62; Knaefler, *Our House Divided*, 40; Matsuo, *Boyhood to War*, 208.

37. Knaefler, *Our House Divided*, first quotation on 40; Brendan Phibbs, *The Other Side of Time: A Combat Surgeon in World War II* (Boston: Little, Brown, 1987), second quotation on 319.

38. "Nisei Veterans Participate in Houston JACL Tribute to Japanese Americans in WWII." www.javadc.org/Press%20release%2005-06-05%20NISEI%20VETERANS%20PARTICIPATE%20IN%20HOUSTON%20JACL%20TRIBUTE%20.HTM.

39. Crost, *Honor by Fire*, 305–306.

40. Crost, *Honor by Fire*, quotations on 301; Hawaii Nikkei History Editorial Board, *Japanese Eyes American Heart*, 398.

41. Rudi Williams, "Japanese American War Hero Recalls Life During World War II," American Forces Information Service News Article, May 25, 2000. www.defenselink.mil/news/May2000/n05252000_20005252.html. Interview with Victor Izui, April 29, 2000, The Go For Broke Educational Foundation, Tape 5; Interview with Wallace Kagawa, June 9, 1999, The Go For Broke Educational Foundation, Tape 4; Interview with Virgil Westdale, June 30, 2002, The Go For Broke Educational Foundation, Tape 6; Interview with Susumu Ito, January 23, 2000, The Go For Broke Educational Foundation, Tape 8.

# 3

## Does the Sex of the Practitioner Matter?

Nursing, Civil Rights, and Discrimination in the
Army Nurse Corps, 1947–1955

CHARISSA THREAT

The Pentagon's decision in 2013 to integrate women into combat roles
represented the culmination of a long struggle by women to achieve equality
in the military; however, Charissa Threat shows that the fight for gender
equality has not always focused on opening traditionally male jobs to women.
During the 1940s and 1950s, Congress and the Pentagon debated whether men
should be allowed to join the Army Nurse Corps, and the controversy revealed
how gender roles from civilian life shaped the military. Opponents argued that
men were supposed to be fighters and women were supposed to be caregivers.
Female officers in the Army Nurse Corps embraced this argument because
they feared that once men were allowed to become nurses, they would push
women out of leadership roles. At the same time, men seeking to work in
traditionally feminine fields such as nursing were suspected of being unmanly
or homosexuals. The personnel needs of the military, as seen in other
chapters, ultimately led to the integration of men into the Army Nurse Corps
Reserve, but only after nursing shortages coupled with concerns about the
proximity of female nurses to combat provided a place for men in military
nursing.[1]

In a May 1952 letter to the *New York Times*, Registered Nurse (RN) Morris Wolf
lamented the ongoing rejection of male nurses who wished to serve in the
Armed Forces Nurse Corps. Male nurses, Morris pointed out, had the same education and training as most of the female nurses who joined the armed services.
But because of their sex, they could not join the Nurse Corps. Morris ended his
letter by asking readers if the "sex of the practitioner matter[ed]" in the care of men
and women in the armed services and their families. His question highlights a

longstanding gender division of labor that persisted in both the civilian and military nursing profession well into the postwar period. This chapter examines the period between the late 1940s, when female nurses received recognition as full military personnel after a struggle that went back to the beginning of the twentieth century, and the mid-1950s, when men finally gained acceptance into the Army Nurse Corps (ANC). The recognition of female nurses as full military personal renewed male nurses' resolve to serve within the ranks of the ANC. At the same time, it revealed female nurses' worry about loss of opportunities should men join their ranks. In the ensuing debates, both sides used gender roles to support their points. After providing a brief overview of the gendered division of labor in nursing and the push to allow female nurses to become regular members of the army, this chapter investigates this debate to understand why men prevailed in the ANC and to shed light on the role gender played in military nursing during the Cold War.

### Gendered Obligations: Nursing and Military Service in Wartime

Since the end of nineteenth century, ideas about gender have influenced the nursing profession and the practice and identity of caregiving. Gender is defined by the socially constructed characteristics or traits that differentiate individuals based on biological sex. "Historically, nursing has been a profession largely connected to women and seen as an extension of women's allegedly inherent nurturing qualities and duties performed within the home. Well into the twentieth century, as Susan Reverby has observed, training and wage earning potential did not alter, 'the assumption that [nursing work] was based on womanly duty requiring service to others.'"[2] Military nursing developed along these lines. Women encompassed the realm of the caregiver or noncombatant and men that of soldier or combatant. Male nurses challenged this delineation and the belief that men had no role in the military outside the combat zone. The tension between these two understandings becomes more apparent following World War II.

The passage of the 1947 Army-Navy Nurse Act provided female nurses full military recognition, with benefits and a professional future. Permanent inclusion in the military also confirmed for female nurses that caregiving was a universally understood duty of women inside and outside of the home.[3] This recognition for female nurses, however, coexisted with the ongoing rejection of male nurses and the gendered belief that men had no role in caregiving. Attempts by nurse activists and several congressional representatives to strike the word "female" from the1947 law found little support.[4] Almost all agreed that nursing needed to be a permanent part of the Army Medical Department, but few supported the idea that both women and men should serve within nursing ranks. The refusal of Congress or the military to support the removal of "female" from the law in 1947 underscored the gender of "nurse" as female. In the postwar period, this refusal and responses to it provide scholars the opportunity to examine the role of the military in larger conversations about discrimination, integration, and equality. What the male nurse campaign reveals is a civil rights experience beyond racial difference foreshadowing the expansive social justice campaigns of postwar America.

The campaign to integrate men into the ANC was not new in the postwar period; it was part of a conversation about male nurses and military service that had existed since the founding of the ANC in 1901. At the onset, strong lobbying by women and civilian nurse activists succeeded in restricting the Nurse Corps, an auxiliary with the Army Medical Department, to women.[5] Their argument for a female-only nurse corps reflected the appropriation of nursing as a female duty, responsibility, and obligation that superseded private and public boundaries in the late nineteenth century. This did not mean that male nurses ceased to practice nursing. In the first decades of the twentieth century, the few men in nursing were largely restricted to psychiatric institutions, asylums, and a few other small areas of the evolving civilian nursing profession. Nevertheless, male nurses continued to push for acceptance among civilian professions and within the military nursing infrastructure.

By the advent of World War II, the question of integrating male nurses into the armed forces gained some traction with the passage of the Selective Services Act of 1940. The act mandated the drafting of all eligible men between the ages of twenty-one and thirty-five. Male nurses saw in the Selective Services Act the opportunity to use their training in aiding the war effort. Even with desperate nursing needs from the beginning of the war, the possibility of male nurse integration diminished as the war continued. Commenting on this failure early in the war, one male nurse lamented, "male nurses expect to assume their part of the country's defense with the rest of the men . . . [but] their proper place in national defense is denied them."[6] Throughout the war, gender ideals hindered men's access to the ANC. Yet similar gender ideals helped African American female nurses mount a successful campaign against race discrimination in their employment in the ANC. African American female nurses used the typing of nursing as a female occupation to argue against race restrictions that kept the number of black female nurses serving in the armed forces well below the number of qualified and available nurses in the country. By 1945, both the Army and Navy Nurse Corps had ended all restrictions in employing these women.[7] For male nurses, however, the Army Medical Department, the surgeon general, and even the American Red Cross argued that male nurses had opportunities to work as medical technicians or corpsmen that allowed them to use their training without complicating the administrative organization of the ANC or the daily duties of army nurses.[8] What was unsaid, but significant, was an assumption about just what type of man would demand to work in a job traditionally viewed as feminine.

Scholars such as Allen Berube, Leisa Meyer, Margot Canaday, and Timothy Stewart-Winter have noted the marked increase in concerns about homosexuality in the ranks of the armed forces during World War II.[9] In fact, in early 1941, Tracy J. Putnam, a neurologist, wrote to members of the Committee on Neuropsychiatry suggesting rearranging the way draft board examiners classified men as fit or unfit for service based on personality deviations, including appearance and behaviors leaning towards homosexual proclivities. While aware of the possibility of homosexual behavior or sexual perversion within military ranks before World War II, the military lacked a clear definition of either and therefore had no clear policies to deal with them. By 1940, however, psychiatrists had begun listing effeminate traits and mannerisms, among others, to help establish clear characterizations of deviant behavior; it was to these definitions that Putnam made his recommendations to the military in 1941.[10] Working in a field traditionally characterized as feminine left male nurses particularly susceptible to charges of homosexuality and, as Berube points out, "stigmatized as sissies" for being "attracted to women's work.[11] Yet at the same time, members of the War Neuroses Subcommittee, psychiatrists, and other doctors argued for the availability of "psychiatrically trained male nurses" as especially needed in the care of soldiers dealing with severe psychological trauma. In early 1941, they recommend that the Red Cross enroll these male nurses for army service.[12] Regardless of their sexuality, male nurses found themselves in difficult position, struggling to find a place between the nurse and soldier divide. By war's end, male nurse integration into the Army Nurse Corps remained where it had been before the war; male nurses continued to serve in the US Army in a variety of areas, including within the medical departments but not within the ANC.

## Gender Equality and the Campaigns for Male Nurse Integration

The push for the integration of male nurses into the ranks of the Army Nurse Corps gained strength from circumstances in the late 1940s. These circumstances included the possibility of war between the United States and the Soviet Union, the reinstatement of the universal draft in March 1948, the passage of Truman's Integration Act, and even the strengthening of the civil rights movement. While nursing activists did not cite the Integration Act or the draft directly as a reason to end restrictions on male nursing in the ANC, there was a marked increase in their campaign after 1948.[13] In late 1949, the American Nurses' Association notified the Army Nurse Corps that it intended to support legislation to permit the commissioning of male nurses.[14] They argued that the inclusion of men in the ANC was necessary to ensure an adequate reserve of care providers. Nurse activists hoped that the permanency of the ANC and the president's support of nondiscrimination in the armed forces would finally translate to success for integrating male nurses. For these activists, integration was a broad ideal that would strengthen the United States and its military in a time of growing global tensions.

Female nurses tempered male nurse hopes of integrating the ANC at the start of the new decade. In response to the American Nurses' Association's announcement in 1949, Colonel Mary G. Phillips, chief of the ANC, solicited comments from nurse officers on the inclusion of men within their ranks.[15] By early 1950, Philips had received dozens of responses. These responses expressed concerns about the addition of male nurses and outlined the possible effects that male nurses might have on the life and work experiences of female nurse officers.[16] Female nurse officers also revealed that plenty was at stake for them. Women dominated only one area in the military: the Nurse Corps. It was the one space that women had carved out to participate in the nation's defense. As Lt. Colonel Katherine Jolliffe suggested, the ANA's move was "not much of a surprise," but "I am sure it is something we have all hoped would never really come up."[17] Jolliffe's response, similar to others, revealed the trepidation that some women felt about the inclusion of men in an occupation that female nurses had struggled to claim and professionalize. By keeping male nurses out of the Army Nurse Corps, female nurses hoped to protect their economic security and professional autonomy.

Female nurses expected only a few advantages from including male nurses in the Army Nurse Corps.[18] First, the majority of respondents agreed that men could fill existing vacancies in the corps. This would make the ANC more efficient and mean that the military could use male nurses in conflict zones, where many doubted that women could live and work. Second, most female officers agreed that assigning male nurses to patient care that mirrored what male nurses did in civilian hospitals would be advantageous to both patients and their providers.[19] Finally, a few nurses conceded that there were no good reasons male nurses should not join the Army Nurse Corps. Lt. Col. Ruby Bryant, for example, pointed out that because the "majority of patients in Army hospitals are male patients . . . the sex of a nurse should be of no consequence so long as efficient nursing care is rendered."[20] These opinions were in the minority, however. Most female nurse officers adamantly believed that the acceptance of men would negatively affect the Nurse Corps.

Female nurses' objections clearly defended women's gains in a male-dominated milieu, especially because they understood the tangible differences in the treatment of men and women in the armed forces. They were alarmed at possible distinctions between duty assignments, responsibilities, and benefits for male and female nurses. Female nurses who wished to join the ANC, for example, could not be married or have dependent children under the age of eighteen. Those already serving in the ANC needed army approval to marry.[21] Women could not receive dependent pay unless they could prove their spouse was completely dependent upon them. Finally, single female nurses stayed in nurses' quarters, where the chief nurse saw that "the morale of the nurses is kept at a high standard."[22] In contrast, male officers could marry, have dependents, and receive dependent pay and allowance for housing. Single men in the army had the option of staying in single officers' housing or living off base.[23] Thus, morale figured high on the list of disadvantages to male nurse inclusion. Many officers believed that female nurses would become dissatisfied if men were treated advantageously. This was a real possibility, if, according to one nurse, one considers that the least attractive assignments—caring for women and obstetrics—might become the sole responsibility of women. Assignment to these areas indicated monotony, little flexibility, and few opportunities to provide service across the Army Nurse Corps and Army Medical Department. Given accepted gender notions of intimate care and male and female responsibilities, female nurses believed it unlikely that male nurses would be assigned to these areas. Major Francis C. Gunn put it succinctly when she wrote, "Utilization of male nurses I feel is going to prove to be a source of annoyance to female nurses" and "will ultimately lead to dissatisfaction among the female nurses."[24] In short, the inclusion of male nurses would come at the risk of alienating the majority of nurses, women.

After a long struggle to find a permanent place within the Medical Department hierarchy, women were extremely protective of an occupation in which they had established autonomy and authority. Nursing was a rare occupation where women, regardless of race, assumed some power over men. Unfortunately, while protecting their domain, these women supported the preservation of the same gendered system they had fought. Lt. Colonel Rosalie D. Colhoun, for example, wrote that, "the recent war convinced most doctors, as well as the patients, that the female nurse inspired and contributed comfort and courage, which the male nurse could not give."[25] Lt. Col. Augusta L. Short pointed out that the "male population of the Army are the greatest objectors . . . [because] any place where a male nurse would be better, we have well-trained enlisted men."[26] Colhoun's and Short's focus on the alleged deficiencies of male nurses was not new. Nursing advocates had used this gendered argument to establish the Nurse Corps as female.

Colhoun's and Short's objective was to bolster the position of female nurses and, more importantly, to keep men out of their organization. They used gender roles to make their argument: Men would not work well within this female environment, nor did they really have a right to. Major Mabel G. Stott was even more emphatic when she questioned the ability of men to take orders from women. "What would be the attitude of male officers serving under the command and leadership of female officers?" She "felt that male officers would [not] be satisfied, happy, or co-operative in serving under this authority."[27] Assuming their institution was under attack, some female officers claimed that the wider nursing profession did not truly support male nurse integration but that a small minority pursued the issue. Lt. Col. Short, for example, ended her letter to the chief of the Army Nurse Corps by stating: "Miss Dietrich does not believe that changing the law to include male nurses is the opinion of the ANA but it is because the male Section is bringing pressure on them."[28] Again, Short's stress on the push for male nurse integration coming from a minority within the nursing profession suggests a general gender division in the belief of who can and should nurse.

If the female nurse officers' judgments on accepting male nurses into the organization revealed their determination to protect their own authority and economic security, even more so did their recommendations for alternatives, which reiterated the gendered nature of the profession and focused on protecting women's position within it. Many nurse officers suggested that the addition of men would lead to a loss of authority for women. Lt. Col. Colhoun worried, for example, that although men "would eventually expect to hold administrative positions . . . this would be resented by the majority of female nurses."[29] To protect themselves, many of the female officers recommended that the chief of the Nurse Corps should always be female, as should the chief nurse at each hospital and each unit. Since women made up the majority of the organization and since the duties of chief nurses encompassed much more than nursing, these officers believed that requiring female leadership would be the most practical solution if males joined the organization.[30]

The female nurse officers further suggested three options intended to keep men as a minority in the organization. These options, evoking memories of the policies limiting black female nurses during World War II, attempted to institutionalize a marginal role for men in the profession and hinted at concessions meant to sustain the status quo. First, they suggested that male nurses be reservists, commissioned only in the event of emergencies. This allowed men short-term duty tours but no permanent place in the Nurse Corps. This would deny male nurses job security, and it revealed a distinct lack of respect from the female nurse officers. Second, and even more disconcerting, was the suggestion of a quota system that based the number of males nurses accepted into the Nurse Corps on the "estimated needs and positions to which male nurses may be assigned to the best advantage."[31] The idea that the army could set parameters by which only the smallest percentage of men would be used as nurses, even when nursing shortages were great, was profoundly reminiscent of the experiences of African American female nurses earlier in the century.[32] Finally, several nurses suggested that male nurses receive commissions in alternate areas of the Medical Department. They looked to the Medical Allied Science or Sanitary Engineering Sections as places where male nurses could use their training and gain officer status. In these areas, male nurses would gain the recognition and status they desperately wanted, but they would not be members of the Army Nurse Corps.

While the chief of the ANC continued to receive responses from her officers, members of Congress moved to introduce legislation to integrate men into the Army Nurse Corps. In August 1950, Congresswoman Frances Payne Bolton introduced H.R. 9398, a bill "to provide for the appointment of male citizens as nurses in the Army, Navy, and Air Force, and for other purposes."[33] Bolton, a longtime advocate of the nursing profession, had devoted both her personal and professional resources to professionalizing nursing, including the integration of men and minority women in both civilian and military nursing.[34] She had unsuccessfully introduced similar legislation on several occasions throughout the 1940s.[35] This new bill, however, had the momentum of the successful Army-

Navy Nurse Act of 1947, strong support from national nursing groups, and mounting Cold War tensions. Bolton and the American Nurses' Association hoped these factors and well-placed campaigns would make the 1950 bill a triumph.[36] Initially, the surgeon general's response was favorable. He stated that the Department of the Army was not opposed to the enactment of the bill but was studying the subject closely.

From every indication early in the process, it appeared that male nurses would finally gain acceptance into the Nurse Corps without many of the limitations suggested by female nurses. Male nurses rejoiced at what they viewed as the most "progressive action" taken to date on their behalf. RN Earl McDowell wrote that he hoped the passage of Bolton's Bill would finally end "sex discrimination" and prove how invaluable male nurses were to the Army Nurse Corps.[37] With the United States involved in the Korean War, the passage of such a bill seemed imminent since the army faced nursing shortages.[38]

Lobbying, including the opinions and information about male nurse integration received from female nurse officers, effectively diminished the momentum of the support for male nurses. In October 1950, the Department of Defense and Army announced it had reconsidered its initial opinion on the matter. The Department of Defense reported to Carl Vinson, chairman of the Committee on Armed Services, that it opposed ratification of H.R. 9398. All three branches of the military, in fact, rejected the male nurse bill. Although each branch suggested that the major reasoning behind this decision centered on the Army-Navy Nurse Act of 1947, equally apparent was the continued negative view of male nurses and the championing of gender-specific occupations. In fact, Colonel Mildred I. Clark remembers that many in the public and military viewed male nurses as having "something wrong with 'em."[39] Military officials argued that the 1947 changes to the Army-Navy Nurse Act rested, in part, on the assumption that the Nurse Corps would remain a female-only group.

The Army Nurse Corps serves as a good example of the social instability in postwar America. Cold War fears, coupled with a growing civil rights movement and the reality of combat in the Korean War era, made the subject of integration about more than the racial desegregation in the ANC. The long-debated question of male nurses continued even after the 1950 and 1951 attempts by Congresswoman Bolton and the American Nurses' Association to alter sex restrictions stalled in the Armed Services Committee. Beyond ensuring a unified military by desegregation, as the country moved into the 1950s, the defense of the nation also meant re-evaluating how gender shaped opportunities in the United States military. For the Army Nurse Corps, that meant re-evaluating the placement of female nurses near combat. For example, while the chief of the Army Nurse Corps' Far East Command commended the job of her nurses in the Far East, she reminded newspaper readers that "in oriental warfare, woman nurses have no place near the battlefront . . . bitter experiences prove the enemy ruthless and unprincipled—we know too well what would happen if nurses were captured."[40] Her opinion that army nurses were "a distinct liability and hazard to themselves and the troops" was just the sort of information that male nurse supporters needed to continue pressing their own cause in the early 1950s.[41] Comments such as these were dangerous to the future of any women who wanted to serve her country; they suggested that women should be confined to only the most protected locations. The Army Nurse Corps and military historically had been able to reassure those who worried about women's proximity to combat by guaranteeing that nurses were protected well behind front lines. The capture of nurses in the South Pacific during World War II, however, shattered this imagined safety net.[42] These circumstances tested the conventional and traditional understanding that nursing was best suited to the females of the population.

Male nurses and their supporters also decried what they viewed as a double standard employed by the military. RN Morris Wolf reminded readers that the Armed Services "have recognized the existence and professional equality of women physicians by granting them officers' rank and status."[43] Shortly after Wolf's letter to the *New York Times*, Public Law 408 allowed for the appointment of qualified women physicians to the army, navy, and air force in 1952.[44] It seemed that the military had resolved many of the arguments about legal barriers and administrative problems associated with the integration of female physicians into male-dominated medical areas; why not do the same for male nurses? Female nurse officers used the same excuses for the impracticality of male nurse integration to their benefit, pointing out that the jobs of the nurse and doctor were not the same in either responsibilities or interactions with patients. Furthermore, the passage of Public Law 408 did not actually mean equal treatment between female and male physicians. For example, women physicians, like female nurses, had to prove that their husbands and children were completely dependent upon them before the military would grant the female officer dependency pay. This was not something that male officers had to prove. The same gender stereotypes remained: Men needed the dependency pay because they were the family breadwinner, while married women did not.[45] Nevertheless, by mid-1952, the army as well as the other branches of the military did accept female physicians in both their reserve corps and as part of the regular military. So what was different, then, about male nurses? Did the "sex of the practitioner matter?" asked Morris.

Certainly, this was the question that male nurses and their supporters repeatedly asked in their campaign and pointedly answered in the negative. An even more important question and point here, however, is that the failure to integrate male nurses highlights not only an underlying fear about blurring gender roles but also the gender inequalities most often experienced by women in the military and civilian society. As African American female nurses had before them, male nurses wanted acceptance and recognition based on their professional training, not some biological factor they could not change. Nevertheless, attached to American understandings of biological difference was automatic access to benefits not available to their female nurses. Would demand for recognition and acceptance as nurse officers also mean male nurses *expected* the same benefits afforded other male military officers?[46] When female nurses were questioned on this subject many answered in the affirmative, believing the male nurses would expect the same benefits provided to male officers of similar rank in other jobs with the army.

Male nurses and their supporters changed the strategy of their campaign in the wake of negative reports from the Department of Defense by responding to gender issues and emphasizing their masculinity. After several attempts to pass a bill granting commissions to male nurses in the armed forces, Frances Bolton suggested two ways of getting commissions for male nurses. The first was a suggestion that several female nurse officers made during the 1950 campaign. Bolton suggested to the chair of the Armed Services Committee that he consider male nurses for the position of medical assistants. The medical assistant was an officer who served as the administrative assistant to the medical officer. The position required the person to have a medical background, as often the assistant helped the medical officer in emergencies. Bolton believed that such a position would fit the skills and training of male nurses. As an added bonus; they could serve as assistant battalion surgeons at aid stations just behind front lines. This would solve the problem of placing female nurses at the front lines while at the same time relieving fears about territorial overlap with female nurses. Furthermore, it would guarantee that the army could suspend commissioning underqualified men with little more than six weeks' training as medical assistants. Ultimately, Bolton's change in strategy reflected an acknowledgment that the greatest obstacle to male nurse integration remained the fact that in the eyes of many, male nurses were the wrong sex for caregiving.[47]

Unlike African American female nurses, who could and did successfully argue that regardless of race they were women and thus rightful caregivers, male nurses, hindered by gender conventions, faced the implication of being "crooked" or unseemly men. The specter of homosexuality was an even more prevalent concern within the framework of Cold War domesticity as heterosexuality and traditional gender roles became another place in the frontline defense against Communist infiltration. Therefore, the military, the extreme representation of societal beliefs and values, remained firmly entrenched in the perception of the "fiction of the women's touch," as one male RN labeled it.[48] High-ranking military officers perpetuated this stereotype. One medical officer remarked to the chief of the ANC, "when I get sick I want a nurse that will bring a woman's touch and if it is a male nurse that brings a woman's touch, I don't want him."[49] The sense that something was wrong with male nurses underlined the pervasive anxiety about homosexuality among military and civilian society. The military command, like many in civilian society, feared that male nurses were in fact sexual deviants propagating taboo behavior. Congresswomen Bolton clearly understood this when she suggested her compromise to Chairman Vinson.

> I am aware of the thought in the minds of many high officials that male nurses exhibit a high incidence of homosexuality, and that this would be a tragic thing for the armed forces. Actually . . . the incidence of sexual deviants among this group was no higher, was lower in fact, than among other groups . . . The charge is certainly unfair to the overwhelming percentage of well adjusted normal healthy male nurses.[50]

By stressing the normality of male nurses and, earlier in the letter, the use of these nurses as medical assistants, Bolton hoped to get male nurses commissioned in a way that made everyone comfortable with their presence. In other words, as the specific gendered connotations attached to the definition of nurses made men's role in this profession suspicious, Bolton hoped renaming their duties would led to officers' commissions. Bolton introduced no bill to support this suggestion, however, and male nurses who attempted to gain commissions through the Medical Service Corps failed.[51] Bolton's only option was to reintroduce the bill to commission men in the Army Nurse Corps.

Bolton's second strategy for the appointment of male nurses into the ANC shifted the focus away from the regular army to the reserve corps. In theory, the army used the reserve corps in times of emergency or personnel shortages. As with her suggestion to commission male nurses as medical assistants, the shift to commission in the reserve corps was viewed as a preliminary step in gaining male nurses recognition in the military. In early 1954, Bolton addressed the House of Representatives to introduce the bill that would authorize the appointment of male nurses as reserve officers. Unlike her previous attempts, the new bill had some support from the Department of Defense. It would focus on all three branches of the military and was not mandatory: It did not force any branch to accept the change but allowed them to use the new law to bolster their numbers in times of peace and war. Bolton and male nurse leader LeRoy Craig pointed out that the passage of such a bill would help increase the supply of nurses to the armed forces, especially during emergencies. It would also reduce the drain on civilian nursing and would help increase the number of men enrolled in nursing schools.[52] In light of the recent hostilities in Korea and the shortages of nurses in both civilian hospitals and in the military, proponents believed that appointing male nurses in the reserve corps was the best and most forward-thinking move the armed forces could take. Interestingly, events taking place outside both the military and the United States helped strengthen support for the bill.

Half a world away, the fall of Dien Bien Phu in 1954 provided some additional support for the argument in favor of male nurses.[53] Among those who faced the horrifying events that unfolded at the fortress was a stranded female airborne nurse. The experiences of this nurse, later known as the "Angel of Dien Bien Phu," represented to Bolton and others the single most important reason for training and accepting male nurses: the possibility of placing women's lives in jeopardy. This was not a new argument about gender conventions and responsibilities in the military. The very same argument had gained attention during the early part of the Korean hostilities, when the question about nurses in combat emerged in public discourse. Bolton, however, saw the Dien Bien Phu incident as a needed dose of reality for those who still argued against the addition of male nurses. After all, the army was lucky to have avoided similar circumstances in Korea, but this might not be the case in the future. No "young women of 29 [should] witness the tragedy of the wounded of Dien Bien Phu," Bolton reminded Congress. Instead, in times of war, male nurse reserve officers could be called upon to "apply their training in areas where we should never ask a woman to serve."[54] In short, Bolton relied on the old argument that the defense of the nation and the protection of female nurses demanded the addition of male nurses. This was one argument and viewpoint that male nurses and supporters had promoted since World War II, although with little success.

In the summer of 1955, several merging factors succeeded in finally getting the bill passed by Congress. According to Nurse Corps historians, major factors included the continuing difficulty of recruiting female nurses into the armed forces during the postwar period, the backing of professional nursing organizations, and the support of individual nursing activists. These factors, however, were not the sole reasons the Bolton Bill of 1955 finally passed. Instead, these factors, coupled with the manipulation of fears, beliefs, and events during the postwar period, eliminated the remaining barriers and prejudices against male nurses in the Army Nurse Corps. Male nurses remained suspect to many, but Bolton, LeRoy Craig, and others could and did play on fears about nursing shortages, strong beliefs that women should never face combat, and Cold War tensions to negotiate men into the Army Nurse Corps.[55] Bolton went even further to connect the male nurse question to a larger debate and fight over discrimination and equal rights taking place in the United States.[56]

Bolton viewed the passage of what she later identified as "my equal rights for men bill," in much the same way she viewed the end to barriers for African American female nurses a decade earlier. In fact, she understood discrimination against male nurses as one more case of inequality in the profession that had to be remedied for the health of the entire country. By recognizing the legitimate place of male nurses in the Army Nurse Corps, Bolton hoped the legislation would help end discrimination in the occupation as a whole. While she saw this as an example of a reversal in "the normal problem of discrimination between men and women in the occupations," she did not view it as any less discriminatory.[57] Instead, she focused on the fact that there was a place and need for every qualified, trained nurse within the nursing profession; out-of-date beliefs on race and gender capabilities had no role in the modern profession. Responding to Bolton's view on gender equality, one reader responded, "she is probably right . . . If we're going to have equality of the sexes, it must work both ways."[58]

Examining the experiences of female and male nurses and military service complicates traditional understanding of the social justice movements that emerged in the postwar period. It would be easy to define gender equality as a women's issue that emerged in its modern incarnation during the second-wave feminist movement of the 1960s and 1970s, yet military nursing suggests a broader history that affected both men and women. Additionally, integration, often defined solely in terms of race, becomes part of larger questions of gender roles and responsibilities, citizenship obligations, and military service when examined through the lens of military nursing in the postwar civil rights period. While gender integration will remain a decisive issue for years to come, recent changes in the military's policies on women in combat units suggest that the US military continues to respond to the changing nature of warfare, changing gender ideals, and the changing social and cultural beliefs that shape our society. Far from examining this change within the isolation of military history, military nursing provides a unique space to reevaluate our understandings of some of the most pressing issues at debate in the latter half of the twentieth century.

NOTES

1. From *Nursing Civil Rights: Gender and Race in the Army Nurse Corps.* Copyright 2015 by the Board of Trustees of the University of Illinois. Used with permission of the University of Illinois Press.

2. Charissa Threat, "'The Hands That Might Save Them': Gender, Race, and the Politics of Nursing during World War II," *Gender and History* 24, no. 2 (August 2012): 458.

3. Earl Lomon Koos, "What Society Demands of the Nurse," *American Journal of Nursing* 47, no. 5 (May 1947): 306.

4. Margaret Chase Smith actually introduced the 1947 bill, but Frances P. Bolton had suggested the striking of "female" from the law. This was in line with her goal of opening the Armed Forces Nurses Corps and expanding the nursing profession to women and men of all races, creeds, and ethnicities. Mary Sarnecky, *A History of the US Army Nurse Corps* (Philadelphia: University of Pennsylvania Press, 1999), 219–292.

5. Sarnecky, *A History of the US Army Nurse Corps*, 49–58.

6. "Nurse or Soldier," *American Journal of Nursing* 4 (December 1941): 1449. Quoted in Threat, "The Hands That Might Save Them," 463.

7. Darlene Clark Hine, *Black Women in White: Racial Conflict and Cooperation in the Nursing Profession 1890–1950* (Bloomington: Indiana University Press, 1989), and Threat, "The Hands That Might Save Them."

8. Threat, "The Hands That Might Save Them," 461–465.

9. Allen Berube, *Coming Out under Fire: The History of Gay Men and Women during World War II* (New York: Free Press, 2000); Leisa D. Meyer, *Creating GI Jane: Sexuality and Power in the Women's Army Corps during World War II* (New York: Columbia University Press, 1998); Timothy Stewart-Winter, "Not a Soldier, Not a Slacker: Conscientious Objectors and Male Citizenship in the United States during the Second World War," *Gender and History* 19 (November 2007): 519–542; Margot Canaday, *The Straight State: Sexuality and Citizenship in Twentieth-Century America* (Princeton, NJ: Princeton University Press, 2009), 57.

10. Dr. Tracy J. Putnam to members of the Committee on Neuropsychiatry, "Suggested Rearrangements of M-R 1–9 (Sections XIX & XX) and A-R 40–105 (Section XX)," Record Group 215, Entry 61, Box 5, p. 10, National Archives Records Administration (hereafter NARA); and Canaday, *The Straight State*, 57.

11. Berube, *Coming Out under Fire*, 62.

12. The Red Cross did offer enrollment to male nurses but not for acceptance into the Nurse Corps. Instead, men enrolled for placement as medical technicians and corpsmen with the starting rank of private. War Neuroses Subcommittee, "Minutes 1 May 1941," Record Group 215, Entry 61, Box 5, pp. 8–9, NARA. See also Threat, "The Hands That Might Save Them," 461–465.

13. RN Earl McDowell praises Bolton's bill to "eliminate sex discrimination in the Armed forces." "FBP Comments: Nursing-Health," *France Payne Bolton Papers*, Folder 61, pp. 248, 258, and 261, Western Reserve Historical Society (hereafter WRHS), Cleveland, OH; and Earl McDowell to France Bolton [typed ltr.], 1950, *France Payne Bolton Papers*, Folder 140, WRHS, Cleveland, OH; see also "Sex Discrimination," *RN Magazine* 13 (September 1950): 46–59; and "Male, Negro Nurses Urged in Emergency," *New York Times*, March 14, 1951, 8.

14. The American Nurses' Association noted in a summer issue of its journal that steps were being taken to "initiate legislation granting military rank to male nurses." In December 1949, Colonel Mary G. Phillips, chief of the Army Nurse Corps, solicited her chief officers about the possible addition of men in the corps. "Congress Considers Nursing," *American Journal of Nursing* 49, no. 7 (July 1949): 429.

15. Female officers' responses to Colonel Phillips' notification mentioned her December 30, 1949, letter to them. "Gender-Male Nurses," Box 110a, Army Nurse Corps Archives, Office of the Surgeon General (hereafter ANCA, OSG), Falls Church, VA.

16. Colonel Mary G. Phillips's request yielded several dozen letters from female nurse officers. See Boxes 110 and 110a, ANCA, OSG, Falls Church, VA.

17. Lt. Col. Katharine V. Jolliffe to Col. Mary G. Phillips, January 9, 1950, Box 110a, ANCA, OSG, Falls Church, VA.

18. "Acceptance of Male Nurses in Army Nurse Corps" [memo], January 1950, Box 110a, ANCA, OSG, Falls Church, VA.

19. Some of the areas mentioned included psychiatric wards, genitor-urinary clinics, and prison wards. Ibid.; see also Lt. Col. Ruby F. Bryant to Col. Mary G. Phillips, January 6, 1950, Box 110a, ANCA, OSG, Falls Church, VA.

20. Ibid.

21. It was not until 1964 that women who were gaining initial appointment in the ANC could be married and the age of dependents was lowered to fifteen. Sarnecky, *A History of the US Army Nurse Corps*, 272; and Carolyn M. Feller and Constance Moore, *Highlights in the History of the Army Nurse Corps* (Washington, DC: US Army Center of Military History, 1995), 18, 38.

22. Major Naomi J. Jensen to Col. Mary G. Phillips, January 10, 1950; and Lt. Col. Daisy McCommons to Col. Mary G. Phillips, January 18, 1950, Box 110a, ANCA, OSG, Falls Church, VA.

23. Ruby F. Bryant to Colonel H. W. Glattly [memo], July 22, 1952, "Study of Utilizing Graduate Professional Male Nurses Within the Army," Box 110, ANCA, OSG, Falls Church, VA.

24. Major Francis C. Gunn to Col. Mary G. Phillips, January 16, 1950, Box 110a, ANCA, OSG, Falls Church, VA.

25. Lt. Col. Rosalie D. Colhoun to Col. Mary G. Phillips, January 3, 1950, Box 110a, ANCA, OSG, Falls Church, VA.

26. Lt. Col. Augusta L. Short to Col. Mary G. Phillips, January 16, 1950, Box 110a, ANCA, OSG, Falls Church, VA.

27. Stott and Lt. Col. Schneider in another letter stress the traditional view of nursing of the sick as a women's, not men's, prerogative. Major Mabel G. Stott to Col. Mary G. Phillips, January 23, 1950, Box 110a, ANCA, OSG, Falls Church, VA.; see also Lt. Col. Elsie E. Schneider to Col. Mary G. Phillips, January 26, 1950, Box 110a, ANCA, OSG, Falls Church, VA.

28. Short to Phillips, January 16, 1950.

29. Colhoun to Phillips, January 3, 1950.

30. "Acceptance of Male Nurses in Army Nurse Corps" [memo], January 1950, Box 110a, ANCA, OSG, Falls Church, VA.

31. Ibid.

32. Hine, *Black Women in White*, and Threat, "The Hands That Might Save Them."

33. The other purposes of the bill included the "appointment and utilization of qualified male dietitians, physical therapists, and occupational therapists in the Women's Medical Specialist Corps on the same basis as females now appointed therein." Major General R. W. Bliss, Surgeon General [memo], August 31, 1950, Box 110a, ANCA, OSG, Falls Church, VA; see also Congresswoman Frances P. Bolton to Major General R. W. Bliss, Surgeon General, August 14, 1950, Box 110a, ANCA, OGS, Falls Church, VA; and "A Bill," *Frances Payne Bolton Papers*, Folder 140, WRHS, Cleveland, OH.

34. Frances Payne Bolton was a congresswoman from Ohio who was a member of the House of Representatives from 1940–1969. She originally served the remainder of her husband, Chester C. Bolton's, term in the House when he died in 1939.

35. For a detailed discussion of Frances Payne Bolton's legislative attempts, see Susan Cramer Winters, "Enlightened Citizen: Frances Payne Bolton and the Nursing Profession" (PhD dissertation, University of Virginia, 1997), 299–301; and Sarnecky, *A History of the US Army Nurse Corps*, 297.

36. Representatives from the American Nurses' Association among others met with the surgeon general's office and other members of the United States military to discuss the possibility of male nurse inclusion and the provisions of the bill introduced by Congresswoman Bolton. Maj. George Armstrong to Satterlee, Warfield, and Stephens, August 15, 1950, Box 110a, ANCA, OSG, Falls Church, VA.

37. A word on references to gender "discrimination" throughout this chapter: There is some debate about whether male nurses faced discrimination or convention. According to Alice Kessler-Harris, sex discrimination was not acknowledged until after the passage of the 1964 Civil Rights Act. However, the use of the word "discrimination" here refers to the use of the word by male nurses themselves. They employed this language to describe their attempts at fair and equal access to the profession. Male nurses understand discrimination from their own experiences within the profession, not from a larger understanding of the sexual discrimination faced by women. Earl McDowell, RN, to Congresswoman Frances P. Bolton, n.d., *Frances Payne Bolton Papers*, Folder 140, WRHS, Cleveland, OH; see also "Sex Discrimination," *RN Magazine* (September 1950): 60.

38. Hostilities in Korea began on June 25, 1950. "Women and War," *RN Magazine* (October 1950): 56–57.

39. Mildred I. Clark, interviewed by Nancy R. Adams, 1986, Project No. 86-2, transcript, ANC Collection, ANCA, OSG, Falls Church, VA. Secretary of the Army Frank Paco, Jr., to Honorable Carl Vinson, October 5, 1950, Box 110a, ANCA, OSG, Falls Church, VA; and MBH to Bolton [memo], October 17, 1950, *Frances Payne Bolton Papers*, WRHS, Folder 140, Cleveland, OH.

40. There is an underlining sense of racism in the Nurse Corps chief's use of the term "oriental" and her reference to the experiences of nurses during World War II. This is meant to differentiate the respectable and civilized white nurse from the ruthless and unprincipled other.

41. Lt. Col. Alice M. Gritsavage as quoted in Dorothy Brandon, "Calls Army Nurse 'Hazard to Troops,'" *Washington Post*, June 1, 1952, 17; see also Dorothy Brandon, "Men to Replace Nurses Up Front Urged by Korean Nurses' Leader," *New York Herald Tribune*, May 5, 1952, n.p.; and Dorothy Brandon, "Nurses Prove They Can Take Korea in Stride," *New York Herald Tribune*, June 29, 1952.

42. Sixty-eight female nurses were captured by the Japanese in 1942 and held as prisoners of war for two and half years on the island of Santo Tomas. The women reported fear, degradation, unsanitary living conditions, and physical and psychological abuse at the hands of their captors. The country was reminded of this experience when questions were raised about the acceptance and use of male nurses during the Korean War. Sarnecky, *A History of the US Army Nurse Corps*, 186–194.

43. Morris A. Wolf, "Male Nurses in Services," *New York Times*, May 5, 1952, 22.

44. For information on the experiences of women doctors during World War II and the Cold War, see Judith Bellafaire and Mercedes Herrera Graf, *Women Doctors in War* (College Station: Texas A&M University Press, 2009), chapters 3–5; and Linda Witt, Judith Bellafaire, Britts Granrud, and Mary Jo Binker, *A Defense Weapon Known to Be of Value: Servicewomen of the Korean Conflict Era* (Hanover, CT: University Press of New England, 2005): 132–134.

45. The military resolved many of its problems with the commissioning of women physicians, in large part because of the dearth of available doctors. Witt, Bellafaire, Granrud, and Binker, *A Defense Weapon Known to be of Value*, 132–134.

46. Katherine E. Baltz, December 28, 1949, Box 110a, "Policies and Laws Governing Male Nurses," ANCA, OSG, Falls Church, VA.

47. Frances P. Bolton to Honorable Carl Vinson, September 8, 1951, *Frances Payne Bolton Papers*, Folder 140, WRHS, Cleveland, OH.

48. Wolf, "Male Nurses in Services." See also George Chauncey, *Gay New York: Gender, Urban Culture, and the Making of the Gay Male World 1890–1940* (New York: Basic Books, 1994).

49. "Meeting and Workshop at the Historical Unit, Fort Detrick, Maryland," February 3, 1975, ANCA, OSG, Falls Church, VA, 34–35.

50. Bolton to Vinson, September 18, 1951.

51. In August 1953, RN Duane Kirby applied for commission as a medical assistant in the Medical Service Corps but was denied because of "lack of qualifications." Duane W. Kirby to Frances P. Bolton, August 25, 1953, *Frances Payne Bolton Papers*, Folder 141, WRHS, Cleveland, OH.

52. Frances P. Bolton [typed statement], February 16, 1954, "A Bill to Authorize Male Nurses and Medical Specialists to Be Appointed as Reserve Officers," *Frances Payne Bolton Papers*, Folder 141, WRHS, Cleveland, OH; LeRoy N. Craig to Anna M. Rosenberg, February 8, 1952, and March 20, 1952, *France Payne Bolton Papers*, Folder 140, WRHS, Cleveland, OH.

53. Dien Bien Phu was the final battle between the French Union Forces and the Vietnamese Viet Minh Communist revolutionary forces in 1954. It ended with the French defeat and withdrawal from its former colony.

54. *Congressional Record*, May 20, 1954, p. 6547; and Bud and Gene to Frances P. Bolton [memo], May 19, 1954, "Suggested Statement on Male Nurses," *France Payne Bolton Papers*, Folder 141, WRHS, Cleveland, OH.

55. Edward L. T. Lyon was the first man to receive a commission in the Army Nurse Corps. He entered active duty on October 10, 1955. Feller and Moore, *Highlights in the History of the Army Nurse Corps*, 28; see also "A Salute to Male Nurses," *Washington Post*, December 30, 1955.

56. President Dwight D. Eisenhower officially signed into law H.R. 2559 on August 9, 1955, which authorized reserve commissions for male nurses in the Army Nurse Corps. Sarnecky, *A History of the US Army Nurse Corps*, 296–297.

57. Frances P. Bolton [typed statement], January 20, 1955, and Gerard Edwards to Frances P. Bolton, August 9, 1965, *France Payne Bolton Papers*, Folders 141 and 142, WRHS, Cleveland, OH.

58. "FBP Comments: Nursing-Health," *France Payne Bolton Papers*, Folder 61, pp. 258 and 260, WRHS, Cleveland, OH.

# 4

## "An Attractive Career for Women"

Opportunities, Limitations, and Women's Integration
in the Cold War Military

TANYA L. ROTH

During World War II, wartime needs for personnel opened military opportunities to women, bringing them into the services in large numbers for the first
time in US history. On the home front, the general assumption was that
women would return to their traditional roles in the home after the war
ended. However, defense needs in the postwar world encouraged President
Harry Truman to sign legislation making women a permanent, if small, part of
the US armed services. During the Cold War, servicewomen faced discrimination, demanded equality, and proved the importance of their contributions to
national defense in spite of cultural and political efforts on the home front
to bolster older gender norms and domestic ideals. Focusing on the Women's
Armed Services Integration Act of 1948, this chapter demonstrates the ways in
which servicewomen launched their own movements for women's equality
long before the second-wave feminist movement of the 1960s.

In 1948, Congress passed an act that permanently opened military service to
women in peacetime. Called the Women's Armed Services Integration Act,
the legislation offered women a chance to pursue military careers, something
previously accessible only to men. Five years earlier, it would have been unthinkable that women would want or should be able to have careers in national defense. Many Americans had believed women should not want careers at all. This
idea re-emerged in the aftermath of World War II as white, middle-class ideals
of stay-at-home mothers took center stage. Yet despite such popular feeling,
members of Congress, military leaders like General Dwight Eisenhower, and
President Harry Truman perceived a need for women's continued defense participation as they eyed ongoing tensions in Europe, planned for postwar occupa-

tions in Europe and Asia, and anticipated personnel needs. However, military and government leaders attempted to reconcile perceived need with prevailing beliefs on proper women's roles, consistently structuring women's military careers on the fundamental belief that women's service should not compromise their femininity or their future roles as wives and mothers. In the next thirty years, such efforts to reconcile personnel needs with social ideals of American womanhood limited women's service opportunities and created diverse problems that have only recently begun to be addressed.

The 1948 Women's Armed Services Integration Act did build on precedent for using women in defense support roles.[1] When the United States entered World War I in 1917, the marine corps and navy both saw opportunities to utilize women and created temporary provisions for women's service while the conflict lasted. Women's military participation, however, remained generally small; by the end of the war, approximately 13,000 women had served in both branches.[2] Not until World War II did women begin to join the armed services in substantial numbers, following the creation of specialized women's service components in the army (Women's Army Auxiliary Corps, later the Women's Army Corps, or WAC), navy (Women Accepted for Volunteer Emergency Services, or WAVES), and marine corps (Women Marines, or WMs). By war's end, at least 350,000 women served in a military capacity.[3] Whether as reserve members in the WAVES or Women Marines or as members of the WAC, by 1943, women serving in these branches had access to the same military benefits and pay structure as their male counterparts. The main difference was that men fought and women did not, a fact that shaped women's training, job utilization, and deployment. While WACs might be deployed internationally, for example, the WAVES and WMs tended to remain stateside.

Despite a push at the federal level to incorporate women into national defense to support total war needs, during World War II many Americans responded negatively to the idea of women in military service because of a basic belief that military service contradicted appropriate roles for women.[4] Americans primarily understood military service as something that entailed guns, fighting, and "making men" of their sons. With that image in mind, the question was whether it was even possible for a girl to remain respectable if she joined an all-male environment with such a mission. Moreover, many wondered whether women who opted to join the services did so in order to gain access to men and thus, presumably, husbands. Even worse in the minds of many Americans was the thought that the armed forces might become a haven for lesbians. In response to such concerns, female military leaders set in place strategies to ensure that femininity and propriety remained at the forefront of servicewomen's minds. All of the women's services practiced femininity in training and appearance to give an air of respectability to servicewomen and to assuage fears of lesbian activity. The *WAC Handbook*, for example, begins by exhorting servicewomen to remember basic rules of how to behave in a ladylike manner, including wearing their gloves, not putting their hands in their pockets, not smoking in public, and not dating officers. In addition to these guidelines, the guidebook also specified that WACs should not dance with other WACs, hold hands with one another, or link arms in public.[5] Such concerns over the appropriateness of women's military participation would be one of the long-term questions with which military leaders would grapple in the Cold War.

By creating a permanent place for women in the military branches, proponents believed it would be possible to reduce draft calls and allow more young men to come home, all while ensuring preparedness in case of future conflict. Indeed, at the same time that members of Congress debated the Women's Armed Services Integration Act, they also considered legislation on extending the draft and creating a Universal Military Training (UMT) program, illustrating that even though the goal was to bring American boys back to the States, there were some concerns about maintaining sufficient numbers of personnel.[6] WAC Director Mary Hallaren was among those who believed such measures were useful, but she argued that one of the lessons of the last two wars had been that there was no place for gender distinctions in times of national emergency. "When the house is on fire, we don't talk about a woman's place in the home. And we don't send her a gilt-edged invitation to help put the fire out."[7] Hallaren's position was that it had been hard enough to get the women's branches—known as the women's components—established quickly in wartime before; by maintaining a permanent place for women in the armed forces, military and government leaders could avoid making the same mistakes as in the past. A peacetime role for women would be the best way to ensure preparedness in case of future conflicts.

After several attempts and missteps, in 1948 both houses of Congress finally agreed to the Women's Armed Services Integration Act, a bill that seemed to allow for the benefits of women's service while also creating clear control mechanisms over women in the armed forces. Signed by President Truman in June of that year, the legislation assented to the need for women in defense but primarily emphasized the limitations on women's military roles now that they could pursue a career in the armed forces. According to the legislation, women could make up no more than 2 percent of the total military strength at any time. The legislation also specified that women could not advance above certain positions. With the Women's Armed Services Integration Act, women could serve in the regular and reserves of all military branches as either enlisted personnel or commissioned officers. However, the highest rank a woman could hold as an officer was colonel or commander, and even then, only one woman per service branch could hold that position (and then only while they served as director of that branch's women's component). Women were not eligible to be generals or admirals, the highest ranks for commissioned officers, nor to hold positions of authority over men.[8]

While rank limitations helped lead to a system of separate promotion lists for men and women, all service members would be placed on the same military pay structure, regardless of sex. In a time when civilian advocates were just beginning to seek equal pay for women in the private sector, equal pay for women in the armed forces followed the precedent set in World War II and in civil service during the interwar years. Secretary of Defense James Forrestal, in particular, argued during the legislation hearings that it made the most sense to him to ensure such an equal pay structure. "If we are going to use women in the armed forces, we should go the whole way and give them identical status and benefits as men. If we do not do this, we will continue to lose our most competent women to other professions and pursuits."[9] His philosophy was not new; the Civil Service Classification Act of 1923 had introduced equal pay in civil service jobs, regardless of sex. Moreover, Hallaren and other female military leaders spoke extensively to the problems that auxiliary status had created for members of the Women's Army Auxiliary Corps early in the war, when women were not granted military pay and benefits.[10]

## Recruiting the "First Ladies of the Land"

After the 1948 legislation passed, military leaders focused on determining how to best attract women now that the war had ended and most American women were being pressured to return to their prewar roles as wives and mothers. Patriotism in wartime could be a large motivator, but now military service would be available to the average American woman just out of high school and college. In keeping with cultural assumptions about what it meant to be a proper young woman, military leaders focused their marketing and training efforts to capitalize on the idea that military service was not only a respectable career opportunity but also one that would enhance a woman's femininity and suitability for later family life. Beginning in the 1950s, marketing materials emphasized that military service would make parents proud of their daughter; appealing to parents was key, as women under age twenty-one needed parental permission in order to join the services.[11] In the 1960s, the brochure "Somebody Special" emphasized the educational and traveling opportunities military service offered women, all while explaining that there was nothing more feminine than a woman in uniform, referring to a new recruit as a "Brand-New Beauty."[12] Alongside messages of equality and opportunity in military careers for women came the idea that military service helped make "The First Ladies of the Land . . . America's Finest."[13] By highlighting servicewomen's femininity, military leaders created a purposeful distinction between women's military service and men's, drawing attention to the fact that there were two very different functions for men and women in national defense. While men might be expected to fight, women provided support behind the lines, where they could remain safely ladylike.

Distinguishing between men's and women's military roles served a dual function, offering a way to illustrate how women could support a modern military that relied on extensive support beyond the battlefield while also emphasizing that such jobs were appropriate for the modern American woman. One popular conception was that military service was a way to become a man, to learn citizenship responsibilities, and to practice courage in the face of extreme stress.[14] The image of young women carrying guns and learning to be strong and manly did not fit with postwar conceptions of what an American woman ought to be. During the war, Americans accepted women's movement into jobs men had once held in the civilian world, embracing Rosie the Riveter as a temporary necessity. In the war's aftermath, however, most Americans believed those jobs should go back to the men who had served their nation and that women should go back to the home. Although women themselves expressed a desire to remain in the workforce, most employers eliminated women workers in favor of men when the war ended.[15]

If the end of the war marked women's return to more gender-appropriate work functions, there was a simultaneous movement of women back into the home as well, further emphasizing popular ideas that the most appropriate roles for women were as wife and mother. Femininity was key to this formulation, as only the most ladylike would be desirable for those roles. Marriage rates rose, with more Americans marrying at younger ages than ever, and birthrates led to the midcentury baby boom. Accompanying these statistics, popular magazines portrayed idealized white, middle-class families, with wives and mothers who appeared perfectly poised and entirely feminine no matter what household work they might be doing. Such women were symbolized in popular culture by TV moms such as June Cleaver and Donna Reed.[16] These were the role models for young American women. Thus, the question at stake for military leaders was how to market military service as a career that would make young women into ladies and ultimately more attractive as wives and potential mothers when they were ready to assume such roles in the future. Moreover, military leaders also wanted to ensure that the women who found military service attractive would also want to move on to lives as wives and mothers one day.

By structuring women's military service as an appropriately feminine civic activity, these leaders hoped to attract heterosexual women and preemptively weed out applicants deemed unsuitable: women with homosexual tendencies. If the World War II WAC Handbook had emphasized avoiding public displays of even friendly affection between women, during the Cold War recruiting materials for the women's services played up the idea of military careers as an opportunity for intimate heterosexual relationships. Through images of women holding hands with men (with both partners in and out of uniform), as well as sightseeing and playing sports with young men, recruiting brochures consistently emphasized military careers as an avenue for engaging with members of the opposite sex, rather than showcasing the camaraderie between women that the women's services might enable through living arrangements, training, and job assignments.[17] Although wartime leaders had been concerned about rumors of women joining the services just to meet and sleep with men, such concerns were far less prominent during the postwar decades. In the era of June Cleaver, the bottom line was that it was better to have servicewomen looking for dates and husbands than to have units full of young lesbians.

Despite such efforts, however, many women did engage in homosexual relationships while in the military, a fact that many officials knew and tried to combat time and again.[18] In addition to investigating allegations of homosexual activity in the women's ranks, by the late 1950s the navy's Crittenden Report on homosexuality in that service branch had concluded that servicewomen had a higher rate of homosexual activity than servicemen but acknowledged that it was "difficult to detect." At the same time, the study's authors noted that homosexual activity between servicewomen "appeared to be more disruptive of morale and discipline" than male homosexual activity in the armed forces and suggested that more studies were needed to better understand homosexuality among military women.[19] Nearly a decade after women became permanent members of the armed forces, the Crittenden Report suggested that efforts to keep lesbian women out of military service were not working—a fact that remained unchanged for the rest of the twentieth century, despite efforts to the contrary.[20]

Just six weeks after signing the Women's Armed Services Integration Act in 1948, President Truman issued Executive Order 9981 to desegregate the armed forces.[21] The timing of this order and the postwar permanent establishment of women's military service meant that the women's units pursued racial integration as policy from the outset in 1948, racially integrating women's training and job assignments. However, recruiting efforts never focused on minority recruitment and retention in particular. The military's education and behavior standards embodied in these recruiting materials, moreover, corresponded with white, middle-class standards of the time. Military leaders particularly sought young women who either fit or aspired to fit that model. The military leaders of the women's components theoretically practiced color-blind policies that assumed all accepted recruits were capable of attaining the military's feminine ideals.

African American women were nonetheless paying attention to the new career opportunity and respectability that military service promised to provide. In 1962, the staff at *Ebony* magazine featured a multi-page spread about military service as a career opportunity for women. Until this time, African American women had been absent from military recruiting brochures. *Ebony*'s writers emphasized that even if visual representations remained nonexistent, plenty of African American women were taking advantage of military careers and succeeding.

> Negro women have been in the forefront of the women's services and . . . have gained high rank—Lt. Col. Ruth A. Lucas of women in the Air Force [WAF], the nation's highest ranking Negro woman officer, holds a rank only one degree lower than the head of the entire 10,000 member Women's Army Corps. Negro captains and majors are found throughout the WAC, WAF and the service nursing corps. There are fewer and less high ranking Negro members of the women Marines [sic] and SPARS [Coast Guard], but these units are much smaller.[22]

Like military leaders did with recruiting materials, the *Ebony* staff capitalized on the importance of femininity in shaping women's military service as an acceptable career. In particular, the authors wrote, "the women's services never make the mistake of considering WACs as soldiers or WAVES as sailors."[23] The point was clear: not only were African American women excelling in this new career field open to all women, but they were doing so specifically as women—or, more specifically, ladies. Military service would not compromise their femininity or make them become more masculine. According to this article, in the military, any woman could have an interesting career and remain respectable.

### Training the Lady in Uniform

Each branch's initial training program included elements to help women better understand what it meant to be a woman in the armed forces. Much of this training focused specifically on maintaining feminine ideals. While male recruits might learn how to clean, handle, and fire a gun or participate in intensive physical training, women's basic training included makeup application classes, instruction on proper diet and exercise, and admonitions about how to wear their uniforms correctly.[24] Clothing and behavior were two important ways to maintain the gender difference of women's military careers, and rules governing these became key strategies for delineating women's military careers in the Cold War era. By 1958, the Women Marines emphasized the connection between physicality and military service: "[e]ven a casual glance at the Woman Marine will reveal that she is well-groomed, poised and confident of her abilities. She knows that her Marine training not only fits her for duties in the Corps, but also helps bring out all her latent qualities as a woman."[25] In this career path, one was a woman first and a member of the military second.

Military leaders' vision of proper American womanhood entirely shaped servicewomen's careers and expectations about their roles in national defense. However, some argued that training servicewomen in how to be ladies was simply the newest iteration of older traditions of imbuing service members with a sense of gender-appropriate behavior. A 1948 conference on planning women's postwar naval service included the following announcement about training:

> The courses in Military Drill, Physical Training, Hygiene and First Aid contain a surprise package—approximately five hours devoted to the topic, 'On being a Lady.' Do not, I ask you, look askance at this phase of the curriculum, for the germ of the idea is as old as our Navy itself. It was John Paul Jones who stressed the need of the service for gentlemen—defined as men of liberal education, refined manners, punctilious courtesy, and the nicest sense of personal honor. It is less than problematical that the history of the Navy is so glorious because its officers and men were first gentlemen and secondly officers and sailors . . . May our women both continue and enrich this tradition.[26]

While training courses on such matters would take on a variety of topics and themes in decades to come, the general idea remained the same.[27] A 1954 hand-book for new Women in the Air Force (WAF) personnel included thirty-nine out of eighty-seven pages devoted to information on beauty, fashion, and uni-forms.[28] By 1969, a revised version of this book included more than one hun-dred pages of advice on being ladylike.[29] As with recruiting materials that emphasized heterosexual social opportunities in the services, training materi-als and procedures underscored the importance of servicewomen's heterosexu-ality. Learning to accentuate one's femininity and to become more ladylike was an additional strategy to help make servicewomen more attractive as potential mates and ideally better able to showcase their charms to future boyfriends and husbands.

By the late 1960s, the impetus to teach servicewomen how to be proper ladies had increased. Military leaders also employed new strategies to address this issue as servicewomen's experiences challenged the practicality of femininity above all else. The Women Marines, for example, went so far as to create a part-nership with the grooming experts used by Pan American Airways to train stew-ardesses. With the goal that they would take their training back to the Women Marines' base, six personnel were dispatched to attend cosmetology classes and other courses led by Revlon makeup professionals in addition to more hands-on training at the Pan Am facilities.[30] Within a year, however, members of the Women's Army Corps stationed in Vietnam vociferously objected to requirements that servicewomen maintain a feminine appearance at all times. Focusing particu-larly on their concerns over clothing, several WACs argued that femininity regula-tions relegated women to a status as "morale-boosters" for men rather than useful members of the armed forces. "There is hardly any doubt that the Wacs here are aware that a small part of their femininity has been sacrificed. But then, are we here to satisfy the desires of the male ego which prefers women in dresses or are we here to do a job?"[31]

Despite such concerns, the emphasis on femininity persisted. New recruit booklets for Women Marines in the same era reveal that out of all the boot camp training subjects, they received the most instruction in grooming and image development—thirty-one hours, with drill clocking in closest at thirty hours.[32] In general, women and men did receive much of the same type of instruction during training throughout the 1950s, 1960s, and 1970s; the key difference was that where men received courses in weapons use and marksmanship, women participated in image development and grooming classes.

### Defining Women's Defense Work

Officially, the only jobs definitively off limits to women were those in combat or combat-support roles. But in reality, through the 1970s servicewomen tended to be confined to jobs deemed most acceptable for women on the basis of their sex alone. This trend was in keeping with the theme of femininity and promoting military service as a way to become an ideal American woman. Consistently through the first three decades of the Cold War, it was in the area of job utilization that servicewomen and military leaders most frequently encountered the challenges of structuring women's military service through gender difference criteria. There were no such problems when it came to men's utilization because men could serve in any military occupation. In the early 1950s, initial conversations about women's career fields emphasized the need for thorough consideration in women's utilization. In assessing which jobs women could perform, leaders needed to take into account such issues as these detailed by one subcommittee report:

1. All steps in career field on promotion ladder must be open to women.
2. Physical demands of job.
3. Psychological factors.
4. Training of enlisted women as economical as that of men.
5. Replacement of men on one to one basis.
6. Job in undesirable or isolated field location.
7. Culturally acceptable to American public.
8. Related civilian occupation.
9. Critical personnel needs in particular ratings.
10. Restrictions imposed by PL625 [the Women's Armed Services Integration Act].[33]

If a job or career field did not fit these criteria, it would not be opened to women. Integrating women into the armed services called for careful evaluation and planning to ensure no servicewoman ended up in an inappropriate job, career field, or geographic location.

The trick was to balance women's roles carefully. If women served in the military because their country needed them, then it was equally important to consider where the country truly would need them, not just where it would be easiest to use women to replace men for combat. Air Force Chief of Staff General Hoyt Vandenberg made such an argument when he noted in 1951,

I do not believe that we would be utilizing very intelligent women to the best advantage of the Air Force in driving a bunch of trucks. I do not believe that if we get some highly skilled women that they would be replacing a man if they put gasoline in an airplane. I think those of the men with the lower intelligence rating can do that. Therefore, part of our problem, as I see it, is what are the categories that we would put the women in.[34]

Between the 1950s and 1970s, those categories would be systematically reevaluated, although extensive change was not quick in coming. By the early 1960s, women were concentrated in administrative and clerical jobs, typically performing traditional female career roles. One official noted at the end of the decade that "the actual working conditions in the types of assignments made to women resemble the conditions of civilian employment." Specifically, 75 percent of all female officers held positions in the administrative, personnel, or information job fields, while 70 percent of enlisted women had jobs in administrative or clerical positions.[35]

Although women might be concentrated in such traditional career roles, President Lyndon Johnson emphasized that the nature of military service, with its diverse roles and duties across a spectrum of job fields, also offered women more nontraditional options. According to him, military service was "an attractive career for women," one that no longer meant limiting women to clerical or nursing roles. "[T]oday women are making important professional and technical contributions to the military as scientists, engineers, as mathematicians, as administrators, and managers, as accountants, as teachers, as lawyers, as linguists."[36] What was common to all these positions, however, was that none of them involved combat or necessitated commanding men. Statistically, some were also fields in which servicewomen were least likely to be found in comparison to other career fields; they were nontraditional, but also exceptional, with fewer women likely to find such opportunities. Moreover, Johnson drew attention to these roles in a time when numbers of women in military service had declined overall, with only around thirty thousand women serving in all military branches.[37]

### Limits to an "Attractive" Career

While some women certainly viewed military service as an "attractive" opportunity, a number of practices and policies limited women's military careers in a practical sense. Beyond the tendency to utilize women in traditional job fields, rank limitations and policies on marriage and family life played important roles in constraining women's career options in national defense. With rank limitations still present from the 1948 Women's Armed Services Integration Act, female officers found career advancement difficult because very few women were permitted to the highest ranks. By 1964, women who had stayed in the services since World War II—while their numbers were small—faced the reality of not being able to advance further in their careers due to such limits. This meant that many officers held jobs technically only available to higher-ranking officers. While military officials clearly found these women important, legal restrictions from the 1948 Women's Armed Services Integration Act prevented women from receiving promotions simply because they were women.[38] On the other end of the spectrum, military leaders found it difficult to retain women until the end of their first enlistment term or beyond, in part because the military structure allowed women the possibility of giving up their careers for the most traditional role of all: wife and mother.

While femininity and careful definition of women's military job roles both helped with defining women's military status, provisions for discharging women upon marriage or pregnancy and motherhood ensured that many women saw military service as an attractive career opportunity only temporarily. During the 1950s, for example, the women's components typically allowed a woman to be discharged early if she married. However, the practice diminished during the Korean conflict. By the Vietnam War in the next decade, a woman could only receive discharge upon marriage if she could not be stationed near her husband.[39] Even with the tightening of such options, the numbers of women leaving service before finishing their enlistment remained high. A 1967 policy review indicated that between 70 and 80 percent of women did not complete their first enlistment; on average, women spent fourteen months in military service before leaving altogether.[40] In the same decade, however, it was not uncommon for 80 percent of men to leave after their first enlistment, even among men who had been drafted into the services.[41] While the turnover rate for enlisted men and women was similar, one key difference is that all women's service was voluntary. In 1967, many men served because their number had been called.

Regardless of whether a newly married servicewoman sought out early discharge or desired a long-term military career, until the 1970s one thing in particular spelled the end of a woman's military career: motherhood. Most women left the military under this policy when they learned they were pregnant, and women who married into parenthood and would, with their partner, maintain at least 50 percent custody of the children by marriage were automatically discharged.

Indeed, during the original debates over the Women's Armed Services Integration Act, the idea was to ensure that military service would not interfere with women's roles as mothers. As Representative Carl Vinson (D-GA) argued in 1948, "we should not put anything in the law which should cause them [servicewomen] to hesitate getting married or to raise a family; on the contrary, we should encourage it."[42] For nearly thirty years, then, military practice and policy ensured that no woman would face a conflict between career and family; according to military leaders, family trumped everything else for women.

Few women challenged this assumption in the 1950s and 1960s, either because they shared the same belief, did not care to stay in service, or did not believe such a challenge was possible. In the early 1960s, Alba Martinelli fought back against her own discharge, to no avail.[43] Ruth Brown, discharged from the WAC in 1955, let her own parents adopt her children and returned to service in 1960.[44] Woman Marine Joan Gerichten faced mandatory discharge when she became a stepmother to her marine corps husband's three children in 1961, even though when he was widowed a year earlier, the marines had made allowances for him to be stationed near family who could provide support. The message was clear: fatherhood did not interfere with military duties, but motherhood—even by marriage alone—was incompatible with service.[45]

### Redefining Appropriate Roles

During the 1970s, however, standards began to change, with women first being able to apply for waivers if they wished to stay on duty after becoming mothers. In 1975, a new Department of Defense policy specified that all pregnancy and parenthood discharges would occur only if requested by the service member.[46] Such changes reflect overall trends in adjustments to women's military service in the 1970s, the decade when women's military service began to move closer to what it is today. In light of new beliefs about women's social and economic roles ignited by the second-wave women's movement and the initial success of the Equal Rights Amendment, military leaders across all branches and the Department of Defense revisited the place of the women's services in national defense. As the draft finally ended, and as mandatory pregnancy and parenthood discharges gave way to an acceptance of mothers in the military, military officials began reassessing women's places in the armed forces. By 1978, the women's service components of each branch had also disappeared in favor of integrating women more completely into each military branch's organizational structure. All three military academies—West Point, the Air Force Academy, and the Naval Academy—opened enrollment to women for the first time. The navy began allowing women to serve at sea for the first time.[47] Out went lipstick and nylons for servicewomen, and in came camouflage fatigues, weapons training, and, in the army, experiments with coed basic training. In 1971, women constituted 1.6 percent of total military strength, but by 1979 this figure had increased to 5.7 percent of total military strength, their numbers tripling in eight years.[48]

Yet even as women's opportunities expanded in some ways, one assumption continued to guide women's service roles: the idea that men performed combat duties and women did not. Even in the midst of changing policies in the 1970s in response to the ERA and the end of the draft, military and congressional leaders continually stressed that adopting sex-neutral standards would not mean necessarily admitting women to combat roles. "The greatest efficiency in utilization of personnel in the Army is achieved by assigning men to combat duties and women to all duties except those involving physical contact with the enemy," noted one official.[49] In the early 1980s, backlash against women's expanded service roles took such beliefs further, introducing new arguments that the 1970s movement toward more sex-neutral standards had not improved military efficiency but instead impaired it, causing larger questions about whether the all-volunteer military could truly be ready for and effective in combat. In short, some questioned whether women's larger presence in the military had weakened, rather than strengthened, defense goals.[50] Such questioning led to increased caution regarding women's utilization in the final decade of the Cold War but did not eliminate all opportunities. During the 1980s, for example, army women deployed to Grenada and Panama in sex-integrated units, experiences that would pave the way for servicewomen's participation in the Persian Gulf War in 1991.

Even as military officials continued to classify women's roles on the same basic principles of combat exclusion, experiences such as the Gulf War illustrated the challenges of such efforts in light of both women's capabilities and the military's practical needs during conflict. Secretary of Defense Dick Cheney acknowledged that women had been vital to the conflict, noting that the United States "could not have won [the war] without them."[51] In further recognition of women's roles in the conflict, the National Defense Authorization Act allowed women to fly in combat missions for the first time. Within a few years, new policies opened combat surface ship and air combat unit positions to women.[52] Despite such changes, it remained clear that servicewomen would not be allowed to engage in direct combat with enemies, particularly on the ground and in face-to-face battle. Even with such goals, stories of women prisoners of war such as Rhonda

Cornum, Jessica Lynch, and Shoshana Johnson brought into question whether such exclusion policies could really protect women from the harshest aspects of war.[53]

Women's military experiences since the 1980s have continually brought into sharp relief the challenges of meeting modern utilization needs in wartime while trying to protect women on the basis of their sex. Government and military leaders can no longer make convincing arguments for utilizing women only in the most sex-appropriate jobs in light of the fact that such distinctions no longer exist for civilian women, who work in all career fields. Moreover, while combat exclusion policies and other sex-based military job restrictions have long been based on ideas that women are physically incapable of the demands of such jobs, servicewomen's contributions in the last thirty years belie such assumptions. As early as 1971, advocates for the Equal Rights Amendment pointed out that in the modern military, strength and brawn are no longer the primary indicators of a soldier's capability. "The effectiveness of the modern soldier is due more to equipment and training than to individual strength."[54] Women today routinely demonstrate their abilities to carry heavy weights and endure extreme physical stress. Certainly, not every servicewoman may be capable of such demands, but neither is every serviceman.

In the twenty years since the end of the Cold War, much has changed, but many of the Cold War–era attitudes toward women's roles in national defense linger. Women's current work in the armed forces testifies to their ability to assume any job role opened to them. Today, women serve on submarines in the navy, advance to four-star generals, and fill nearly any job outside of combat. Servicewomen's equality with men as members of the armed forces remains elusive, however, because discrimination, sexual harassment, abuse, and even career limitations still affect many women in service. Such problems demonstrate the key consequence of the Cold War military structure that emphasized gender difference ideals: far from creating a separate-but-equal military, Cold War policies created a military in which women's service remains less valued than men's and women's capabilities more likely to be called into question.

The issue of sexual assault in the military is one way to understand how servicewomen are perceived as lesser contributors to national defense. Current estimates indicate that between 20 and 25 percent of servicewomen become victims of sexual assault during their military careers, but most cases of sexual assault are believed to remain unreported. In recent years, greater media attention has increased awareness of this problem. However, women note that reporting sexual assault often has negative impacts on their own careers. Additionally, justice for victims in reported cases tends to be uneven.[55] As the overall numbers of servicewomen have grown in recent decades, as servicewomen have expanded into more career fields than ever, such problems demonstrate an institutional lack of respect for and recognition of women's rights as individuals. Sexual violence against servicewomen is, at its root, an example of men both asserting power over women and their right to maintain a privileged place over women.

On January 24, 2013, Secretary of Defense Leon Panetta announced the end of the combat exclusion policy that applied to women specifically. "Success in our military based solely on ability, qualifications, and performance is consistent with our values and enhances military readiness," the memo announced, further noting that the new plans "will fully integrate women without compromising our readiness, morale, or war-fighting capacity."[56] Until recently, combat exclusions for women have only served to perpetuate ideas that women should participate in national defense in distinct ways from men, even though women continued to demonstrate their abilities in the Iraq and Afghanistan conflicts in the early twenty-first century. In the immediate aftermath of the policy announcement, a Gallup poll indicated broad support for such a measure, finding that three-quarters of Americans would support allowing women in combat.[57] Certainly, attitudes regarding appropriate roles for women in national defense have changed greatly since the Cold War. The removal of combat exclusion policies suggests women could have unprecedented access to military careers that once would have been entirely unthinkable. However, Panetta's announcement also specified that the military branches may request to keep some jobs closed to women.

While the end of combat exclusion is an important step in expanding servicewomen's career opportunities, Panetta's announcement is only the beginning of change. Cold War limitations on women's service have left a significant mark and remain a powerful influence for many within the armed forces. Such limitations become apparent in light of the experiences of women whose career progression stalled because of such limits. Moreover, the problem of military sexual assault provides a consistent reminder that sexual integration does not mean that individuals perceive both sexes as equal. The long history of relying on gender difference to structure military service illustrates how such a program worked to impede progress and limit women's effective utilization. Whether military service will continue to be an "attractive career" to women depends on how well military personnel at all levels can move beyond assumptions that gender difference does matter to national defense.

NOTES

1. Beginning in 1901, the Army Nurse Corps made the army the first branch to create a permanent place for women. The establishment of the Navy Nurse Corps followed in 1908. The Army and Navy Nurse Corps began on the assumption that nursing was a woman's profession and that consequently, the military had no choice but to employ women in such capacities. This chapter focuses on women's military employment in all service branches except for the nursing corps. For specific information on these branches, see Mary T. Sarnecky, *A History of the US Army Nurse Corps*, Studies in Health, Illness, and Caregiving (Philadelphia: University of Pennsylvania Press, 1999), or Doris M. Sterner, *In and Out of Harm's Way: A History of the US Navy Nurse Corps* (Seattle, WA: Peanut Butter Publishing, 1997).

2. Mattie E. Treadwell, *The Women's Army Corps* (Washington, DC: Office of the Chief of Military History, Department of the Army, 1954), 10.

3. Jeanne Holm, *Women in the Military: An Unfinished Revolution*, rev. ed. (Novato, CA: Presidio Press, 1992), 100. The air force did not exist as a separate branch until 1948 but remained part of the army before that.

4. Historian Leisa D. Meyer explains the negative response to women in uniform in World War II in her analysis of the Women's Army Corps. See chapter 2, " 'Ain't Misbehavin'?' The Slander Campaign against the WAC," in Meyer, *Creating GI Jane: Sexuality and Power in the Women's Army Corps during World War II* (New York: Columbia University Press, 1996), 33–70. Meyer suggests that WAVES and Women Marines encountered a few minor problems along the same lines, but only women in the army seem to have been subject to a systematic opposition to women in service. This may be because the WAVES and WMs components were much smaller and classified with reserve status only. Treadwell also provides coverage of the same image concerns; see chapter 11, "The 'Slander Campaign,' " in Treadwell, *The Women's Army Corps*, 191–218.

5. *WAC Handbook*, Item WV0436.2.003, Idele Singletary Meng scrapbook, Betty H. Carter Women Veterans Historical Project, Jackson Library, The University of North Carolina at Greensboro. http://library.uncg.edu/dp/wv/results28.aspx?i=4708&s=2.

6. Linda Witt, Judith Bellafaire, Britta Granrud, and Mary Jo Binker, *"A Defense Weapon Known to Be of Value": Servicewomen of the Korean War Era* (Hanover, CT: University Press of New England, 2005), 29.

7. Hallaren Statement on S.1103, 1947, 1–2, Mary Hallaren Collection, US Army Women's Museum, Fort Lee, VA.

8. Public Law 625 in *United States Statutes at Large*, vol. 62, part 1, 360. Major General Jeanne Holm also specifies the legislation's provisions; see Holm, *Women in the Military*, 119–120.

9. Statement of Secretary of Defense James V. Forrestal, S1641 (No. 238) Subcommittee Hearings on S. 1641, 5573, Record Group 287, National Archives Building, Washington, DC.

10. For more on the Civil Service Classification Act of 1923, see US Office of Personnel Management, Strategic Compensation Policy Center, "Evolution of Federal White Collar Pay." www.opm.gov/strategiccomp/html/HISTORY1.asp#1923.

11. Public Law 625.

12. "Somebody Special," Department of the Army Materials, Box 6. Files of the President's Commission on Equal Opportunity in the Armed Forces, Lyndon B. Johnson Presidential Library, Austin, TX.

13. "Take Your Place among the First Ladies of the Land . . . America's Finest!" advertisement, *New York Times,* April 24, 1952.

14. For more on male military service as a masculinization process, see Michael S. Nieberg, *Making Citizen-Soldiers: ROTC and the Ideology of American Military Service* (Cambridge, MA: Harvard University Press, 2000), and E. Anthony Rotundo, *American Manhood: Transformations in Masculinity from the Revolution to the Modern Era* (New York: Basic Books, 1993). Historian Melissa Herbert has also observed the benefits of distinguishing between masculine and feminine military roles, noting that "by requiring women to maintain a degree of femininity, perceptions of masculinity remain intact." See Herbert, *Camouflage Isn't Only for Combat: Gender, Sexuality and Women in the Military* (New York: New York University Press, 1998), 10.

15. Cynthia Harrison notes that although 3.25 million women did quit or were laid off at the end of World War II, 2.75 million also took jobs, which primarily indicates that "Rosie the Riveter had become a file clerk." Harrison, *On Account of Sex: The Politics of Women's Issues, 1945–1968* (Berkeley: University of California Press, 1988), 5.

16. For more on the postwar emphasis on domesticity, see Elaine Tyler May, *Homeward Bound: American Families in the Cold War Era,* rev. ed. (New York: Basic Books, 1999); see also Jessica Weiss, *To Have and to Hold: Marriage, the Baby Boom, and Social Change* (Chicago: University of Chicago Press, 2000).

17. "An Adventure in Belonging . . . a modern Odyssey," "Somebody Special," and "A New World of Opportunity" offer examples of men and women engaged together in leisure activities, often with romantic undertones, as does "Everything You Ever Wanted to Know about Navy Waves" (no page numbers given). Department of the Army Materials, Box 6. Files of the President's Commission on Equal Opportunity in the Armed Forces, LBJ Library. WAC Brochures Folder, Background—WAC, Record Group 319, NACP. Women in the Military Folder, Box 7, Ready Reference Files, Operational Archives Branch, Naval Historical Center, Washington, DC.

18. By 1949, homosexuality was officially a reason for military discharge. See Allan Berube, *Coming Out under Fire: The History of Gay Men and Women in World War Two* (New York: The Free Press, 1990), quoted on 261.

19. "The Crittenden Report: Report of the Board Appointed to Prepare and Submit Recommendations to the Secretary of the Navy for the Revision of Policies, Procedures, and Directives Dealing with Homosexuals" (Upland, PA: Defense Information Access Network, DIANE Publishing Company, 1993[1957]), 42–43.

20. For more on the military's efforts to identify and oust lesbians from the services, see Margot Canaday's work on the 1950s WAC witch hunts to identify lesbian servicewomen, *The Straight State: Sexuality and Citizenship in Twentieth-Century America* (Princeton, NJ: Princeton University Press, 2009). Additionally, journalist Randy Shilts notes that some estimates place the number of lesbians in service as high as 80 percent during World War II and asserts that "[t]he highest-ranking officers in the military

services well into the 1980s came largely from this group. Until the late 1960s, when the first rumblings of the women's movement made nontradilional jobs attractive to women from all walks of life, women's military units tended to include a large propor-tion of lesbians." Shilts, *Conduct Unbecoming: Gays and Lesbians in the US Military* (New York: St. Martin's Griffin, 2005), 140.

21. President Harry S. Truman, Executive Order 9981, July 26, 1948. John T. Woolley and Gerhard Peters, *The American Presidency Project*, Santa Barbara, CA. www .presidency.ucsb.edu/ws/index.php?pid=60737.

22. "Women in Uniform," *Ebony*, December 1962, 63.

23. Ibid., 64.

24. For examples of men's training programs, see John Patrick Mora, "Historical Data of the 3700th Air Force Indoctrination Wing, Lackland Air Force Base, San Antonio, Texas, Volume Seventeen, October 1951 to December 1951," with training-specific details on multiple pages; K229.72-16, Air Force Historical Research Agency (AFHRA), Maxwell Air Force Base (AFB), AL.

25. "Share a Proud Tradition," 1958, Rose Kirwin Collection (1019), Women's Memorial Foundation Collection, Alexandria, VA.

26. Lieutenant Sybil A. Grant on "Plans for the Training of Enlisted Women," 24–25, Miscellaneous District Directors Conference 1948 Folder, Reel 2, WAVES, Records of the Assistant Chief of Personnel for Women 1942–1973, Scholarly Re-sources, Inc.

27. Several examples of training documents and programs include the 1950 guide "You in the Service (Notes on Good Manners, Appearance, and Good Grooming Prepared for Women Recruits in the Armed Forces)," "You in the Service" Research Evaluation 1950 Folder, Box 17, Records of the Bureau of Personnel Special Assistant for Women (BuPersooW), Operational Archives Branch, Naval Historical Center, Wash-ington, DC; a 1955 WAF handbook by Myra N. Conklin, "Good Grooming for the Women in the Armed Forces," produced by The Toilet Goods Association as a public service for the Department of Defense; Jane Sewell Collection, 168.7172, AFHRA, Maxwell AFB, AL; and a WAC "Personal Standards and Social Concepts" segment of basic training in the late 1960s, profiled in SP5 Richard A. Dey, Jr., "WAC: Training for Army Service," *Army Digest*, June 1969, 43, 401–407 Magazine/Newspaper Articles Folder, Background—WAC, Record Group 319, National Archives, College Park, MD (NACP).

28. "WAF: A Handbook for Air Force Women," Training Command ATRC Manual 13.2, 1954, K220.716035-2, AFHRA.

29. "Personal Development: A Guide for Women in the Air Force," Air Force ROTC/Air University, 1969, Joanne Rodefer Collection (4288), Women's Memorial Foundation Collection.

30. "Women Marine Newsletter," Spring 1967, 3, Women Marine Newsletter, 1966–69, Headquarters—Marine Corps (HQMC) Folder, Records Relating to Women Marines, History and Museum Division, Record Group 127, NACP.

31. Memorandum from Captain Joanne Murphy—Problem: The advisability of enlisted WAC personnel, WAC Detachment, USARV, being required to wear Class A

Uniform, to Director of the Women's Army Corps, 1 and 2, June 26, 1968, Vietnam Uniform Problems Folder, Background—WAC, Record Group 319, NACP.

32. "Woman Recruit Training Syllabus," in US Marine Corps Women Marines (document with information for new recruits), dated "late 1960s," Boot Camp Folder, Stremlow Women Marines, Record Group 127, NACP.

33. "Criteria Used in Peacetime in Determining Jobs for Enlisted Women," in Sub-Committee Project Report Number M-7-51, "Maximum Utilization of Military Womanpower," April 9, 1951, 77; Subcommittee to the Military Personnel Policy Committee Project Report: Maximum Utilization of Military Womanpower, April 9, 1951, Folder, Military Operations, Programs, and Organizations, Marine Corps History and Museum Division, Record Group 127, NACP.

34. "Minutes of WAF Meeting," January 24, 1951, 2; WAF Meeting Minutes, January 24, 1951, Folder, Box 6, Papers of Jackie Cochran, Air Force Series (1948–1971), Dwight D. Eisenhower Presidential Library, Abilene, KS.

35. "Civilian-Military Substitution and Other Utilization Programs to Increase Voluntary Manpower," circa 1969, 7–8, Gruenther Collection, All-Volunteer Forces Series, Presidential Commission on the All-Volunteer Armed Forces—2, Eisenhower Presidential Library, Abilene, KS.

36. "Remarks of President Johnson to DACOWITS at White House," April 28, 1964, 1–2, Government Policy and Guidelines for Women in the Military, 1964–1965 Folder, Box 1, Papers of Dr. Lynne Dunn, Operational Archives Branch, Naval Historical Center.

37. Holm, *Women in the Military*, 177.

38. Ibid., 193. In 1967, the passage of Public Law 90–130 removed arbitrary rank limitations on the basis of sex.

39. According to Holm, military leaders made exceptions for "joint assignments to the southeast Asia war zone and to certain isolated locations where family accommodations were not available. Even with these exceptions, the system worked so well that roughly 90 percent of married couples were able to establish joint homes." Holm, *Women in the Military*, 289–290. For history on the marriage discharge policy in the Korean War, see Witt et al., *"A Defense Weapon Known to Be of Value,"* 2–3.

40. Holm, *Women in the Military*, 163, and Colonel Elizabeth Hoisington (WAC) testimony, "Enlisted Promotion Policy Review," Subcommittee on Enlisted Promotion Policy Review, House Armed Services Committee, October 5, 1967, 1307; Pre Public Law 90-130 Hearings Folder, Military Operations, Programs, and Organization, Marine Corps History and Museum Division, Record Group 127, NACP.

41. Charles C. Moskos, *The American Enlisted Man: The Rank and File in Today's Military* (New York: Russell Sage Foundation, 1970), 52.

42. House Armed Services Subcommittee Hearings on S.1641, February–March 1948, 5667, Publications of the US Government, Record Group 287, National Archives Building, Washington, DC.

43. Witt et al., *"A Defense Weapon Known to Be of Value,"* 90–91.

44. Ruth Virginia Payne Brown Papers, Ruth Payne Brown interview with Eric Elliott, 2000, WV0193.5.001, the Betty H. Carter Women Veterans Historical Project. http://library.uncg.edu/dp/wv/results5.aspx?i=2687&s=5&c=3.

45. Joan E. Gerichten Papers, Joan Gerichten interview with Eric Elliott, October 29, 1999, WV0109.5.001, The Betty H. Carter Women Veterans Historical Project. http://library.uncg.edu/dp/wv/results5.aspx?i=2628&s=5. A little more than a decade later, Gerichten returned to the reserves. Holm notes two additional examples from the Vietnam War era that demonstrate the alternate standards for men with children. One widowed sergeant received praise for going to Vietnam even after his wife's death left him in charge of his children, while a single male chaplain was lauded for adopting two Vietnamese children. Holm, *Women in the Military*, 293–294.

46. Holm, *Women in the Military*, 300–303.

47. "Women on Sea Duty," *All Hands*, November 1978, 8. Ready Reference Files on Women in the Military, Box 2, Women in the Military Post 74 Folder, Operational Archives Branch, Naval Historical Center.

48. While overall numbers of women and women as a percentage of all forces increased in the 1970s, the size of the military did decrease in the 1970s with the withdrawal from Vietnam and the end of the draft. For sources on manpower numbers, see The Office of the Deputy Assistant Secretary of Defense (Equal Opportunity), "Women in the Armed Forces: A Statistical Fact Book," August 1, 1973, chart: Strength of Women in the Armed Forces. WAC Statistics Folder, Background—WAC, Record Group 319, NACP. Office of the Assistant Secretary of Defense (Manpower, Reserve Affairs and Logistics), *America's Volunteers: A Report on the All-Volunteer Armed Forces*, 69, Records of the Bureau of Personnel, Special Assistant for Women's Policy (PERS-00W), Box 18, A Report on the All-Volunteer Armed Forces "America's Volunteers" 1978 Folder, Operational Archives Branch, Naval Historical Center. Ed Gates, "Women in the Service," *The Retired Officer*, November 1977. Papers of Louise Wilde, Box 4, Sea Duty 1970s Folder, Operational Archives Branch, Naval Historical Center.

49. Office of the Deputy Chief of Staff for Personnel, Department of the Army, Report of the Committee to Study the Proposed Equal Rights Amendment, December 1972, iv, Study—"Impact of Passage of ERA on Women in the Army," December 1972 Folder, Background—WAC, Record Group 319, NACP.

50. For more on the "womanpause" of the early 1980s, see Holm, *Women in the Military*, 387–388.

51. Quoted in Holm, *Women in the Military*, 470.

52. Darlene Iskra, *Women in the United States Armed Forces: A Guide to the Issues* (Santa Barbara, CA: Praeger, 2010), 107.

53. For more on female prisoners of war in the Gulf War and the Iraq War, see Holm, *Women in the Military*, 455–459; Rhonda Cornum and Peter Copeland, *She Went to War: The Rhonda Cornum Story* (Novato, CA: Presidio Press, 1992); Shoshana Johnson, *I'm Still Standing: From Captive US Soldier to Free Citizen—My Journey Home* (New York: Touchstone, 2010); Rick Bragg, *I Am a Soldier, Too: The Jessica Lynch Story* (New York: Alfred A. Knopf, 2003).

54. Barbara A. Brown, Thomas I. Emerson, Gail Falk, and Ann E. Freedman, "The Equal Rights Amendment: A Constitutional Basis for Equal Rights for Women," *The Yale Law Journal* 80, no. 5 (April 1971): 968.

55. A 2012 documentary, *The Invisible War*, focused on the current problem of sexual assault in the military, earning an Academy Award nomination. For a recent

account of military sexual assault and the problem of justice, see Quil Lawrence and Marisa Penaloza, "Sexual Violence Victims Say Military Justice System is 'Broken,'" NPR, March 21, 2013. www.npr.org/2013/03/21/174840895/sexual-violence-victims-say -military-justice-system-is-broken.

56. Secretary of Defense Leon Panetta and Chairman of the Joint Chiefs of Staff Martin Dempsey, "Memorandum for Secretaries of the Military Departments Acting Under Secretary of Defense for Personnel and Readiness, Chiefs of the Military Services," January 24, 2013. www.defense.gov/news/WISRJointMemo.pdf.

57. Alyssa Brown, "Americans Favor Allowing Women in Combat: Men and Women Equally Likely to Support Policy," January 25, 2013. www.gallup.com/poll/160124 /americans-favor-allowing-women-combat.aspx.

# 5

## African Americans, Civil Rights, and the Armed Forces during the Vietnam War

JAMES E. WESTHEIDER

In 1968, the Defense Department's annual report declared that institutional racism had been eliminated from the armed services. However, that same year, several events took place that called this confident declaration into question. As the Vietnam War grew more and more unpopular, Dr. Martin Luther King, Jr., began counseling black men to avoid service, citing inequities in the Selective Service System and lingering racial discrimination in the military establishment. Whereas in earlier wars, African Americans considered military service a path to full citizenship, during the Vietnam War, black enlisted men found themselves in increasingly isolated and disillusioned. This chapter examines the contradictions of the 1960s in the relationship between African Americans and the military, where images of black achievement contrasted with evidence that racism persisted both institutionally and among service personnel.

The war in Vietnam and the civil rights movement were two of the seminal events of the mid-twentieth century, and from the beginning, their fates were intertwined. This symbiotic relationship was initially a positive one but eventually deteriorated into a destructive entity that helped destroy the once-successful civil rights coalition and call into question black America's historic belief that military service could lead to greater equality and civil rights. Within the armed forces, the civil rights movement contributed to the rise of racial violence and friction, but it also helped convince the Pentagon to make race relations and discrimination a priority, leading to a series of reforms that once again established the military as a model of racial opportunity and cooperation.

## The Civil Rights Movement and Vietnam

On July 15, 1966, Whitney Young, executive director of the National Urban League, met with President Lyndon Johnson at the White House to debrief him on his recent five-day fact-finding trip to Vietnam to evaluate the treatment and attitude of black serviceman. Young gave the president an "encouraging report," stating that morale was "extremely high" among the black troops, that an "unprecedented, unparalleled" degree of integration existed among the American troops in Vietnam, and that white Southerners "willingly and respectfully" followed orders from black officers.[1] Less than a month later, in early August, the Urban League expressed pride in "the part played by Negro Americans in the armed services in Vietnam" at its fifty-sixth annual convention in Philadelphia. The convention praised "This loyalty to America and continued service in its defense by Negro citizens . . . it "is yet another moral claim on the nation to strive for a true equality of condition, to the end that equality on the battlefield is matched by equality in housing, employment, and education for all, regardless of race, creed, religion or national origin."[2]

The feelings expressed by Young and his colleagues at the National Urban League fit well into a historical precedent. African Americans have long been aware of the connection between the right to bear arms and the ability to exercise the privileges of citizenship. Frederick Douglas commented on it during the Civil War, and in the twentieth century both conservative and integrationist leaders and organizations in the black community supported military service as a way to secure equality and civil rights. Both believed it was essential for African Americans to serve in the armed forces and prove their capabilities to a skeptical white America. For example, as the United States acquired an imperial empire, the accommodationist Booker T. Washington expressed hope that it would include expanded opportunities for African Americans.[3] During World War I, W. E. B. DuBois predicted that out of Allied victory would emerge "an American Negro with the right to vote and the right to work, and the right to live without insult."[4] In World War II, the *Pittsburgh Courier* originated the "Double V" program, which called for victory over fascism abroad and over racism at home. The Double V was endorsed by more than two hundred black newspapers and the National Association for the Advancement of Colored People (NAACP).[5] The NAACP Papers relating to World War II state that "African-Americans, recognizing that military service provided both opportunities not otherwise available and a claim for full citizenship, sought such opportunities."[6]

Initially, Vietnam was no different: civil rights leaders as well as black military personnel supported military service and the war as opportunities for African Americans to excel in an egalitarian environment. A black officer serving in Vietnam stated proudly that "The brother does all right here . . . you see its just about the first time in his life that he finds he can compete with whites on an equal or very close to equal basis." Journalist David Llorens observed that "Negroes find the Armed Forces just about the most productive, rewarding, and racially congenial experience that they can have."[7] Sgt. Willie E. Burney, Jr., said that by fighting in Vietnam, African Americans were "earning the right to call the United States 'our' country, and when we return home, we will earn the right to keep it 'ours.' . . . We now fight two separate wars in Vietnam, and as long as we share a predominately white society we will always fight two wars— one for freedom, the other for equality."[8] Whitney Young claimed that "Vietnam will have a profound and far-reaching effect on the whole race situation in America during the next decade. For in this war there is a degree of integration among black and white Americans far exceeding that of any other war in our history as well as any other time or place in our domestic life. The impact of this experience on both white and Negro servicemen in Vietnam has formidable ramifications for the future of all Americans."[9]

Not all African Americans shared this belief that military service would translate into greater civil rights, and in every war of the twentieth century there were those who criticized black participation. In World War I, Socialist and labor leader Asa Philip Randolph ridiculed the notion that black participation would lead to more civil rights in the January 1918 edition of the *Messenger.* "Since when has the subject race come out of a war with its rights and privileges accorded for such participation," he asked. "Did not the Negro take part in the Spanish-American War? . . . and have not prejudice and race hate grown in this country since 1898?"[10] During World War II, historian Benjamin Quarles questioned the importance of military service and belittled black leaders who naively expected white gratitude in return.

There were, of course, voices of dissent among black rights leaders concerning Vietnam, and early on the war began to cause tension within the civil rights movement. The public image of the movement tended to be as a monolithic entity led by the charismatic Dr. Martin Luther King, Jr. King was indispensable to the success of the movement, but the reality was that the coalition was not a unified entity under the control of any one leader or organization. It was a loose alliance of organizations and individuals that had in common the desire to ex-pand black rights and eliminate discrimination. Within this framework, there was a lot of disagreement as to philosophy, tactics, and ultimate goals. Those who were most committed to an integrationist philosophy and willing to work through the system to achieve it included many of the veterans of the movement such as Randolph, Bayard Rustin, the NAACP and its executive director Roy Wilkins, Young and the National Urban League, and Dr. King and his Southern Christian Leadership Conference (SCLC). The two other major organizations in the coalition, however, the Student Nonviolent Coordinating Committee (SNCC) and the Congress of Racial Equality (CORE), were more radical. By 1964, they were already beginning to question their commitment to nonviolence and inte-gration in favor of embracing the more militant philosophy of black power, which emphasized self-determination and cultural, political, and economic indepen-dence from the dominant white power structure. Ideologically SNCC and CORE were a link between the integrationists and the Black Nationalists, such as the Nation of Islam and later the Black Panther Party (BPP). By 1964 Malcolm X had also embraced many of the tenants of the civil rights movement and displayed a willingness to work with Dr. King. He was also one of the early critics of black participation in the Vietnam War.

On December 31, 1964, Malcolm X denounced the war in the strongest of terms in a speech at McComb, Mississippi. Several members of SNCC, includ-ing James Forman and Robert Moses, had criticized the war in Vietnam and collaborated in the antiwar movement, but they did so as individuals and not as representatives of SNCC. In July 1965, the Mississippi Freedom Democratic Party published a newsletter critical of the war, claiming that African Ameri-cans from Mississippi should not "fight in Vietnam for the white man's free-dom, until all the Negro people are free in Mississippi."[11] But early in the war, the civil rights movement was divided over Vietnam, and most of its leaders were reluctant to criticize President Lyndon Johnson's handling of the conflict considering everything he had done to help the movement. At the same time, Forman and Moses were active in antiwar demonstrations. For example, SNCC officials John Lewis and Marion Barry worked with organizers of the White House Conference on Civil Rights, to be held in June 1966. Eventually, Lewis and most others would align themselves with the antiwar activists, but the con-troversy over the war would be a major factor in the demise of the civil rights coalition.

### Military Service as a Path to Full Citizenship

Whites, of course, were well aware African Americans hoped to translate military service into civil rights gains in civilian society and, until the 1950's, were generally adamant about preventing it. During World War I, Secretary of War Newton D. Baker, who generally supported greater opportunities in the armed forces for African Americans, declared the army would not be used as a social laboratory and that "there is no intention on the part of the War Department . . . to settle the so-called race question."[12] In World War II, the War Department was very critical of the Double V program. Assistant Secretary of War John McCloy complained that the emphasis on the Double V in "papers like the *Pittsburgh Courier* . . . serve to take the mind of the Negro soldier . . . off what you term the basic issues of the war . . . I bespeak greater emphasis on the necessity for greater out-and-out support of the war, particularly by the Negro press."[13]

Unlike during previous conflicts, the military was at first boastful of its record on racial equality and the fact it was held up as a model for civilian society; it was very happy to be considered a social laboratory. It was in part the failure of the military to actually live up to these claims that contributed to the racial friction and violence that marred the armed forces in the latter stages of the Vietnam War.

Despite the resistance of white leaders and the skepticism of many black ones, mainstream civil rights leaders continued to support patriotism and military service because the tactic generally did work to their advantage, especially when pressuring the military and government to enact reforms. In World War I, civil rights advocates led by DuBois and the executive director of the NAACP, Joel Spingarn, successfully lobbied the government for a wider black role in that conflict, including the establishment of a black officers' training camp at Des Moines, Iowa, the first of its kind in American history. During World War II President Franklin Roosevelt and his military leadership refused to consider officially desegregating the armed forces, but FDR was sympathetic to black aspirations and enacted numerous reforms to give African Americans much greater opportunities. Previous all-white domains such as the army air force, the navy, and the marine corps were opened to African Americans, and the navy even began training black officers. Unofficially, segregation was also slowly fading. In March 1943, the War Department ordered integrated recreational facilities, post exchanges, and transportation facilities on all stateside bases and all of its officer training camps, with the exception of those training pilots. By late 1944, the army was operating twenty desegregated Officer Candidate School camps and had also begun to desegregate its specialist training schools. The integrated camps were more efficient and cost effective, and they reported far less racial friction than the segregated ones.[14]

Most of the reforms had come after intense lobbying and pressure from civil rights leaders. Newton Baker and President Woodrow Wilson had agreed to the training of black officers and the raising of black combat divisions in World War I only after civil rights advocates and black colleges had staged a nationwide campaign. FDR was far less racist than Wilson and far more receptive to supporting black civil rights, but it still took pressure from black leaders, in particular Walter White of the NAACP, T. Arnold Hill of the National Urban League, and A. Philip Randolph of the Brotherhood of Sleeping Car Porters, to get him to act.

The civil rights advocates scored their greatest victory in 1948. That year, Randolph organized the "Committee Against Jim Crowism in Military Service and Training" and began a concerted campaign to force the federal government to desegregate the armed forces. On March 22 he warned President Harry Truman, "Negroes are in no mood to shoulder a gun for democracy abroad as long as they are denied democracy here at home." Later that month he told Congress he would actively urge young men of all races to resist a Jim Crow draft and service in a segregated military.[15] Truman had been a lifelong racist and almost joined the Ku Klux Klan years earlier to benefit his political career, but he was honest and open minded, and as a United States senator, he had consistently supported legislation favored by the black community, including a federal antilynching law. He had also recently had something of an epiphany on race and civil rights. In 1946, Walter E. White and the National Emergency Committee against Mob Violence met with the president and briefed him about the racist treatment accorded African American veterans after the war. Truman was deeply disturbed by the accounts of murders and lynchings, but what moved him most was the account of Sgt. Isaac Woodward, a decorated veteran who had his eyes gouged out by police in Aiken, South Carolina, only hours after being discharged from the army. "My God. I had no idea it was as terrible as that," the president replied. "We've got to do something." On 5 December 1946, he announced the formation of the President's Committee on Civil Rights, also called the Fahy Committee after its chair, Charles Fahy. In October 1947, the Fahy Committee released its landmark report, *To Secure These Rights*. The report stated there were a wide discrepancy between America's ideals of equality and freedom for all and its racial policies in practice. It also warned that in the heightening tensions of a developing Cold War, the Communists could use racism in America as fruitful propaganda. Most importantly, the report was a blueprint for change, making nearly three dozen specific recommendations, including desegregating the armed forces.[16] On July 26, 1948, Truman issued Executive Order 9981, calling for "equality of treatment and opportunity for all persons in the Armed Services without regard to race, color, religion or national order." Without ever actually stating it, Truman effectively ordered the desegregation of the armed forces.[17]

Black leaders were elated. A major barrier had been destroyed, and here was a long-awaited opportunity to use the military as a social laboratory and to demonstrate the merits of integration and equal opportunity to a still-segregated civilian society. But opposition to integration remained strong in the military. In 1949, the newly independent air force took immediate steps to comply with the directive, but it was obvious that the other services were reluctant to implement desegregation in any meaningful way. The marines, for example, had abolished segregated training but still maintained all-black units. The army agreed in March 1950 to drop all objections and comply with Truman's executive order, but a NAACP investigation of racial conditions in Korea and Japan in early 1951, led by Thurgood Marshall, found rigid patterns of segregation the norm in the army's Far East command. Marshall was convinced that most of the senior command were diehard segregationists, General Douglas MacArthur in particular.[18] As late as 1953, there were only 23,000 African Americans in the navy, and over half were still in the racially exclusive steward branch.[19]

In both world wars, military officials had argued against attempting to integrate the armed forces during hostilities, but just the opposite occurred with the Korean War. In August 1950, two months after hostilities began, the army began integrating training units and implemented what best could be described as "battlefield integration" in Korea as replacements were shipped out to combat units regardless of race. Far from hampering military efficiency, the integrated units performed quite capably in the field. Project Clear, conducted in 1951, concluded that "Integration enhances the effectiveness of the Army." A study conducted by the Operations Research Office at Johns Hopkins University found that integration was generally well accepted by both whites and blacks, and most believed it increased efficiency. The army dropped its opposition to integration, and on October 30, 1954, the Pentagon announced that the last all-black units were officially integrated.[20]

The army's announcement came less than six months after the Supreme Court, by unanimous opinion in *Brown v. Board of Education*, struck down the doctrine of "separate but equal" and legalized segregation in America in May 1954. After decades of resisting racial change, the armed forces now embraced their new role as a social laboratory, presenting the services as a shining example of racial cooperation and equal opportunity. Integration did increase efficiency and reduce costs, and it made wonderful Cold War propaganda, both at home and abroad.

The Pentagon even began to take proactive measures to combat discrimination. A June 1961 directive from Secretary of Defense Robert MacNamara encouraged all stateside base commanders to work vigorously to integrate nearby off-base housing and recreational spots. In July 1963, MacNamara charged base commanders with fostering equal treatment both on and off the base. Next, he established the post of assistant secretary of defense for civil rights, to oversee the Pentagon's equal opportunity compliance. A year later, the secretary of the navy banned navy or marine corps participation in any event or organization that practiced racial segregation or discrimination. By the mid-1960s, the services had made such progress that sociologist Charles C. Moskos could refer to stateside military installations as "Island[s] of integration in a sea of Jim Crow."[21]

In return, many civil rights organizations purged their leadership cadres of members who still espoused radical philosophies that could be construed as unpatriotic. By the early 1950s the NAACP and Walter White, for example, had ousted DuBois, denounced his Pan-African and anti-colonial positions, and embraced anti-Communism. Many activists, like former Communist Party USA member Bayard Rustin, distanced themselves from their socialist past and counseled younger members of the civil rights coalition, particularly from SNCC, to avoid any connection with Communists or Communism.

### Fighting Discrimination during the Vietnam War

But support for the military and American foreign policy did not mean that the civil rights organizations would cease advocating for the rights of black service personnel. The armed forces may have established a laudable record on integration and opportunity, but numerous problems still existed, and personal and institutional racism were still endemic to the system. African Americans faced discrimination in virtually every facet of military life, but it was especially egregious in the areas of testing and assignment, promotion, and the military justice system. These were not new problems, and civil rights organizations had intervened on behalf of black service personnel in the past.

The NAACP, in particular, had a long history of investigating racism and injustice in the armed forces. In 1919, W. E. B. DuBois made an extensive tour of

American bases in Europe to document the racism, discrimination, and in many cases violence that black troops were subject to while serving in World War I. In World War II, NAACP Executive Secretary Walter White went on a similar mission, visiting and interviewing African American soldiers serving in the European, Mediterranean, and Pacific theaters of operation.[22] Stateside, the NAACP responded to dozens of complaints ranging from attempts to demote black officers at Camp Breckenridge, Kentucky, to charges of racial discrimination by the commanding officer of Fort Benning, Georgia.[23] Though they could not directly represent black military personnel in a military court, they aided them in courts-martial; probably the most famous case was the Port Chicago Mutiny, where fifty African American sailors were court-martialed for refusing to unload ammunition ships after an explosion aboard one on July 17, 1944, killed 202 black ammunition handlers.

During the Vietnam War era, the NAACP would again find itself involved in the military justice system. Many of the cases stemmed from the widespread racial violence that racked the armed forces after 1967. The NAACP successfully defended black service personnel accused of rioting and assault at Millington Naval Air Station, Tennessee, and at Fort Knox, Kentucky, as well as the so-called Darmstadt 43 in Germany.[24] General Counsel Nathaniel Jones not only got all of the charges dropped against five black airmen accused of inciting a racial gang fight at Goose Bay, Labrador, but also managed to get the base commander, Colonel Benton Fielder, transferred. In January 1971, Jones led an NAACP investigative team to Europe to investigate charges of racism in Germany, particularly in the administration of military justice.[25]

Most of the problems faced by black service personnel were due to the nature of the military justice system and the wide latitude for abuse inherent in the system. The military justice system is somewhat different from its civilian counterpart in that in the armed forces, justice is administered at two distinct levels. Petty offences such as minor insubordination, uniform code violations, or being late for duty were handled through a process known as nonjudicial punishment (NJP). Commonly called an Article 15 in the army and air force and a Captain's Mast in the navy and marine corps, it was administered by one's commanding officer, who had wide latitude in handing down punishment. A penalty could be nothing more than a written reprimand in your service file or as severe as thirty days' correctional custody in the stockade, forty-five days of extra duty, or sixty days' restriction plus forfeiture of half a month's pay for two months. In addition, enlisted grades up to E-4 could be reduced to E-1, the lowest enlisted rank.

The wide discretion officers had in dispensing nonjudicial punishment meant the system was ripe for abuse by racist officers and noncommissioned officers (NCOs).

Most African Americans were convinced there was a racial double standard in the administration of NJP, and nothing generated more complaints from black military personnel. Jones found that black soldiers in Germany were "convinced that white soldiers are not punished for behavior which, on the part of a black, would bring an Article 15 action. Whites, they said, were not dealt with for wearing long hair while blacks were punished for long hair. There seemed to be two sets of rules: one for whites and the other for blacks."[26] Blacks were given Article 15s in disproportionate numbers. The numbers for the 193rd Infantry Brigade were typical for most units. African Americans constituted 27.5 percent of the enlisted strength of the brigade, but between June 1, 1970, and July 31, 1971, they received 39 percent of the Article 15s decided in that unit.[27]

Serious offenses were dealt with by courts-martial. Under military law someone can be held in confinement for up to thirty days without being formally charged, or even longer at the court's discretion. There was no appeal process or chance for bail. African Americans were also far more likely to be given pretrial confinement than were whites. In 1970, nearly 40 percent of African Americans charged with the offense of being absent without leave (AWOL) were incarcerated, compared to only 15 percent of whites.[28] African Americans made up roughly 50 percent of all prisoners held in pretrial confinement in West Germany but accounted for less than 10 percent of the army's enlisted strength in that country.[29]

Not surprisingly, there was a disparity based on race in the percentages of service personnel brought to court-martial. A 1972 Department of Defense investigation of military justice at several bases revealed that African Americans made up over 34 percent of the courts-martial.[30] At Camp Casey, Vietnam, African Americans accounted for 57 percent of all general courts-martial. The Defense Department study found that blacks were more likely to be court-martialed for lesser offences than were whites. Once convicted, black defendants typically served longer sentences than did whites; the average sentence for white offenders was about two and half years, whereas for African Americans it was three years.[31]

Another area where institutional racism was a problem was in testing and placement. All of the services administered aptitude tests to new inductees which were crucial to their future training and assignment. The standard exam given to all new recruits, regardless of service branch, was the Armed Forces

Qualification Test (AFQT), which was similar to a civilian IQ test. Each service also had its own specialized exams, with the army and marine corps utilizing the Army Qualification Battery, the navy the Short Basic Test Battery, and the air force the Airman Qualifying Examination. Higher scores on these exams meant a recruit had more latitude in choosing a Military Occupational Specialty (MOS) and could request more lucrative assignments, such as intelligence or a technical specialty. A low score relegated the recruit to the infantry or a service MOS. In 1965–1966, 40 percent of the African Americans tested ended up in the lowest category.[32] As a result of poor testing, blacks were assigned in disproportionate numbers to the infantry and to service and supply units, making up 16.3 percent of enlisted personnel assigned to combat specialties and nearly 20 percent of the service and supply troops in 1972.[33]

One of the problems, substandard education for African Americans in civilian society, was outside the control of military authorities. As early as 1949, the Fahy Committee observed that even if military policy was unbiased, "through no fault of their own," African Americans "do not have the skills or education required for many of the Army's occupational specialties."[34] One black sergeant explained to the NAACP investigative team in Germany that "When you come in, you take the AFQT. If you haven't had a good background and a good high school or college education, or experience in electronics, into Supply and Transportation you go. I graduated from high school in 1955. I got substandard education, compared to the white NCOs my age."[35]

The other problem with testing and placement, however unintentional, was the fault of the armed forces. Though the battery of tests given to new recruits was supposed to be culturally neutral, it did contain an inherent Eurocentric bias, or as the NAACP report characterized it, "a bonus for growing up white."[36] Sociologist Donald F. Hueber considered the AFQT to be "a measure of the individual's participation in the culture" and not a true measure of intelligence.[37]

African Americans faced discrimination in promotion, field and advanced military school assignments, and off-base housing, among other issues. They also felt that the military ignored their cultural needs. There were few black products, such as hair care products, magazines, and clothes, for sale at the post exchange, and most of the recreational facilities on military bases were geared to the interests of whites. As one black marine observed, "You don't see many of the brothers out on the skeet range."[38] The NAACP found that "Base clubs, never the favorite serviceman's hangout in any case, were viewed as alien and often hostile places for blacks."[39] The clubs often featured country-and-western music during the busiest weekend hours, for example, and only occasionally played soul music. Marine Corps Lt. Colonel Hurdle L. Maxwell summed up black frustration by noting, "The Corps says it treats all men just one way—as a Marine. What it actually has done is treat everybody like a white Marine."[40]

During the Vietnam War one of the problems the NAACP and other advocacy groups encountered in their attempts to help black service personnel was the stubborn refusal of military authorities, at least initially, to admit that institutional racism was still a major problem. Officially, authorities claimed it had been eradicated. According to the *Department of Defense Annual Report for 1968*, "Defense manpower policy has long required that equal treatment and opportunity be afforded all servicemen without regard to race, color, creed, or national origin. The application of this principle, established in 1948, has officially eliminated racial discrimination in the Military Services and led to major breakthroughs in advancements in rank based on merit alone."[41] When challenged, white authorities defended the system and dismissed the complaints as unwarranted. In 1968, Major Harry Fancher, representing the United States Army Europe's Judge Advocate Division, claimed that "We often hear complaints that a Negro soldier believed he has received an Article 15 or court-martial for an offense that a white soldier would only have been slapped on the wrist for . . . It is bad that many people believe this and it hurts the Army's image," adding, "Most of the time there is no validity to complaints of racial inequity in the military justice system."[42]

Black officers tended to be more conservative and promilitary than black enlisted personnel, and many of them defended the system against charges of racism. One of the few African Americans to hold high rank in the military justice system during the Vietnam War, Colonel Willard C. Stewart, an inspector general stationed at army headquarters in Heidelberg, dismissed racial discrimination complaints as unjustified and self-serving. "Unfortunately, the colored soldier bases his complaints on his race too frequently . . . he uses it as a crutch."[43] General Daniel "Chappie" James, the first black full general in the armed forces and an outspoken defender of the armed forces and American involvement in Vietnam, took issue with the Congressional Black Caucus's hearings on racism in the military, disparaging the "criticism from the black side of the house" and labeling it "unfortunate" considering that on the issue of race the armed forces had "made more progress than in the whole history of the United States."[44] Brigadier-general Frederic Davison praised the army for making "unbelievable progress against prejudice."[45]

Most African Americans, however proud of the military's record on race relations, still supported and appreciated the efforts of the civil rights movement. This support was generally strongest early in the war and among the career officers and NCOs. Colin Powell recalled that when he was an advisor in Vietnam in 1963, "there occurred the eighteenth bombing of black neighborhoods in Birmingham. While I was fighting the VC, a young Baptist minister, Dr. Martin Luther King, Jr., had been arrested for leading a protest march on Birmingham's city hall . . . while I was patrolling the A Shau Valley for communists, R. C., my father-in-law, sat up nights, a shotgun across his lap, ready to defend his home against fellow Americans of a different color."[46] Sp. 4 Charles C. Park stationed at Long Binh, Vietnam, in 1968 supported "what some of our fellow Soul brothers are doing in an effort to bring about equality for the black men of America, the land of the free . . . Though I'm in Vietnam I'm with the patriots of Milwaukee a 100 per cent in their efforts to obtain a fair housing law."[47] Sgt. Allen Thomas, Jr., a veteran of three tours of duty in Vietnam, was a lifelong supporter of the movement, and he admired King and A. P. Randolph. As late as 1970, with Vietnam all but lost and the movement in disarray, Major Robert E. Jones still expressed support for the war and the civil rights movement. "I support the black community in its non-violent movements, the NAACP and the rest and about one fourth of the demonstrators," he explained.[48] Many saw a connection between the efforts of the movement and the military's positive record on race. Two decades after Dr. King's assassination, General Colin Powell kept a framed poster of King, given to him by Coretta Scott King, in his office at Fort McPherson, Georgia. The poster was there to remind him and anyone who came to his office of "the leading role the Army had played in defending freedom and advancing racial justice."[49]

Irrespective of their support for the movement, most black careerists chose to remain silent on the issue of civil rights. Historian Isaac Hampton II has argued that "black officers tended to be politically conservative and generally avoided identification with any movement that could potentially damage their image as excellent soldiers and their chance for promotion—most avoided identification with either the Civil Rights Movement or Black Power."[50] For example, despite being a pioneer and role model, Lt. General Benjamin O. Davis, Jr., was never considered to be a "racial reformer." One observer lamented that "because of the general's neutral position on civil rights and his noninvolvement policy, his tremendous Air Force record has had little impact" on race relations.[51]

No matter much they admired—and often defended-—the armed forces record on race, black officers and NCOs were under no illusion that things were perfect.

They were well aware that racism still pervaded the armed forces. But they had faith in the system that had given them much more opportunity to succeed than they could have found in the civilian sector and chose to change it from the inside by becoming super soldiers, working through existing channels, and leading by example. General Davis was known to work quietly behind the scenes on behalf of black military personnel.[52] Colin Powell greatly admired "the black officers from the South. After a lifetime of second-class treatment, segregation . . . Most of them simply refused to carry the baggage that racists tried to pile on their backs. Fortunately, they had joined the most democratic institution in America, where they could rise or fall on merit."[53]

As the war in Vietnam progressed, however, the younger, black enlisted personnel entering the armed forces were far less complacent and trusting in the system than were the officers and NCOs. Many were unwilling conscripts, drafted into the army by a Selective Service they considered racist. They were more sensitive to real or perceived instances or racism and expected to encounter it in their military careers. They felt out of place in what was essentially a white institution. There were few black officers; African Americans made up only 2 percent of the officer corps during the war, and enlisted African Americans tended to distrust them. Black enlisted men reacted by closing ranks and developing a black culture within the military based on racial solidarity and racial pride. They self-segregated and called each other "blood," "soul brother," and "brother." They greeted one another with a black power salute—a clenched fist raised in the air—or by dapping. Dapping, a corruption of the Vietnamese slang for "beautiful," was an often lengthy, ritualized handshake, and each move of the dap had a specific meaning. They also wore the trappings of racial pride and solidarity, such as black power canes and slave bracelets woven from boot laces, and they flew a black power flag proudly over an all-black "hootch" or living quarters in Vietnam. Journalist Wallace Terry observed that when he interviewed black soldiers in Vietnam in 1966, "no Negroes seemed to identify with extreme militants." Three years later, he "noted some extremists and their sympathizers saluting each other with the Black Panther fist when passing on the street."[54]

Black soldiers' views on civil rights and the war in Vietnam had also changed; many now linked the war directly to the issue of civil rights at home. Sergeant Andrew May admitted that "It does make you feel funny sometimes, fighting here for things we're denied at home."[55] Another black soldier thought that "If they can't pass the civil rights bill because it's the just and right thing to do, they should do it in recognition of what the Negro guys have done and are doing in

Vietnam. That's reason enough."[56] Writing in the *New York Times* in May 1969, C. L. Sulzberger observed that "American Negro soldiers in Vietnam used to consider the war and the civil rights movement as separate things but the past three years have had an exacerbating effect. For the first time black GI's ask: 'Why should I defend someone else's freedom if no one defends mine?' "[57]

Prominent African Americans were also questioning many aspects of the war and its negative impact on the black community. They were troubled by inequities in the Selective Service System that largely exempted middle- and upper-classes from military service at the expense of minorities and working-class whites. All were alarmed at the extremely high black casualty rates early in the war. In July 1966, African Americans constituted around 11 percent of the US population. In the armed forces they accounted for 13.9 percent of the army, 10.7 percent of the air force, 9 percent of the marine corps, and 5.8 percent of the navy. African Americans were over-represented among army and marine corps formations in Vietnam and were suffering a disproportionate percentage of the casualties. Blacks made up 15 percent of American forces stationed in Vietnam, but they accounted for 22 percent of the total casualties to date.[58] By the end of direct American involvement in 1973, the 7,241 African Americans killed in the war would constitute 12.6 percent of American casualties in Vietnam.

There was also the economic damage the war was causing to domestic re-form. The problem was that President Johnson had done more for the movement than any president in American history. As part of his ambitious reform program, the Great Society, he had engineered the enactment of the historic Civil Rights Act of 1964, the Voting Rights Act of 1965, and the Civil Rights Act of 1968, aimed at eliminating discrimination in housing. His War on Poverty offered hope at alleviating the economic woes facing a majority of black Americans and offering previously unavailable educational opportunities. But these initiatives were expensive, and the costly war in Vietnam drained resources away from the Great Society programs. Between 1964 and 1973, the war accounted for over $111 billion in direct costs and untold billions more in military aid to South Vietnam and to subsidize contingents from allied nations. The total cost of the war is controversial, depending on how one calculates such things as veteran benefits or interest on loans, but the estimates range from a total cost of $350 billion to $900 billion.[59] By comparison, the government appropriated only $1 billion for the War on Poverty in 1964 and $2 billion in both 1965 and 1966. Disagreeing with the president over Vietnam was also complicated by Johnson's notions concerning political loyalty. Johnson had supported the civil rights movement, and he fully expected civil rights leaders to back him on Vietnam. There was little middle ground on the issue. They also had to worry about possible retaliation; LBJ's wrath and sense of vengeance could be formidable if he felt betrayed.

At the same time that Vietnam was becoming a major concern, CORE and SNCC were undergoing metamorphoses. Their members tended to be younger than those of the other major civil rights organizations, and they had provided the majority of the activists involved in such daring operations as the sit-ins, the freedom rides, and the freedom summer in Mississippi. In the words of historian Clayborne Carson, they were the "shock troops" of the movement. They were the ones who had largely been arrested, jailed, bombed, beaten, and shot. They had rejected their commitment to nonviolence and integration and embraced the more militant black power movement. They no longer viewed military service positively but as a burden imposed on African Americans in support of white hegemony. Instead of being separate from the civil rights movement, the war in Vietnam had in fact become the foremost civil rights issue.

## The War in Vietnam as a Civil Rights Issue

CORE and SNCC now began to more actively support the antiwar movement. In April 1965, SNCC's executive committee endorsed a large antiwar rally in Washington, DC, organized by the leftist Students for a Democratic Society (SDS). In July, delegates at CORE's annual convention, in Baltimore, Maryland, endorsed resolutions supporting black power, rejecting the doctrine of nonviolence, demanding the withdrawal of US forces from Vietnam, and supporting resistance to the draft. They narrowly defeated another resolution officially opposing the war. On January 6, 1966, SNCC became the first civil rights organization to officially oppose the war. John Lewis issued a statement condemning American involvement in Vietnam and the use of the draft to raise the manpower needed in the conflict. Lewis stated that SNCC was "in sympathy with and supports the men in this country who are unwilling to respond to a military draft which would compel them to contribute their lives to United States aggression in Vietnam . . . in the name of the 'freedom' we find so false in this country."[60] On August 6, several groups from SNCC and CORE marched in a mass demonstration in New York's Times Square to protest the Vietnam War and to mark the twenty-first anniversary of the dropping of the atomic bomb on Hiroshima in World War II. One group from Harlem carried a long banner reading "Bring Our Black GI's Home. No Fighting For Racist USA. Our Fight Is Here, Not There," while chanting "black power." Lincoln Lynch, associate national director of CORE, was one of the featured speakers at the rally.[61]

The leaders of the moderate civil rights organizations remained reluctant to criticize Johnson and break with him over the war. King still trusted Johnson and believed the president was sincerely trying to negotiate a peaceful solution. As late as fall 1965 he "believed it was essential for all Americans to publicly avoid the debate on why we were waging war in the far-off lands of Vietnam . . . The president's strong declaration to negotiate, to talk peace, and thus end the death and destruction, had to be accepted, honored and implemented." For these reasons, King said he "did not march, I did not demonstrate, I did not rally." In private meetings, King petitioned the president and other officials to seek peace, but for a time he left it up to his wife, Coretta Scott King, to carry the antiwar banner and "make the meetings on the peace issue, and leave me to concentrate on civil rights."[62] King did comment on the war, although usually in muted terms. He questioned among other things the inequities in the draft and the diversion of funds from the Great Society programs to the war but fell short of indicting Johnson or condemning the war. By February 1967, however, King had reached the conclusion that he could no longer contain his protest. The civil rights giant had continued to agonize "a great deal" over the war in the preceding months, but finally, "Something said to me, 'Martin, you have got to stand up on this. No matter what it means.'" It was an article he had been reading one night entitled "The Children of Vietnam" that convinced him, "Never again will I be silent on an issue that is destroying the soul of our nation and destroying thousands and thousands of little children in Vietnam."[63]

King openly broke with LBJ on Vietnam on April 4, 1967, in an impassioned speech at the famous Riverside church in New York. He really did not say anything he had not stated before, but on this occasion the great orator articulated it with more power, depth, and poetry. King began his sermon by pointing out the linkage between the war and the civil rights movement, stating there was a "very obvious and facile connection between the war in Vietnam and the struggle I and others have been waging in America." He pointed out that the war, "like some demonic, destructive suction tube," sucked precious resources away from the movement, and with the "buildup in Vietnam . . . I watched this program broken and eviscerated as if it were some idle political plaything of a society gone mad on war." It was sad but ironic that "we have been repeatedly faced with the cruel irony of watching Negro and white boys on TV screens as they kill and die together for a nation that has been unable to seat them together in the same schools."[64]

King understood fully the dangers in speaking out against the war. Recriminations and retaliation had come quickly to the individuals and organizations that had previously taken a stand. Just four days after Lewis issued SNCC's press release opposing the war in January 1966, Julian Bond, a member of SNCC, was refused his duly elected seat in the Georgia legislature over his and the organization's antiwar stance.[65] Other SNCC leaders, such as John Lewis and Cleveland Sellers, found themselves the targets of the Selective Service System, despite having already been granted conscientious objector status. Several black newspapers, including the *Atlanta Daily World* and the *Pittsburgh Courier*, slammed SNCC for jeopardizing the movement. That summer, Whitney Young threatened that the Urban League would cease associating itself with any civil rights organization that advocated black power or linked the war in Vietnam to the civil rights movement domestically.[66]

Despite King's immense stature in the movement, the criticism was both immediate and severe. On April 11, the NAACP issued a statement distancing itself from King and the antiwar movement. The press release read in part, "Civil rights battles will have to be fought and won on their own merits, irrespective of the state of war or peace in the world. We are not a peace organization nor a foreign policy association. We are a civil rights organization. The NAACP remains committed to its primary goal of eliminating all forms of racial discrimination and achieving equal rights and equal opportunities for all Americans."[67] *Life* magazine categorized Dr. King's antiwar pleas "demagogic slander that sounds like a script for radio Hanoi."[68] An editorial in the *New York Times* on April 7, 1967, accused him of fusing "two public problems that are distinct and separate. By drawing them together, Dr. King has done a disservice to both." The editorial claimed that "to divert the energies of the civil rights movement to the Vietnam issue is both wasteful and self-defeating" and concluded by warning King that "linking these hard, complex problems will not lead to solutions but to deeper confusion."[69]

King, of course, did have his supporters. Stokely Carmichael was elated and publicly called King his hero.[70] An open letter by Rev. James Bevel defended Dr. King's assertion that the peace and civil rights issues were " 'fused' into a single concern," adding it was only appropriate, for "they have experienced firsthand the Government's disrespect for humanity and dignity at home and are compelled to voice their outrage at this calculated destruction abroad of their Vietnamese brothers."[71] In 1968, Executive Director of CORE Roy Innis released a rough draft of his organization's "Proposed Statement on Vietnam and the

Draft" which read, "We of CORE wish resolutely to state our total opposition to our country's continued intervention in Vietnam, and our complete endorsement of Martin Luther King's five point program for ending the war."[72]

In 1967, the New York State chapter of the NAACP adopted a resolution opposing the war in Vietnam. This was in direct defiance of the national leadership of the organization, which never would take a stance opposing the war. Beginning in 1967, however, their annual convention would issue a statement "deploring the war" and hoping for a speedy settlement.[73] By 1969, Andrew Young, like King, became convinced that the war was killing the civil rights movement. In October, the once-hesitant director of the Urban League joined the ranks of the opposition and finally condemned the war in Vietnam. At a conference at the Urban League's headquarters he called it a "moral and spiritual drain." Young said developments in the last several months due to the war endangered "both the black and white American communities," but he was "totally convinced that this war had an extra dimension for black people that it does not have for many whites. We are suffering doubly. We are dying for something abroad that we do not have at home." He ended his news conference with a plea similar to Dr. King's, to "turn away from Vietnam. We must terminate this war as soon as possible. We must pour our vital resources back into our own land, our own cities, our own people." Young further shocked supporters of the war by announcing plans to attend and support an upcoming "moratorium" for peace on the Vietnam War.[74]

Many African Americans in the armed forces had also experienced a change of heart. Allen Thomas, Jr., remained a committed supporter of the civil rights movement. But by his second tour of duty in 1967–1968, he, like King, had concluded the war was a lost cause and that US involvement was a mistake, a "big lie."[75] Jerry Brown went to Vietnam "believing strongly in the war," but the twenty-seven-year-old student said he came back believing it to be immoral and futile. "Why fight a war for freedom in a country far away when at home the civil rights war in not yet won," he asked.[76]

African Americans in Vietnam were becoming disillusioned with the war and with the pace of reform back home. This was never more so than after the assassination of Dr. King on April 4, 1968, in Memphis, Tennessee. King symbolized everything they hoped for in the movement, and the sense of loss, shock, and despair among African Americans was manifold. Specialist 4 Reginald Daniels, speaking for many, observed, "That was a man we believed in, we trusted in. If anybody was the liberator, he was the man."[77] A lot of African Americans were furious. Sgt. Allen Thomas, Jr., remembered that "Some of the younger guys were angry and just wanted to hurt someone, and there were some fist fights between whites and blacks."[78] Private Morocco Coleman, an insightful observer and sensitive to the changing dynamics among black military personnel, observed, "Almost everywhere here you can see the unity which exists among the Negro soldiers. After the assassination of Dr. M. L. King you could also feel the malcontent."[79]

Although a host of factors contributed to the problem, King's death proved to be the catalyst for the explosion of racial discontent and violence throughout the military establishment. It began that August with riots at the Danang Brig and the Long Binh Stockade in Vietnam. One of the largest incidents occurred at Camp Lejeune, North Carolina, on July 20, 1969, leading to the death of a white corporal. For the next several years there were racial gang fights or major incidents of violence throughout the military establishment, including prominent examples at Millington Naval Air Station near Memphis, Tennessee; the naval installation at Cam Ranh Bay, Vietnam; Kaneohe Marine Corps Air Station in Hawaii; and Fort McClellan, Alabama, in late 1971. Low-intensity violence, including individual encounters and ambushing or "headhunting" unsuspecting individuals, occurred on most bases, whether stateside or in Germany, Vietnam, or Okinawa. In 1972, violence would erupt on two aircraft carriers, *Constellation* and *Kitty Hawk*, as well as several other combat and support vessels. The one segment of the military establishment that did not see significant racial violence was the combat units in Vietnam. This was largely due to the cohesion and teamwork needed to stay alive during operations and the fact that everyone was heavily armed.

Military authorities blamed the racial problems on radical changes in civilian society, including discontent over the war and a growing militancy among young African Americans. For example, the House Armed Services Committee's investigation into the racial disturbance at Camp Lejeune concluded that "the racial problem at Camp Lejeune is a reflection of the nation's racial problem."[80] A host of senior defense officials and military officers, including Assistant Secretary of Defense Roger T. Kelley, General William Westmoreland, Deputy Assistant Secretary of Defense L. Howard Bennett, and Admiral Samuel Gravely, the first African American admiral in the US Navy, all blamed "outside agitators' and "external influences" for the military's racial woes.

There was some truth to the assertion. Though support for the civil rights movement remained strong among black service personnel, many had lost faith in the movement's ability to continue to affect change. Many African Americans were more militant, spoke in terms of black power, and admired Malcolm X. Instead of the civil rights movement, they looked to Black Nationalist organizations to bring about change, particularly the Black Panther Party. A survey of four hundred black servicemen in Vietnam in 1970 by *Time* found that 45 percent were willing to engage in armed struggle to secure black rights when they returned to the United States.[81] The Black Panthers were the most popular choice among armed revolutionary groups; nearly a third of the black troopers interviewed by Wallace Terry in Vietnam said they were considering joining the Panthers or another militant black organization once they got home.[82] One black sailor was very eager to "join em, and I'd help them kill all those honky muther fuckers because do unto him before he do unto you."[83] Ronald Washington also planned to join the BPP after his discharge from the armed forces and claimed that many others were planning to do the same. Some actually did. Reginald "Malik" Edwards served nearly seven years in the marine corps before getting a bad conduct discharge for fighting with a white marine. He joined the Black Panther chapter in Washington, DC, because the Panthers "were the only organization that was fighting the system."[84]

Panther officials, including cofounder Bobby Seale and Katharine Cleaver, encouraged black veterans to join the party as well as those currently serving in the armed forces. There were some Black Panthers in uniform, and there were apparently organized chapters at some bases including Camp Lejeune and Goose Bay, Labrador. Journalist Michael Herr claimed he had met some in Vietnam.[85] But their influence, and the fear the Panthers inspired in white officials, was all out of proportion to their actual numbers. The Panthers were stylish and cool, and it was not difficult to imitate their trademark uniform of black leather jacket and black beret. There were a lot more black men claiming to be Panthers than actually belonged to a legitimate chapter. Malik Edwards, for example, admitted he dressed like a Panther before he ever joined the party.[86] One African American who claimed there were a dozen Panthers in his platoon and that he was a recruiter for the BPP subsequently told Herr he was only joking.[87]

Much like the Panthers, the overall impact of the militants was more apparent than real. Though many African Americans embraced the sense of brotherhood and wore proudly the outward expressions of black pride, they were not revolutionaries. Allen Thomas, Jr.'s, response was fairly typical. "You've got to understand where I came from," he explained. "Malcolm X scared the hell out of me, just like he scared a lot of white folks, he scared the hell out of a lot of black people too. Proud . . . but fear at the same time . . . Anything out of the main-stream was out if you were going to be a professional in the army."[88]

## Military Reform to Address Racial Discrimination

The racial problems and violence, the discontent of black service personnel, and investigations and pressure by the NAACP, the Congressional Black Caucus, and other advocacy groups had a profound effect on senior military and civilian leaders and forced them to come to grips with the fact that they had a serious problem. There was also new leadership in many cases that took the issue of race relations and equal opportunity seriously, such as Chief of Naval Operations Admiral Elmo Zumwalt. By the early 1970s they were willing to admit that many of the racial problems in the armed forces were internal and that personal and institutional racism were still major issues that needed to be eliminated. They were also far more receptive to taking advice on how this could be accomplished. For example, in May 1971, Nathaniel Jones and an NAACP investigative team submitted their formal report on racial conditions in Germany to Secretary of Defense Melvin Laird and Army Chief of Staff William Westmoreland. Both men expressed appreciation for the team's efforts, and many of the military's subsequent reforms were based at least partially on the NAACP's recommendations.[89] The military justice system was reformed, and much of the discretionary power commanding officers exercised in NJP cases was curtailed. In 1972, the army replaced the AFQT with the Army Classification Battery, which was designed to be more culturally neutral than the previous exam. This change alone led to a rise from 33 percent of African Americans testing into the higher placement categories in 1972, the last year for the old AFQT, to over 42 percent in 1973. White scores remained virtually the same.[90] There was now greater African American representation in 137 different military occupational specialties.[91] Cultural needs were also addressed. More black music was programmed for the club jukeboxes, and black bands were hired for dances and mixers. By the end of the Vietnam War military barbers were being trained in cutting African Americans' hair, and black service personnel had several officially sanctioned haircuts from which to choose, including a modified Afro.

A lot of factors had contributed to the reforms, and influence and pressure from civil rights and Black Power advocates—almost acting out "good cop" and "bad cop" roles—certainly did its share to convince military authorities to enact meaningful change. The armed forces have somewhat regained their reputation for fairness and opportunity. The civil rights movement and the issues it raised also helped change the way black Americans view military service. While black participation in the armed forces is still disproportionately higher than African Americans' share of the US population, widespread disenchantment among African Americans with the recent war in Iraq indicates that the traditional model of black support for military service to further political and cultural agendas is no longer valid. The war in Vietnam contributed directly to the demise of the classic civil rights movement, but the movement influenced antiwar activism and inspired military reforms aimed at improving the conditions for African American troops.

NOTES

1. John W. Finney, "Johnson Backs Negro Promotion," *New York Times*, July 27, 1966, 24.

2. M. S. Handler, "Negro GI Hailed by Urban League," *New York Times*, August 4, 1966, 16.

3. NAACP, *Papers of the NAACP, Part 9: Discrimination in the US Armed Forces, 1918–1955* (Bethesda, MD: University Publications of America, 1989), viii.

4. "War," *The Crisis*, May 1917, 37; W. E. B. DuBois, "Close Ranks," *The Crisis*, July 1918, 111.

5. Lee Finkle, *Forum for Protest: The Black Press during World War Two* (Canbury, NJ: Associated University Press, 1975), 110–112.

6. NAACP, *Papers of the NAACP, Part 9*, vii.

7. Gene Grove, "The Army and the Negro," *New York Times Magazine*, July 24, 1965, 50; David Llorens, "Why Negroes Re-enlist," *Ebony*, August 1965, 87.

8. Sgt. Willie E. Burney, Jr., "Our Men in Vietnam," *Sepia*, August 1968, 69.

9. Whitney M. Young, Jr., "When the Negroes in Vietnam Come Home," *Harpers*, June 1967, 66.

10. Jack D. Foner, *Blacks and the Military in American History* (New York: Praeger, 1974), 110.

11. Clayborne Carson, *In Struggle: SNCC and the Black Awakening of the 1960s* (Cambridge, MA: Harvard University Press, 1981), 185–186.

12. Lou Potter, William Miles, and Nina Rosenblum, *Liberators: Fighting on Two Fronts in World War Two* (New York: Harcourt Brace Jovanovich, 1992), 23; Richard M. Dalfiume, *Desegregation of the Armed Forces* (Columbia: University of Missouri Press, 1969), 13.

13. Lee Finkle, *Forum for Protest: The Black Press during World War Two* (Canbury, NJ: Associated University Press, 1975), 110–112.

14. Foner, *Blacks and the Military*, 149–151; Ulysses Lee, "The Draft and the Negro," *Current History*, July 1968, 32.

15. Foner, *Blacks and the Military*, 181.

16. William E. Leuchtenburg, "The Conversion of Harry Truman," *American Heritage*, November 1991, 55–58.

17. Russell F. Weigley, *History of the United States Army* (New York: Macmillan, 1967), 555.

18. Carl T. Rowan, *Dream Makers, Dream Breakers: The World of Justice Thurgood Marshall* (Boston: Little, Brown, 1993), 161–169.

19. Foner, *Blacks and the Military*, 187–189; Martin Binkin and Mark J. Eitelberg, *Blacks and the Military*, Studies in Defense Policy Series (Washington, DC: Brookings Institution, 1982), 27–30.

20. Foner, *Blacks and the Military*, 187–189; Binkin and Eitelberg, *Blacks and the Military*, 27–30.

21. James E. Westheider, *Fighting on Two Fronts: African-Americans and the Vietnam War* (New York: New York University Press, 1997), 68.

22. "NAACP: A Century in the Fight for Freedom, World War II and the Postwar Years," online exhibition of the Library of Congress. www.loc.gov/exhibits/naacp/world -war-ii-and-the-post-war-years.html.

23. NAACP, *Papers of the NAACP, Part 9*, 1–2.

24. "Air Force Jim Crow," *The Crisis* 77 (June–July 1970): 227–229; Foner, *Blacks and the Military*, 232.

25. NAACP, *The Search for Military Justice* (New York: NAACP, 1971), 19.

26. Ibid., 6.

27. Hon. Ronald V. Dellums, "Institutional Racism in the Military," *Congressional Record*, March 2, 1972 (Washington, DC: Government Printing Office, 1973), 36584, hereafter cited as "Black Caucus Report."

28. Department of Defense, *Task Force on the Administration of Military Justice in the Armed Forces*, vols. 1–5 (Washington, DC: Government Printing Office, 1972), vol. 1, 29, and vol. 4, 8.

29. NAACP, *The Search for Military Justice*, 9.

30. Department of Defense, *Task Force on the Administration of Military Justice*, vol. 1, 30.

31. Department of Defense, *Task Force on the Administration of Military Justice*, vol. 4, 57–61.

32. Department of Defense, *Task Force on the Administration of Military Justice*, vol. 1, 48; Lawrence M. Baskir and William Strauss, *Chance and Circumstance: The Draft, the War, and the Vietnam Generation* (New York: Random House, 1978), 125–126.

33. "Black Caucus Report," 36583.

34. Morris J. MacGregor and Bernard C. Nalty, *Blacks in the United States Armed Forces*, vol. 11, Fahy Committee Report (Wilmington, DE: Scholarly Resources, 1977), 1343–1345.

35. NAACP, *The Search for Military Justice*, 2.

36. NAACP, *The Search for Military Justice*, 3.

37. Llorens, "Why Negroes Re-enlist," 90.

38. Steven Morris, "How Blacks Upset the Marine Corps," *Ebony*, December 1969, 57–60.

39. NAACP, *The Search for Military Justice*, 18–19; Richard Halloran, "Air Force Racism Charged in Study," *New York Times*, August 31, 1971, 1; "Black Caucus Report," 6741.

40. Morris, "How Blacks Upset the Marine Corps," 57.

41. *Department of Defense Annual Report for Fiscal Year 1968* (Washington, DC: Government Printing Office, 1971), 74.

42. Curtis Daniell, "Germany: Trouble Spot for Black GIs," *Ebony*, August 1968, 127.

43. Daniell, "Trouble Spot for Black GIs," 127.

44. Brigadier General Daniel James, Jr., "Rapping with Chappie," *Air University Review*, July 1972, 12.

45. "No Admirals," *Newsweek*, September 30, 1968, 35.

46. Colin Powell with Joseph E. Persico, *My American Journey* (New York: Random House, 1995), 93.

47. Charles Porter, "Letters to the Editor," *Sepia*, March 1968, 6.

48. Garven Dalglish, "Black and Back from Vietnam," *Enquirer Magazine*, July 19, 1970, 12.

49. Powell, *My American Journey*, 399.

50. Isaac Hampton II, *The Black Officer Corps* (New York: Routledge, 2012), ix.

51. "Lt. General Benjamin O. Davis, Jr.," *Ebony*, August 1968, 58.

52. Ibid.

53. Powell, *My American Journey*, 114.

54. Wallace Terry, "Bringing the War Home," *Black Scholar*, November 1970, 7–8.

55. Whitney M. Young, Jr., "When the Negroes in Vietnam Come Home," *Harpers*, June 1967, 66.

56. Young, "When the Negroes in Vietnam Come Home," 66.

57. C. L. Sulzberger, "Foreign Affairs: The Spin-Out," *New York Times*, May 21, 1969, 46.

58. John W. Finney, "Johnson Backs Negro Promotion," *New York Times*, July 27, 1966, 24.

59. Paul Shannon, "The ABC's of the Vietnam War," *Indochina Newsletter*, Special Issue 93–97, 1996. www.vn-agentorange.org/edmaterials/cost_of_vn_war.html.

60. "Viet Rebuke Stirs Storm," *The Baltimore Afro-American*, January 22, 1966, 14; John Lewis, "SNCC Statement on Vietnam," *Freedomways*, first quarter, vol. 6, 1966, 6–7.

61. Douglas Robinson, "Thousands over Nation March to Protest War and Hiroshima," *New York Times*, August 7, 1966, 1, 3.

62. Clayborne Carson, *The Autobiography of Martin Luther King, Jr.* (New York: Warner, 1998), 334.

63. Carson, *The Autobiography of Martin Luther King, Jr.*, 335.

64. Ibid., 337–343.

65. Carson, *In Struggle: SNCC and the Black Awakening of the 1960s*, 187.

66. Ibid., 220.

67. "NAACP Decries Stand of Dr. King on Vietnam," *New York Times*, April 11, 1967, 1, 17.

68. "Dr. King's Error," *New York Times*, April 7, 1967.

69. "NAACP Decries Stand of Dr. King on Vietnam," *New York Times*, April 11, 1967, 1, 17.

70. "Dr. King Accuses Johnson on War," *New York Times*, May 1, 1967, 1, 12.

71. James Bevel, "Dr. King Is Backed," *New York Times*, April 12, 1967, 46.

72. Congress of Racial Equality, "Rough Draft of Proposed Statement on Vietnam and the Draft," 1968. www.aavw.org/protest/civilrights_core_abstract08.html.

73. Thomas A. Johnson, "Whitney Young, Ending Silence, Condemns War," *New York Times*, October 14, 1969, 24.

74. Ibid.

75. Allen Thomas, Jr., interviewed by the author, July 25, 2000.

76. Dalglish, "Black and Back from Vietnam," 11.

77. Bernard Weintraub, "Rioting Disquiets G.I.'s in Vietnam," *New York Times*, April 8, 1968, 35.

78. James E. Westheider, "Sgt. Allen Thomas, Jr.: A Black Soldier in Vietnam," in *Portraits of African American Life Since 1865*, edited by Nina Mjagkij (Wilmington, DE: Scholarly Resources, 2003), 230–231.

79. "Letters to the Editor," *Ebony*, August 1968, 17.

80. House Armed Services Committee, *Inquiry into the Disturbances at Marine Corps Base, Camp Lejeune, N.C. on July 20, 1969* (Washington, DC: Government Printing Office, 1969), 5052.

81. Brendan Gallagher, "The Vietnam War and the Civil Rights Movement," *American Studies Online Today*, February 20, 2014. www.americansc.org.uk/online /vietnam_civil_rights.htm#_ednref46.

82. Grant, "Whites against Blacks in Vietnam," *The New Republic*, January 18, 1969, 15; Terry, "Bringing the War Home," 10, 14.

83. Grant, "Whites against Blacks in Vietnam," 15; Terry, "Bringing the War Home," 10, 14.

84. Wallace Terry, *Bloods: An Oral History of the Vietnam War by Black Veterans* (New York: Random House, 1984), 13.

85. Michael Herr, *Dispatches* (New York: Vintage, 1991), 180.

86. Terry, *Bloods*, 13.

87. Herr, *Dispatches*, 180.

88. Westheider, "Sgt. Allen Thomas, Jr.: A Black Soldier in Vietnam," 231.

89. NAACP, *The Search for Military Justice*, 19; "A Black Admiral for U.S. Navy," *The Pittsburgh Courier*, May 8, 1971, 11.

90. William Bowman, Roger Little, and G. Thomas Sicilia, *The All-Volunteer Force after a Decade* (Washington, DC: Pergamon-Brassey, 1984), 78.

91. General William Westmoreland, *Report of the Chief of Staff of the United States Army, 1 July 1968–30 June 1972* (Washington, DC: Department of the Army, 1977), 66.

# 6

## Reform in Ranks

The History of the Defense Race Relations Institute, 1971–2014

ISAAC HAMPTON II

The Defense Race Relations Institute was little known but was, without
question, the most important organization created by the Department of Defense
to combat racism within the armed forces. The Institute opened its doors in
1971. Isaac Hampton II sheds new light on the Institute's history by drawing on
oral history interviews he conducted with five individuals who worked as
instructors and directors at the Institute between 1971 and 2014. These
interviews explain how the Institute overcame initial resistance both inside
and outside the military and why the focus of the curriculum shifted from
tamping down racial tension to addressing gender issues and the dynamics of
human relations in the armed forces.[1]

By the mid-1960s, the outlook of African Americans on the military attitude
had taken a far-reaching shift in comparison to ten years prior. In the 1950s,
Black America largely took a guarded, patient outlook toward reform in the
military, but several factors changed the outlook in the 1960s to anger and protest,
all against the backdrop of the Vietnam War. These factors were continued
police violence against blacks across America, an unfair draft that systemically
targeted poor and disadvantaged youth, unfair assignment and promotion policies in the military, and the perception that federal government would not guarantee the constitutional rights of African Americans within the military justice
system. All of these factors assumed greater importance due to the number of
African Americans fighting and, more importantly, dying in Vietnam. From 1961
to 1967, African Americans formed more than 14 percent of American casualties
in Southeast Asia. The height of black casualties was reached in 1965, when one
out of four American soldiers who died in combat was black. Although the black

casualty rate declined after 1967, the overall death rate for black soldiers was approximately 30 percent higher than for all US forces fighting in Southeast Asia.[2]

This pent-up energy and disillusionment manifested itself in numerous ways such as anger, impatience, resistance, and a mosaic of racial expression in the forms of music, cultural dress, hair styling, race riots, and the daring notion of Black Power. Collectively this led African Americans to redefine who they were and challenge the status quo. In January of 1966, the Student Nonviolent Coordinating Committee (SNCC) released a statement that called for ending the war in Vietnam, and Dr. Martin Luther King, Jr., supported SNCC's position. In April of 1967, Dr. King delivered a widely reported speech that condemned the war and its handling by President Lyndon B. Johnson's administration. Then 1968 began with the surprise attack by North Vietnamese and Viet Cong forces on more than one hundred South Vietnamese cities, towns, and villages during the Tet holiday. Although US forces repelled the invasion, the American public grew skeptical of claims from General Westmoreland and President Johnson that victory was in sight. Unrest ensued in the armed forces among soldiers of all races, but the confluence of ongoing racial discrimination with the declining popularity of the war made a sizeable minority of black soldiers into black militants.[3]

### The Road to DRRI

The racial disturbances at the marine corps' Camp Lejeune in North Carolina in 1969 led the military to create a program that would keep the country's most hallowed institution from tearing apart itself from the inside. This riot left one soldier dead and dozens injured. One factor that caused the riot was the hard feelings stirred up by white soldiers who openly celebrated the assassination of Dr. King. The problems with race relations at Camp Lejeune made the national news and prompted the creation of a special House Armed Services Committee to investigate racial tension on United States military bases. On December 15, 1969, the committee's report, titled the "House Committee Report on Disturbances at Military Bases," suggested that the military "institute a program of education in race relations at all levels of command with an emphasis on the platoon and company levels." The findings in the report influenced Secretary of Defense Melvin Laird to issue a memo on January 28, 1970, that established the Inter-Service Task Force on Education and Race Relations.[4]

Lucius Theus, an African American who was then a colonel in the air force, led the task force with Judge L. Howard Bennett of the Office of the Deputy

Assistant of Defense for Civil Rights. Both of these men and fourteen other members from the military service branches researched and developed a comprehensive education and race relations program that would eventually be used throughout the entire military to combat racial tension. The task force spent four months visiting instructors and researched the curriculum of various armed forces training centers to find the best combination of teaching and learning techniques that were already in use by the military. The task force's five-volume final report to Laird called for the establishment of a Defense Race Relations Institute (DRRI, pronounced "dry") that would "educate, train instructors in race relations, develop a doctrine and curricula, conduct research, perform evaluation of program effectiveness and disseminate educational guidelines and material for the use throughout the armed forces."[5] Theus was arguably the most influential and persuasive member of the task force because he was able to incorporate the culture and the values of the military into the final report and effectively discuss its important findings among the decision makers in the Pentagon.[6]

When a race riot broke out at Travis Air Force base in California on May 25, 1971, that left one killed, ten injured, and 115 arrested, the urgency to curb racial tensions grew to an unprecedented level.[7] This incident required the air force to reevaluate its race relations policies. On June 24, 1971, Deputy Secretary of Defense David Packard signed Directive 1322.11 establishing the Race Relations Education Board. This board was composed of specialists from the Department of Defense and fell under the auspices of the Assistant Secretary of Defense, Manpower and Reserve Affairs and the Defense Race Relations Institute. The Race Relations Education Board set guidelines and established policy for education in race relations for the armed forces. It would be DRRI's responsibility to implement this training and education guidelines. What made Directive 1322.11 unique was its focus on race relations education for military personnel and not equal opportunity compliance.[8]

The armed forces believed that they had sufficient controls in place, in the form of regulations and the inspector general, to monitor their own progress in the area of compliance for equal opportunity and affirmative action. The special task force led by Theus and Bennett concluded that race relations education needed to anticipate problems and not be a static curriculum. The task force strongly believed that race relations instruction should target the root causes of racial tension, inequality, injustice, and prejudice.[9] However, military leaders were adamant that all programs that sought to bring more equality, affirmative action, and racial harmony to the armed forces do so with the primary goal of maintaining military efficiency and combat effectiveness.[10] Secretary of Defense Laird stated, "The primary purpose of the program . . . is to achieve a more harmonious relationship among all military personnel so that organizational efficiency and combat readiness will not be impaired by racial unrest, tension, or conflict."[11]

Laird was not only a politician (R-WI) but also a practical businessman who insisted on efficiency and fair-mindedness. According to those who worked with Laird, he was quite genuine in his belief in DRRI.

Surprisingly, some of the greatest strides in equal opportunity and race relations in the armed forces took place under a Republican administration with conservatives such as President Richard Nixon and Laird. Nixon's administration continued President Lyndon B. Johnson's Executive Order 11246, which prohibited federal contractors and subcontractors from discriminating against workers and enforced affirmative action ensuring equal opportunity because of race, color, religion, sex, or national origin.[12] Although Colonel Clarence Miller, who served as DRRI's second director of education, never worked directly with Laird, he had direct contact with Laird concerning DRRI. Miller stated, "you are never going to make a bleeding heart liberal out of him [Laird] [but], he was a fair guy and had an appreciation of what was needed at that time" in regards to moving a program forward on race relations.[13]

### The Early Years and Growing Pains

In September of 1971, DRRI officially opened its doors at Patrick Air Force Base near Cocoa Beach, Florida. The initial training classes at Patrick AFB lasted seven weeks. Army officers and noncommissioned officer (NCO) trainees who attended DRRI were given the title of equal opportunity advisor. This was a career identifier but not a military occupational skill (MOS) with a clearly defined career path. The air force established what was known as social action officers, which included NCOs and commissioned officers. Depending on the size and scope of the organization, the chief of social actions could rank as a major (O-4) or lieutenant colonel (O-5) in the air force. The navy and marines officers who graduated from DRRI were titled race relations instructors once they returned to their units.[14] The staff at DRRI consisted of approximately twenty-five military personnel, eight from the army and navy, nine from the air force, and nineteen civilians. There were also two marines on staff at the ranks of lieutenant colonel (O-5) and gunnery sergeant (E-7). Marines did not enter as students until at least 1974. The air force provided the initial start-up budget for the fiscal year of 1971, which was $215,000, and by 1972, the budget had almost doubled to $525,000.[15]

When Colonel Clarence Miller took charge of DRRI, there were substantial problems to overcome. One of the biggest enemies of DRRI in the early years was the rumors and falsehoods about the school started by those who wanted to see it closed. This included much of the local population in and around Cocoa Beach, who derogatorily referred to DRRI as "Watermelon University" or "Razor Blade Tech."[16] From an administrative side it was Theus who masterfully interpreted what the staff at DRRI was attempting to do and headed off calls to close the school with his influential written reports to the Department of Defense, which quelled much of the anxiety about the institute.[17]

Colonel Miller, an ROTC Prairie View A&M graduate of 1951 and Vietnam veteran, arrived at DRRI in July of 1972 to replace Colonel Albert Kilby, who was an air force officer.[18] Milton Frances, who was the deputy chief of staff of personnel of the army and the deputy assistant secretary of defense for equal opportunity, handpicked Miller to implement a stronger military bearing at DRRI and to sharpen the instruction program. Miller served as director until the summer of 1974. According to Miller, some civilian members of the early DRRI staff did not fit in and had their own agendas. There were even faculty members who threatened to boycott a visit by Secretary of Defense Laird. According to Miller,

> that was a kind of attitude that was pervasive. They were not all pro-military. When I first went there, I thought it took the services a while to get up to speed on the importance of the race relations mission. By that, I mean the services were not choosing their best people to send down there. That changed over a period of time. Some commander says, "I got to send some guy to the race relations school," and I think that's the way it was viewed at first. I didn't see a hell of a lot of what we call in the Army fast track burners . . . . From my personal perspective, I always thought that I could have done more to make a real change in the curriculum while I was there. We did around the edges. As I look back, I think there were a lot of people who should have been moved out when I got there but we tried to work with them. We should have made much bigger changes in the curriculum, but it evolved over period of time and turned out to be a pretty good curriculum.[19]

Inarguably, one of most influential architects of DRRI's educational model was respected sociologist Richard O. Hope. Prior to coming on at DRRI, Hope was a professor at Brooklyn College, and like many of his contemporaries in academia, he opposed the unpopular war in Vietnam. The first director of DRRI, Colonel Edward Krise, brought Hope onto the faculty at the suggestion of Judge L. Howard Bennett.[20] From Hope's perspective, the mission of DRRI was to develop a curriculum, course, and classes to improve communication between the races. Research findings would give direction to the school. This information established an evaluation component that determined the impact of what the staff at DRRI was proposing. This included evaluations to measure the effectiveness of classes and the program as whole.[21]

The idea of DRRI, not to mention an entire school dedicated to race relations, was a polarizing subject in the 1970s. Whether the institute was a positive or negative mechanism for the armed forces depended on whom one spoke to about this revolutionary concept. A strong minority within the military believed that the armed services needed DRRI to quell racial tension and that education was the best way to achieve this goal. Fortunately for DRRI, the culture of the late 1960s and early 1970s promoted education for dealing with the sensitive issue of race relations.[22] Concerning the early curriculum at DRRI, Hope observed:

> This was a military operation and I was a civilian. Various folks alerted me
> that you have to let this thing evolve and participate in the evolution. In other
> words if I came in and said on first day here is the curriculum. The second day
> here is the test. The third day here is this (laughter). It did not happen that way
> at all. We used a lot of group discussions. We had a lot of experts come in and
> we had a lot of trial and error. Let's say I had a direction I thought should be
> taken. I would try and move it along in an advisory capacity. I had the director
> of instruction or curriculum director [working with me] and what I generally
> did was go through that person. I worked through the evaluations that provided
> timely reaction to certain types of intervention.[23]

Hope had a delicate balancing act while he was at DRRI. If he moved too fast and appeared to dominate the early curriculum model at the school, the military could make his ideas difficult to implement. If he moved too slowly, little progress would be made, and DoD could interpret his measures as ineffective and unguided.

The measures of effectiveness at DRRI quickly took on a combination of sociological and psychological tone under Hope's unobtrusive style of leadership. Drawing on his academic background, Hope collected data so he could assess progress.

> We established a variety of instruments at the institute and at other locations
> to help establish the baseline measures of race relations on military bases
> throughout the world. It was variously referred to as the race relations index,

*race relations indicator . . . it was an attempt through a written survey and
interviews to get a sense of the nature of race relations at that time.*

Hope said participants in the DRRI trainings also had to complete a racial climate indicator [psychological test]. He said it was a challenge to measure the
impact of the training.

*You had folks compelled to attend these seminars and you talk to them at the
beginning and you talk them at the end. Then you would get a reaction. For
example one of the experiences that stands out to me was this officer from
Mississippi who said "I'm still pissed off, but now I am more pissed off because
you made me come to this thing (DRRI)." . . . . This person [officer] who was
upset about attending and typically would be in a state of what we call a
cognitive dissonance, and the cognitive dissonance theory suggest that in this
state the individual is highly motivated to reduce the dissonance.*

Hope said participants were disturbed by what they learned about racial discrimination. and would do things they did not normally do to prove they were not racist.

*To do that you carry out actions that are not typical in your normal behavior,
such as going to the library to read about race or talk to black people if you are
white or talk to white people if you are black. A lot of this type of activity
happens after [DRRI] for no other reason than to disprove what they had
observed or heard or read in the [DRRI] course.*

Because white individuals in the training were given permission to speak freely,
they often exposed racial stereotypes that shaped their thinking.

*For example, there were some who believed that black folks had tails. I
mean literally had tails. We often had to get out anatomical charts. We were
desperate. We tried everything. In this particular case, this person was told
by their grandmother, black people had tails. So, he went to libraries and read
about the anatomy of black people and then it gave him more courage to
interact with black people, but to disprove what he's heard. The more he
interacted with the black people, in a sense if you are talking about psychological testing the more liberal he becomes because the more his grandmother is
disproved by this phenomenon.*

Hope said the DRRI played an instrumental role in diminishing racial tensions.

*Without DRRI [racial tension] would have elevated to a certain kind of chaos
because there was such anger building up on both sides and there was no way
to express this. It became almost the alpha and omega in any mission that
occurred . . . It was very much a part of the 24/7 life. If there had not been a
way to release that tension there would have been quite a calamity.*[24]

## Resistance and Innovative Education

Eugene C. Johnson, an air force veteran of thirty-one years, was one of the original Defense Race Relations Institute staff members who came from Washington, DC, on August 28, 1971, and helped establish the school. Throughout his tenure at the Institute, both as a military officer and as a civilian, Johnson served in many positions such as trainer, deputy director of academics, chief of the curriculum support division, and chief of curriculum management. As of the writing of this chapter, Johnson is the vice president for the Defense Equal Opportunity Management Institute (DEOMI) Foundation, an organization of the founding staff members. Johnson, born in 1932, grew up in Melbourne, Florida, under strict Jim Crow laws and racial segregation.[25]

When Johnson first arrived at Patrick Air Force base in 1963, he was not a part of DRRI. At his new assignment, he would be directing other noncommissioned officers and junior enlisted personnel. When Johnson reported for duty, his superiors were surprised the air force had sent them an African American. Johnson recalled, "They didn't know what to do with me. I was the ranking staff sergeant . . . I had just been promoted to E-6 (technical sergeant). They didn't want me to command white troops, so they sent me down to the weather station, which was a communications facility. It was rough. You had to handle yourself or you would lose out in the end."[26] Johnson was not a part of DRRI during his initial tour at Patrick. He would go on to Washington, DC, and work at the Defense Atomic Support Agency. Later, he applied to DRRI, was sent back to Patrick AFB, and became the chief of community involvement. Like Hope, Johnson as a military leader recalled the need for race relations training and the distinctive interest African Americans had in seeing DRRI become a success:

> DRRI was established to put out the fires immediately because of all of the race riots that were taking place. They, even the military were in need of someone to go out into the field to teach human relations, race relations, and that was a job. The training of black and white, those were the first concepts of training in the classroom. The focus was only on discrimination and racism (sexism did not become a focus at DEOMI until 1980). It was a total military focus. One of the things about it was that most of the people that volunteered for the program were black [trainers] NCOs. Blacks were feeling the heat and the mentality was if I can down there and do something, let me go now to get this training, so I can do something and help my service and help my service in the community.[27]

According to Johnson, some commanders had concerns that students returning to their home bases from training at DRRI would be looked at as troublemakers on and off military installations. Some blacks were seen as asking too many questions and carrying out activities that challenged longstanding racist local customs and behaviors that favored white Americans:

> It was amazing. We had an experience. . . . DRRI was totally focused on putting out that fire (racial tension). You go to Texas we had race riots in San Antonio, race riots in California, at sea, pilots were afraid to fly because they didn't know if they had been sabotaged. Put out the fire! That's all we saw at that time. That's what it was about.[28]

Training at DRRI during the early years was polarizing for many in and out of the program. Most whites and blacks had very little experience with each other beyond casual contact up to the 1970s. As late as 1972, some schools in the American heartland, such as Dayton, Ohio, remained segregated. Racial acrimony was alive and well between both races in the 1970s, and the architects of DRRI's curriculum knew this all too well. Their experience and research led them to design a practical and immersive experience that would expose blacks, whites, and Hispanics to people outside of their ethnic circles and see how they lived. DRRI students would usually spend a three-day weekend with migrant farmers and in city ghettos. This would at best widen students' aperture of cultural awareness, lessen some of their fears about the other races, and give many a first encounter with the hardships minorities experienced in their everyday lives. This educational, but controversial, component of DRRI's training was dubbed the Miami experience.[29] Johnson remembered the following on this exercise and those who wanted the institution to fail:

> In DRRI, we did a lot of introducing for people directly to have activity. For the Miami experience, we would take teams down there for the weekend. Blacks would more or less get assigned to a white component. We had Jewish, Mexican-Americans, and Native Americans. We would assign teams to go out for that weekend and have an experience that they never had growing up . . . Some whites [would say] I don't understand this, or that I am used to doing this or that. We put that person from Friday evening until Sunday morning out there in the fields with Hispanics picking fruit on the farm . . . We were trying to break down that barrier. It was all military. It was not a civilian thing. The military was the only thing we were trying to focus on.[30]
> You see the whole DRRI thing was an appeasement . . . There has to be a school on race relations. Most people thought the school would not last.

*It was not that easy to begin with. In the beginning, we were not totally getting to the root cause of the racism itself. There were many outside of DRRI wondering what are we were teaching these people. There were spies civilian and military who would come down to watch us and they would report back we were brainwashing the students who came through DRRI. We had a conglomeration of issues. We had people that threatened our lives. I was threatened. I bought a .38 Special that I kept in my car when I drove to work. I would close it up at the gate until I would leave at the end of the day. Even in my office, I would have bricks and stones thrown into the office windows at DRRI. So, there were those who did want us there and those that said we weren't going to be there long.*[31]

There is little doubt that there was formidable opposition and rejection to a race relations school at Patrick AFB outside and inside the armed forces. This should come as little surprise even though progress had been made, at least legislatively, up to 1968. Much of white America was suffering from civil rights fatigue and felt blacks had been on an even playing field since the passing of the 1964 Civil Rights Act, the Voting Rights Act in 1965, and a second Civil Rights Act passed in 1968 after Dr. Martin Luther King's murder. Add in the media's focus on black anger, with television images of Black Panther shootouts with police, the kidnapping of the nineteen-year-old media heir Patty Hearst by the Symbionese Liberation Army, and the Black Power messages of Eldridge Cleaver and Angela Davis, and you have a recipe for the American public's rejection of the African Americans' struggle.[32]

## DEOMI Replaces DRRI

In July of 1979, the officials at DRRI changed the school's name to the Defense and Equal Opportunity Management Institute (DEOMI). Was the mission of equal opportunity replacing that of race relations in the armed force? Perhaps, but legislation guaranteeing equal rights for women was taking root, and the military was slowly beginning to reflect the advancement of women. The civil rights and feminist movements pushed the country to practice the philosophies of the Constitution for more than just white males at the end of the 1960s. In November of 1967, President Lyndon B. Johnson signed Public Law 90–130, which lifted the 2-percent ceiling on women in the military. It also removed restrictions on female promotions. Up until the signing of the new law, women were not eligible to be promoted higher than the rank of major (0–4). President Johnson stated, "The bill does not create any female generals or female admirals, but it does make that possible. There is no reason why we should not someday have a female Chief of Staff or even a female Commander in Chief."[33]

One DEOMI staffer recalled the new attention to women's equality in the early 1980s. "The civil rights and antiwar movements politicized and radicalized a growing number of women bombarded with contradictory expectations and images about work and family."[34] The clearest example of this was in women's inability to gain appointments to the service academies. After the women's movement of the 1970s, there was public pressure and legal action to challenge the exclusion of female attendance at the academies. Congress passed Public Law 94–106, signed by President Gerald Ford on October 7, 1975.[35] In the fall of 1976, over three hundred women stepped into the male-dominated worlds of Annapolis, West Point, the US Air Force Academy, and the US Coast Guard Academy.[36] These actions, combined with the end of the draft and shift to an all-volunteer force in 1973, finally began to affect the gender and racial balance of the armed services after only six years.[37]

However, Eugene Johnson and others who were involved at DEOMI felt there were political reasons for the institution changing its name:

*White America was not too much into race relations. They didn't want to hear it because it was true. We still had a racial problem. If we can get away from a name with "race" [in it] then the racial problem is gone. Then we don't have to deal with it. So all of a sudden, we have the Defense Equal Opportunity Management Institution. Nothing about race in there. One thing that hap-pened to us down there is that we got educated and we got smarter . . . The government didn't want to deal with that because they knew it was true. They knew there were still racial problems. That was a concern all of the time. The idea was to get the name away from race. This was the concept that pushed us into the DEOMI thing . . . You will never find that written. You won't find that written [stated boldly]. You would hear all kinds of sophisticated arguments but we knew through the workshops that this [racial tension] was what we were still having the problem with but, equal opportunity is on [in vogue] and we are going to manage it.[38]*

The civilian sector in many cases seemed to mirror DEOMI when it came to the language of race relations. It was during this decade and the 1990s that the term "affirmative action" was slowly replaced by the words "diversity" and "equal op-portunity."[39] However, some of the learning concepts at DEOMI still reflected an outdated analysis of the past, especially when it came to African Americans.

For example, the curriculum at DEOMI in 1980 was directed at those who still believed Black Power ideologies were driving racial tension in the military. Some white commanders incorrectly thought the people who attended DEOMI should only be trained to focus on African Americans based on the troubled race relations of the Vietnam era. DEOMI was surprisingly slow to evolve in this area, and it seemed as if the institution was trying to fight its current battle with the last war's tactics, techniques, and procedures. To its credit, DEOMI knew institutional discrimination (also known as systemic racism) was at the heart of its racial and gender problems. DEOMI's data clearly indicated that a failure of leadership was a major factor in continuing problems with discrimination in the military.[40]

In many cases, commanders did not know or realize they were contributing to the discrimination problem because they did not view racial distinctions as offensive. Many commanders underwent training that made them consider whether their organizational decisions were sexist or racially offensive to others under their command.[41] This type of behavior by commanders could merely be categorized as benign neglect, but it is plausible too that many in the armed forces, black and white, were suffering from cultural and implicit racial bias. "Implicit bias refers to the attitudes or stereotypes that affect our understanding, actions, and decisions in an unconscious manner. These biases, which encompass both favorable and unfavorable assessments, are activated involuntarily and without an individual's awareness or intentional control."[42] Deconstructing and analyzing the sociological tenets of race is outside of the scope of this chapter, but it would be wise for historians to familiarize themselves with the pathology of racial tension when trying to understand the actions of Americans in the military.[43] African Americans spent decades reacting to the effects of unaddressed racism, which often resulted in violence. Fortunately, a few black and white officers stood ready to directly address racial tensions.

Becoming involved in the military's race relations educational efforts had its trade-offs. A number of black officers and civilians were interested in working at DRRI and DEOMI to help bring more equality and racial understanding to the armed services. However, there could be career pitfalls for black and white service members working in this field. For example, Lieutenant Colonel Dennis Michael Collins, who was a 1969 Howard University ROTC graduate, served as a race relations officer at Hurlburt Field, Florida, and he had earned a certificate of completion as an Air Force Human Relations advisor. Collins attended DRRI in

1972, and in 1989, he returned to Patrick AFB as the director of training at DEOMI.[44] On the reaction of black officers to DRRI and DEOMI, Collins said,

> black officers thought it was the right way to go. There were a lot of people who volunteered but they saw it as a big risk to get involved in it because they saw it as being a career hinder or would limit their promotions and did. It ended the careers of a lot of sharp black officers who thought this was more important to do than pursuing some other career. I think in general people were really glad that this came about because of their own experiences. They saw a need for change and needed change agents . . . Overall, the black officer Corps was supportive. Now the white officer Corps that was a different story . . . most of them thought this program was not going to last. It's too crazy and is too wild and is not going to be supported by the establishment because the establishment is going to find it too radical and too militant for the military. They hoped it to be a passing fancy and go away. You had some senior officers who knew this had to work. Those folks like General Robert J. Dixon kept it alive, but a lot of people were trying to undermine it [DRRI].[45]

In the seventeen years that passed from when Collins first entered DRRI as a student, much had changed, including the name of the institution. The length of the course had gone from seven weeks to fifteen weeks. DEOMI became more professional and went from reacting to crises to training people in human relations and equal opportunity. The curriculum began to focus on organizational development to address institutional racism.[46] Collins explained what DRRI and DEOMI accomplished:

> It got to the bigger issue of discrimination and fair treatment. It got people to the point where they could see that fair treatment was something everybody should be afforded. I think it changed the way people were looked at for jobs [and] promotions. It was the forerunner to an increase in minority general officers because it started to change behaviors. The goal of the military was behavioral change. Now we have regulations in place that say [by military order] "you will do it." Our job was to change those attitudes. Change the heart and mind so to speak . . . so, stereotypes that people brought with them could be put away, in that when you looked at me as a black lieutenant, you looked at me as lieutenant that was just as capable as doing the job as any other lieutenant, and be given the same opportunities for promotion and advancement.[47]

Much of Collins' quotation echoes what African Americans have fought for since Reconstruction. The armed forces were a microcosm of American society. The same type of racial inequality found in the civilian world occurred within the military. Since the armed forces draws individuals from society, the biases of the public are introduced into the military. Systemically, these biases were concealed and controlled by military orders. DRRI and DEOMI got members of the armed forces to rethink their positions on race and gender in order to advance organizational change.

The long career of William Yates reflected the changing focus of antidiscrimination efforts in the military. Yates, who grew up under Jim Crow laws in Baton Rouge, Louisiana, was a student in DRRI Class 73-1 from August to September of 1972. He returned to DRRI in 1987 as the director of training and retired in 1989 from the air force as a lieutenant colonel. When the position of dean was created at DEOMI in 2003, Yates took it, and he retired from that position at the end of 2014. For over forty years, Yates was involved in some segment of race relations and equal opportunity.[48] When Yates retuned to DEOMI as dean in 2004, the institution was still looking at race, but the issue of human relations and gender had become more pronounced.[49]

One reason gender took on a greater emphasis than race after 2003 in the military was combat operations in Iraq and Afghanistan. The ongoing exposure to and participation in direct action by women led to casualties. Women shared many of the same experiences with men, no matter if it was driving trucks on roads with improvised explosive devices as part of a convoy, serving as medics, or flying aircraft. The enemy did not care about gender differences on the battlefield. This forced the military to rethink traditional gender roles and the limitations placed on women by the institution.[50]

Gender inequality was not seen as an overt form of discrimination well into the 1970s. During the Vietnam War, blatant racial discrimination in and out of the military was rife in America. As overt racism was brought under control, it quietly morphed into systemic racism by the 1980s that still exists today. Similarly, preconceived notions of gender combined with Western cultural practices greatly shaped the US military's view on what was female space.[51] By 2011, many women felt they had done enough to push back against gender inequality; of over 283,000 female soldiers deployed to Iraq and Afghanistan, approximately 139 had been killed and over 800 wounded.[52]

A long view on gender roles in the army comes from Colonel Douthard Butler, a graduate of Prairie View A&M University's ROTC program in 1955. Butler went on to earn a doctorate in public policy and become an administrator and professor at George Mason University. He worked in the Pentagon with the army personnel system into the 1980s and was quite familiar with how the institution viewed the evolving role of women. While at the Pentagon, Butler worked with Major General George W. Putnam and credits him with raising the awareness level in the army during the late 1970s so women officers would be trained beyond the stereotypical positions they had held historically.

Butler stated:

> What's going on in the Army reflects what's going on outside of the Army. Politics, etcetera. We [general public] never understand the Army draws at random from society. Because we draw at random from society whatever problems and attitudes from out there we get them . . . During the race relations era the focus was on blacks because blacks were the problem. We did very little for women back then. But the focus now in society is women. Not blacks. All the services are doing is reflecting attitudes in society in which they function.[53]

In the early 1980s the Officer Personnel Director and Army Military Personnel Center began to reevaluate the condition of women. Once promoted, many female officers failed in leadership positions. The problem was not with the material but with the system. Historically, women were not given the developmental assignment opportunities that prepared them for more responsibility and management roles. Unsurprisingly, the majority of female officers from the 1960s into the late 1970s were not groomed from day one as lieutenants, as their male counterparts were, so they could one day command companies, battalions, and brigades.[54]

In the 1990s female officers were indeed commanders of companies to brigades, and women were commanders of US Navy ships, but still more work needed to be done. In 2004 the gender theorem became a greater concern, and DEOMI took on other sophisticated issues of sexism and the dynamics behind it. Training expanded to include cross-cultural competence, sexual harassment, hazing, and bullying.[55] Under Yates's leadership, innovation flourished at the institute. For example, the DEOMI Organizational Climate Survey (DEOCS), created by Director of Research Dan McDonald, was established. DEOCS is a confidential, command-requested organization development survey focusing on issues of equal opportunity and organizational effectiveness. It is the survey of choice for all DoD organizational assessments. DEOCS's predecessor was the Military Equal Opportunity Climate Survey. Mickey Dansby, who was the director of research in the 1990s, created this human relations tool.[56]

DEOMI now addresses microaggressions, which create a climate of unhealthy pressure based on race or gender that has a tremendous impact on people's ability to perform.[57] DEOMI is also addressing the complicated world of white privilege. Yates articulated the following on this topic:

*White people will deny that it exists. Some people are becoming more aware of the fact that part of white privilege is that you are white. There are a lot of things that you don't have to think about because you are not affected by some of the things that people of color are . . . white privilege is a difficult concept to teach people because most whites will tell you they think they have not been privileged. It takes some work to get them to understand that we are not talking about something that you did, but we are talking about something that you have benefited from that exists in a social system.*[58]

In the 1960s, ongoing white privilege was at the heart of racial tensions and violence among black and white Americans. The civil rights and Black Power movements challenged this status quo in the civilian sector. In the military, the creation of DRRI and DEOMI fought this battle through education to ease racial tensions and create more awareness and understanding among the races. However, DRRI and DEOMI were tools whose intent was to bring military cohesion and efficiency back to the armed forces during a time of racial unrest while the country was still fighting the Cold War.

In 1972 the United States military was still a troubled institution concerning race relations.[59] Four years earlier in 1968, the Department of Defense's annual report boldly stated the elimination of institutional racism across the armed services. During that interim period, forces in and out of the military were catalysts for deteriorating race relations. Seared into the black consciousness were the assassination of Dr. Martin Luther King, Jr., the Orangeburg massacre in South Carolina,[60] and an unfair conscription process where less than 2 percent of the 16,000 who sat on draft boards were black.[61] The rise of the Black Power movement, the race riots at Travis Air Force base in 1971, and the mutiny of black sailors on the carriers *Kitty Hawk* and *Constellation* in 1972 were the collective culmination of pent-up racial tension that took place across the armed forces near the end of the Vietnam War.

## Conclusion

Much has changed in and out of the military since the high tide of racial tension in the 1960s and early 1970s. The memories of Collins, Hope, Johnson, Miller, and Yates reveal the special challenges that blacks were facing in the military through the 1970s. Initially, the staff of DRRI had to overcome resistance to educating military personnel about race relations even as they jeopardized their careers by working for the Institute. Over time, the curriculum evolved from simply addressing the crises of the day to systematically examining the plight of black soldiers in the military. As the DRRI program advanced its research, the Institute began to move beyond isolated incidents of discrimination and examine institutional racism. Arguably, the military today still has a systemic race problem, but the patterns of racial discrimination are more subtle than in the 1960s and 1970s. In 1980, when the name of the Institute changed from DRRI to DEOMI, so did the emphasis of its mission change. It now addressed the broader problem of the lack of equal opportunity based on organizational structure. In addition, DEOMI expanded its scope to include discrimination faced by other minorities, such as Hispanics and women.

The current state of race relations in the military is good, at least on the surface, with accolades going to the vast majority of men and women associated with DRRI/DEOMI. Put simply, this institution has been an exceptional success in spite of those who tried to derail it in the early and mid-1970s. To this day, it is the only school of its kind in any military across the globe.

With the growing presence of women in the military since the 1980s, it should come as little surprise that gender equality has taken a greater priority. Inequality concerning the status of women in field grade (O-4 to O-6) officer ranks continues throughout the armed forces. While there are more women today who hold admiral and general officer appointments than at any other time in US military history, a new methodology is needed to understand why the current system still suffers from implicit gender biases. Unfortunately, women officers of color are more likely to be discriminated against than men of color. In the workplace and in the community, racial discrimination is inseparable from gender discrimination. Across the US military there is still work to do, and DEOMI will play a major in shaping solutions for the armed forces.[62]

NOTES

1. This chapter is indebted to James E. Lovejoy for his unpublished paper "A History of the Defense Race Relations Institute. Volume 1: The Formative Period" (1977). The only other analysis of the DRRI is found in Charles C. Moskos and John Sibley Butler, *All That We Can Be: Black Leadership and Racial Integration the Army Way* (New York: Basic Books, 1996), 56, 60–61, 71. The history of the DRRI is addressed more comprehensively in Isaac Hampton II, *The Black Officer Corps: A History of Black Military Advancement from Integration through Vietnam* (Routledge: New York, 2012), chapter 8. For an overview of racial tensions in the armed forces during the Vietnam era, see James E. Westheider, *Fighting on Two Fronts: African Americans and the Vietnam War* (New York: New York University Press, 1997); Herman Graham, *The Brothers' Vietnam War: Black Power, Manhood, and the Military Experience* (Gainesville: University Press of

Florida, 2003); John Darrell Sherwood, *Black Sailor, White Navy: Racial Unrest in the Fleet during the Vietnam War Era* (New York: New York University Press, 2007); Kimberly L. Phillips, *War! What Is It Good For? Black Freedom Struggles & the US Military from World War II to Iraq* (Chapel Hill: University of North Carolina Press, 2012), chapter 5.

2.  Westheider, *Fighting on Two Fronts*, 12–13, 41–65.

3.  Kimberly L. Phillips, *War! What Is It Good For?*, 242, 248–249; David Cortright, *Soldiers in Revolt: GI Resistance during the Vietnam War* (Chicago: Haymarket Books, 1975); Westheider, *Fighting on Two Fronts*, 94–115.

4.  Lovejoy, "A History of the Defense Race Relations Institute," 19; Westheider, *Fighting on Two Fronts*, 94–98, 100, 129–130, 140, 159. See also Haynes Johnson and George C. Wilson, *Army in Anguish* (New York: Pocket Books, 1971).

5.  Ibid., 19, 20, 21.

6.  Richard O. Hope, interviewed by the author on December 7, 2007. Tape in author's possession. Richard Hope holds a PhD in sociology from Syracuse University and was the vice president of the Woodrow Wilson National Fellowship Foundation at Princeton University. Also see Hope's book *Racial Strife in the United States Military: Toward the Elimination of Discrimination* (Santa Barbara, CA: Praeger, 1979).

7.  "NBC Evening News for Tuesday, May 25, 1971," Vanderbilt Television News Archive. http://tvnews.vanderbilt.edu/program.pl?ID=457899.

8.  Lovejoy, "A History of the Defense Race Relations Institute," 1.

9.  Ibid., 30.

10.  Morris J. MacGregor, *Integration of the Armed Forces 1940–1965* (Washington, DC: Center of Military History, 1981), 620.

11.  Dana Adams Schmidt, "Classes in Race Relations Ordered for Armed Forces," *New York Times*, March 6, 1971.

12.  The United States Department of Labor, Executive Order 11246. www.dol.gov /compliance/laws/comp-eeo.htm; Herbert S. Parmet, *Richard M. Nixon: An American Enigma* (New York: Pearson, 2008), 109, 110. Melvin Laird served as secretary of defense from January 22, 1969, to January 29, 1973.

13.  Colonel Clarence Miller, interviewed by the author on December 12, 2007. Tape and transcript deposited at Houston History Archives, M. D. Anderson Library, and University of Houston (HMA-UH). See also Dale Van Atta, *With Honor: Melvin Laird in War, Peace, and Politics* (Madison: University of Wisconsin Press, 2008).

14.  Eugene Johnson, e-mail to author, December 14, 2014.

15.  Moskos and Butler, *All That We Can Be*, 49. The air force was ultimately responsible for providing all future operational budgets and funds for DRRI. E-mail from Johnson to author, December 29, 2014.

16.  Moskos and Butler, *All That We Can Be*, 56.

17.  Miller interview; Lovejoy, "A History of the Defense Race Relations Institute," 42, 43.

18.  Lovejoy, "A History of the Defense Race Relations Institute," 127.

19.  Miller interview.

20.  Hope interview.

21.  Miller interview.

22. Hope interview.

23. Ibid.

24. Ibid.

25. Eugene C. Johnson, interviewed by the author on November 5, 2014. Interview in author's possession.

26. Ibid.

27. Ibid.

28. Ibid.

29. Isaac Hampton II, *The Black Officer Corps*, 133–137.

30. Johnson interview.

31. Ibid.

32. Harvard Sitkoff, *The Struggle for Black Equality 1954–1980* (New York: Hill and Wang, 1981), 224, 225.

33. "The Secretary of the Army's Senior Review Panel on Sexual Harassment Executive Summary," vol. 2, Data Report, Pentagon Library, July 28, 1997, 129; John Woolley and Gerhard Peters, "Lyndon B. Johnson XXXVI President of the United States 1963–69, 475—Remarks Upon Signing Bill Providing Equal Opportunity in Promotions for Women in the Armed Forces," November 8, 1967. www.presidency.ucsb.edu/ws/?pid=28533.

34. Kenneth T. Walsh, "The 1960s: A Decade of Change for Women," *US News & World Report*, March 12, 2010. www.usnews.com/news/articles/2010/03/12/the-1960s-a -decade-of-change-for-women.

35. Public Law 94-106, October 7, 1975, Title VIII—General Provisions, Sec. 803(a). www.gpo.gov/fdsys/pkg/STATUTE-89/pdf/STATUTE-89-Pg531.pdf.

36. Women in Military Service for America Memorial Foundation, www .womensmemorial.org/H&C/History/milacad.html.

37. See Beth Bailey, *America's Army: Making the All-Volunteer Force* (Cambridge, MA: Belknap, 2009).

38. Johnson interview.

39. Douthard Butler. Butler holds a PhD in public administration and teaches government at George Mason University. In February 2013, I was invited to attend one of his lectures and traced the transition of how the government and American public, outside of litigation, rarely uses the term "affirmative action" and has replaced it with "equal opportunity" and "diversity."

40. Johnson interview.

41. Hope and Johnson interviews.

42. Cheryl Staats, "State of the Science: Implicit Bias Review 2014," 16. http:// kirwaninstitute.osu.edu/wp-content/uploads/2014/03/2014-implicit-bias.pdf.

43. A good starting point is Michael Omi and Howard Winant, *Racial Formation in the United States from the 1960s to the 1980s* (New York: Routledge, 1986).

44. Michael D. Collins, interviewed by the author on November 6, 2007. Interview in author's possession.

45. Collins interview. General Robert J. Dixon was never the head of DRRI, but Collins served as his race relations officer. Dixon insisted members of his staff attend the DRRI course and believed racial tension was a real problem in the armed forces.

46. Ibid.

47. Ibid.

48. DEOMI, "Biography of Dr. Williams Yates II." http://deomi.org/AboutDEOMI /documents/Yates_William_Dr_CC.pdf.

49. William Yates II, interviewed by the author on December 11, 2014. Interview in author's possession.

50. Information from this section came from a DEOMI graduate still serving on active duty as an equal opportunity officer who wished to remain anonymous.

51. Ibid.

52. David Wallechinsky and Noel Brinkerhoff, "139 Female Soldiers Have Died in Iraq and Afghanistan," AllGov.com. www.allgov.com/news/us-and-the-world/139 -female-soldiers-have-died-in-iraq-and-afghanistan?news=844316. Kirsten Holmstedt, *Band of Sisters: American Women at War in Iraq* (Mechanicsburg, PA: Stackpole Books, 2007), 310.

53. Douthard Butler, interviewed by the author on May 15, 2016. Interview in author's possession.

54. Ibid.

55. Yates interview.

56. William Yates, e-mail to author, December 15, 2014.

57. Yates interview; Derald Wing Sue, *Microaggressions in Everyday Life: Race, Gender, and Sexual Orientation* (Hoboken, NJ: Wiley, 2010), 40. The term "racial microaggression" was first proposed by psychiatrist Chester M. Pierce in the 1970s. Racial microaggressions are brief and commonplace daily verbal, behavioral, or environmental indignities, whether intentional or unintentional, that communicate hostile, derogatory, or negative racial slights and insults and potentially have a harmful or unpleasant psychological impact on the target person or group.

58. Yates interview.

59. Lovejoy, "A History of the Defense Race Relations Institute," 9.

60. On the campus of South Carolina State in Orangeburg the night of February 8, 1968, three African American students were killed by police gunfire with twenty-seven others wounded. None of the students were armed, and most were shot in their backs or the soles of their feet. For more on the Orangeburg Massacre see Jack Bass and Jack Nelson's book *Orangeburg Massacre* (Macon, GA: Mercer University Press, 2001).

61. Lawrence M. Baskir and William A. Strauss, *Chance and Circumstance* (New York: Alfred A. Knopf, 1978), 560.

62. Helen Cooper, "Pentagon Study Finds 50% Increase in Reports of Military Sexual Assaults," *New York Times*, May 1, 2014. www.nytimes.com/2014/05/02/us /military-sex-assault-report.html?_r=0.

# 7

# Men's and Women's Liberation

## Challenging Military Culture after the Vietnam War

HEATHER MARIE STUR

As the Vietnam War grew increasingly unpopular in 1968, American men and women began to express disillusionment with the gender ideals that had defined men's and women's roles in the military and on the home front. Some of this reaction took shape in the GI and veteran antiwar movement, which blamed military "machismo" for atrocities in Vietnam and emphasized the racism and sexism embedded in it. When the Vietnam-era draft was discontinued in 1973, the armed services developed recruiting campaigns that rebranded the military as an institution where both men and women could receive job training, get money for education, and build a career. This was a shift away from the image of military service as an arena in which men demonstrated their masculinity. Yet even as policies opened the armed forces to women, transforming military culture on the ground proved difficult, as is clear in recent discussions about women serving in combat and sexual assault against female personnel. This chapter focuses on the starting point of this ongoing transition, from the late 1960s into the post–Vietnam War era and the transition to the all-volunteer force.

In 1976, the year of America's bicentennial, the United States Military Academy's class of 1980 entered West Point with 119 women in the group. It was West Point's first gender-integrated class following Congressional legislation in 1975 opening the US service academies to women. The move was part of a broader effort to expand the armed forces following the end of the Vietnam War–era draft in 1973. Newspaper headlines reflected the debates in the military and the public about what the full integration of women into the service academies would do to the character of the military. The *St. Louis Post-Dispatch* wondered if women would "threaten West Point's 'manly environment,'"[1] but the

Arlington, Virginia, military newspaper *Pentagram News* later assured readers that West Point's "walls still stand" six months after the "feminine invasion" that occurred when the class of 1980 arrived on campus.[2] Media coverage voiced Americans' anxieties about how servicemen and women would interact with one another, whether women had the physical and mental stamina to handle military service, the issue of unit cohesion, and, most importantly, whether the integration of women into the military would lead to women serving in combat. It was the idea of women in combat, more than anything else, that challenged Americans' beliefs about who should serve in the military and in what roles.[3]

The Vietnam War was the starting point for significant transformation in US military culture and the image of the armed services. Until Vietnam, masculine citizenship and military service had been intertwined in American culture, but as the war grew unpopular, so did the notion that boys became men on the battlefields. When the draft ended, the armed services embarked on recruitment campaigns aimed at drawing both men and women into the ranks in order to fill personnel needs. Because the Vietnam War in many ways discredited the military, no longer could the forces rely on a pro-military culture to drive men into the services. At the same time, women demanded wider access to military specialties and career paths. Yet while military authorities tended to view the integration of women as a pragmatic move to fill personnel needs, critics within both the military and the civilian public asserted traditional ideas about military service.

An examination of the gender integration of the military after 1975 offers a window on the legal, social, and cultural climate of the late twentieth century. Debates about women in the military reflected arguments on the legality of using gender to apply laws differently to men and women. They revealed tensions within the feminist movement over war and militarization and about how far feminists were willing to go to demand gender equality. They illuminated American cultural attitudes about gender and sexuality, and they illustrated the power that culture often has on politics. As historian D'Ann Campbell has argued, discussions of women in combat emphasize law, psychology, and biology but rarely examine the history of women's roles in militaries and wartime. Rather than being based on empirical evidence regarding women's suitability for combat service, restrictions on women in combat have been the results of political decisions that reflected public opinion and congressional attitudes.[4] The expansion of women's military opportunities in the 1970s coincided with efforts to ratify the Equal Rights Amendment, and one of the points of contention regarding ERA was whether it would subject women to the draft. Gender roles and the stability of the family were central to arguments both for and against the expansion of women's military roles. Opponents argued that the trauma of separation from a parent was more difficult for a child to bear when the parent deploying was the mother. Those in favor of the gender integration of the military suggested that the deployment of wives and mothers would contribute to a reshaping of gender roles within the family, leading to a more equitable sharing of childcare and other domestic duties.

The history of women in the US military is one of gradual integration and fairly consistent cultural resistance. Women began serving officially in the armed forces when the army and navy established nurse corps in the early 1900s. Long considered women's work, nursing was an acceptable field in which women could serve. But when American women joined civilian rifle clubs and civil defense groups during World War I, this subversion of traditional ideas about men as protectors and women in need of protection shocked the American public.[5] During World War II, manpower needs led the army to establish the Women's Army Corps (WAC), which opened clerical, intelligence, communications, and other noncombat specialties to women. Critics decried this type of mobilization of women, arguing that women did not belong in harm's way and worrying about women's sexuality.[6] When the Defense Department abolished the draft at the end of the Vietnam War, the armed forces launched recruitment campaigns targeting women in order to help fill the ranks of an all-volunteer force. The US military academies began admitting women in 1976, and the army dissolved the WAC in 1978 and integrated servicewomen into the army.[7] The number of women in the US armed forces increased significantly during the 1970s, from 1.3 percent of the enlisted ranks in 1971 to 7.6 percent in 1979. The army saw an even larger increase, from 1.2 percent to 8.4 percent.[8] In the early 1990s, more than 40,000 American women served in the Gulf War, and in 1993, Congress authorized servicewomen to fly combat missions and serve on combat ships other than submarines.

The changes in women's roles in the military were intricately intertwined with changes in America's racial landscape. Within the increase in women joining the military, by 1987, African American women constituted more than 44 percent of all enlisted women in the army. The number was four times black women's proportion of the civilian female population in the United States. In the total armed forces, black women made up more than 25 percent of all enlisted women. For some young African American women in the Reagan years, the military looked like a rare institution that would provide them with education, job training, health benefits, and pay.[9] Since the warrior myth had declined in popularity due to the Vietnam War, the military sought to emphasize those benefits to service that had nothing to do with proving one's manhood in battle.

Challenges to the links between gender and military service occurred amid broad questioning, and in some ways rejection, of traditional gender roles in the civilian world. In the years after World War II, the women's movement, gay liberation, and black freedom struggles all called for alternatives to the definitions of masculinity and femininity that had characterized the white, middle-class social hierarchy and the suburban family image that had symbolized the American dream for the first half of the Cold War. Because military service was deeply ingrained in American identity, the transformations in military access and culture happened alongside and were influenced by home front social movements. Antiwar GIs called upon their fellow servicemen to support women's liberation, which, by extension, would liberate them from the constraints of militarized masculinity. Black troops pointed out the ways in which the racism and sexism that oppressed African Americans at home shaped US foreign relations. Women demanded increased access to military service as part of the drive for gender equality. In this complex mix of disillusionment, activism, and redefinition, the US armed services attempted to respond to changes in the civilian culture they had, at one time, defined. If many Americans now refused to see military service as the ultimate proof of manhood, and at the same time, a movement demanded that women have equal access to professions and institutions, leaders of the armed forces realized they had to reshape the image of the forces in order to preserve them.

## Gender Roles and American Culture in the Cold War

As the United States embraced its position as one of two superpowers after World War II, Americans used gender to make sense of international relations and their nation's global mission. In the US Cold War worldview, American masculine strength and power would be put to use in the defense of weaker nations that were threatened by Communist insurgencies, the concern that dominated US foreign relations after 1945. The conventional wisdom of the era went that if Communism was allowed to take hold throughout the world, it would threaten all that Americans held dear, including the nuclear family and comfortably appointed suburban homes. Embodying the American dream was the "girl next door," who was innocent, white, middle-class, and in need of protection by a courageous gunslinger.[10] The most visible symbol of the benevolent gunslinger in Cold War American popular culture was John Wayne, whose roles in World

War II films and westerns offered Americans a metaphor for US engagement with the world. Loren Baritz argues that Wayne represented "the traditional American male" who "performs, delivers the goods, is a loner, has the equipment, usually a six-shooter or a superior rifle, to beat the bad guys, and he knows what he is doing."[11] Throughout the 1950s and into the 1960s, novels, television shows, and films glorified the frontier as the "meeting point between civilization and savagery," where toughness and a commitment to absolute truths defined real men.[12]

Wayne became the ultimate cowboy-hero, and in his own life he made it his mission to promote "good, old-fashioned American virtues," which in the Cold War world meant fighting Communist insurrections. In 1966, Wayne toured Vietnam to entertain US troops, and he returned home an outspoken supporter of the war. His experience in Vietnam inspired him to direct and star in *The Green Berets*, a film that critics panned but that grossed $7 million in its first three months.[13] For many of the men who served in Vietnam, cowboys, Indians, and the Wild West shaped the playtime of their youth, and "Indians" stood in for faceless Communism in their childhood war games.[14] Noting the international reach of the John Wayne image, Cynthia Enloe characterizes Wayne as "globalized shorthand for militarized masculinity."[15]

The ideas Wayne embodied played out not only on the big and small screens, but also in the development of US foreign policy. Cowboy movies enforced the notion that the United States had a noble mission to press ahead into the "new frontier" and tame the "savage" world.[16] Immersed in a culture in which the figure of John Wayne symbolized the masculine ideal, US policymakers were influenced, consciously and unconsciously, by these cultural narratives as they plotted the course of America's international relations. John F. Kennedy won the presidency in 1960 with a vision that US-style democracy would touch all corners of the globe. But the new president feared that suburban comforts had made American young men "soft" and thus unfit to compete in Cold War competitions. Robert Dean argues that, in order to justify projects like the expansion of the army's Green Berets, Kennedy exploited the fear that a "crisis of masculinity" could weaken US global power.[17] The president wrote articles for *Sports Illustrated* and hired Bud Wilkinson, a former University of Oklahoma football coach, to be his physical fitness adviser. Kennedy believed that American men must be "tough" and physically fit to endure "military demands in Europe and the jungles of Asia."[18]

Kennedy created the President's Council on Youth Fitness, which set standards for physical education at public schools.[19] He stressed the need for sports and organizations such as Outward Bound and the Boy Scouts to instill masculinity in boys who spent their days under their mothers' indulgent tutelage. The implication here is that, although the ideal post–World War II American family structure featured a breadwinner father and a childrearing mother, mothers could not teach their sons how to be productive, civic-minded men. Jacqueline Lawson contends that military advertisements produced after the Korean War played on the dichotomy of male aggressiveness and female passivity. She maintains that slogans such as "the Marine Corps builds men" assume that a mother cannot teach her son how to be a man.[20] Lucian Truscott, a former *Village Voice* reporter who graduated from West Point in 1969, connected service in Vietnam to ideas about masculinity: "There was always an undercurrent that if you didn't go to Vietnam then there's going to be something wrong with you as a man, because we all know that civilizations have constantly over the course of history called upon people to go and fight wars."[21]

Lyndon Johnson inherited Vietnam from Kennedy, and John Wayne–like concerns about masculinity also informed his policy making. He feared that he would appear "less of a man" than Kennedy if he brought US troops home before winning the war.[22] Reflecting the paternalism of American Cold War foreign policy, Johnson believed the United States had an obligation to help alleviate poverty in the decolonizing world. Lloyd Gardner argues that Johnson and his advisors, such as Walt Rostow, viewed economic development as the means to halt the spread of Communism. Initiatives such as the Mekong Project, which was modeled after the New Deal Tennessee Valley Authority, aimed to bring electricity to and improve irrigation in the Mekong River region. In order to provide a moral justification for US intervention in Vietnam, Johnson sought to extend the "Great Society" into foreign policy by committing money and manpower to modernization and development projects. This strategy reflected his paternalistic conviction that the United States had a duty to aid the development of "backward regions."[23] In Vietnam, war accompanied development aid, and some American troops who served there found themselves questioning the ideology that had informed US intervention. Some of those who began to doubt the war's validity focused on the ways in which sexism and racism had come to characterize many aspects of US engagement in Vietnam.

One of the first introductions servicemen had to the military's oppressive and destructive uses of gender and sexuality was in basic training.[24] Derogatory references to women were used to denigrate recruits and define the enemy during basic training. In his study of US combat troops sent to Vietnam, Christian Appy writes that throughout basic training, drill instructors repeatedly used pejorative terms about women in order to accuse recruits of showing weakness. To be called a woman—or usually, more crudely, a "cunt" or "pussy"—was to be pegged as lacking manhood. Appy quotes novelist Tim O'Brien, who wrote that during basic training, "women are dinks. Women are villains. They are creatures akin to Communists and yellow-skinned people and hippies." Additionally, references to women and femininity were synonyms for homosexuality, an even more damaging accusation because military law prohibited homosexual relations. Recruits who were called "faggots" or "queers" by drill instructors faced more vicious treatment.[25] In this climate, proving masculinity through aggressive displays of heterosexuality became part of the rite of passage.

Racism also had a role in basic training during the Vietnam War. At Quantico, Virginia, in 1966, a drill instructor told Don Mitsuo, a Japanese American marine, to don a pair of loose black pants, a black shirt, and a conical straw hat. After he put on the costume, the drill sergeant handed Mitsuo a rifle, directed him to a stage in front of the other marines, and said, "This is what your enemy looks like. I want you to kill it before it kills you."[26] Mitsuo's experience encapsulated the ways in which race, along with gender, shaped the culture of basic training during the Vietnam War. But as the war became increasingly unpopular, some troops began to speak out against what they saw as links between the sexism and racism that drill sergeants perpetuated in basic training and US foreign policy in Vietnam. To them, the John Wayne ideal of manliness was revealed to be a warrior myth.

### The GI Antiwar Movement

For some GIs, basic training and the war stripped the glorious veneer from the military's version of masculinity and revealed "the mentality that turns human beings into . . . murdering soldiers."[27] The warrior myth as played out in the realities of war left them feeling not like men at all, if being a man meant killing a man—or a woman or child. They were what the troops psychiatrist Robert Jay Lifton called "antiwar warriors," who attempted to redefine the myths that US policy makers employed to enforce existing power structures and justify America's Cold War scramble for global domination.[28] Antiwar GIs opposed not only the Vietnam War but also the gendered ideology that defined it. Servicemen demanded an end to sexism in the military, and some even reached out to women's groups, adopting the rhetoric of women's liberation and applying it to their situations. On stateside military posts and overseas bases, as well as among civilians, antiwar GIs found ways to express their opposition to the war by writing in antiwar newspapers and frequenting GI coffeehouses. Among the main issues antiwar GIs and veterans addressed was their belief that both women and men had to be liberated from their socially constructed roles in order to stop war.

Coffeehouses and antiwar newspapers provided some of the most important support and voices for GIs and veterans who opposed the war. GI coffeehouses were typically run by civilians in towns and cities that were homes to military posts. In 1967, civilian antiwar activists Fred Gardner and Donna Mickleson founded the first GI coffeehouse, the UFO, in Columbia, South Carolina, near Fort Jackson. By 1971, there were as many as twenty-six coffeehouses where GIs could discuss the war, get legal counseling on issues such as going AWOL and obtaining conscientious objector status, and learn about ways to protest the war.[29] Many of the coffeehouses published antiwar newspapers aimed specifically at GIs and veterans with exposés on poor conditions in military prisons, articles on GI antiwar activities, and testimonials from disillusioned soldiers. The papers, along with antiwar newspapers published by soldiers on bases, provided a forum for soldiers to speak out against the war.[30] The Defense Department knew about the papers but chose to not crack down on antiwar expression, reasoning that stifling dissent in print form might encourage more damaging expressions of opposition to the war.

Gender liberation—the liberation of both men and women—was a recurring theme in the GI antiwar press. Soldiers wrote articles arguing that gender roles oppressed them by equating masculinity with fighting and sexual aggression. The rejection of the type of masculinity the military promoted was part of a broader opposition to military authority, to the Vietnam War, and to the ideology that some GIs believed underwrote it. Articles discussed the need for men and women to unite rather than view each other as adversaries and called on soldiers to resist military imagery and language that degraded women. The GI antiwar rhetoric denouncing sexism reflects the influence of the American women's and civil rights movements and of international movements against imperialism. In his book on the GI antiwar movement, historian Richard Moser estimates that about 25 percent of GIs participated regularly in antiwar activism.[31] Certainly, not all antiwar soldiers criticized the military's version of masculinity, but antiwar newspapers and coffeehouse activities indicate that a significant number of antiwar GIs specifically opposed the masculinity of the warrior myth.

James Daniel, an ex-GI who attended the University of California at Berkeley after he was discharged, referred to military masculinity as the "manhood

game," criticizing it for its glorification of drunkenness, fighting, and sexual pro-
miscuity. In a letter to *Ally*, Daniel argued that true manhood means learning "to
truly love—a woman, an idea, a place, a time, because they have had an inner
vision which makes these real along with a recognition that a man will fight if he
or his is attacked."[32] Some GIs who wrote for antiwar newspapers argued that
the military actively exploited men through its criteria for masculinity. Writers
for Fort Hood's *Fatigue Press* maintained that most lonely GIs simply wanted
"a meaningful relationship with a member of the opposite sex . . . and someone
to talk to and be with," while drill sergeants inundated them with the judgment
that the "sign of manhood is the number of women you've made love to."[33] An
article in the paper noted that GIs were "subject to constant propaganda on
sex" from the moment they entered the military. The blatant sexism alienated
some GIs from the military establishment and, in some cases, from the military's
overall mission. An article in *Fatigue Press* encouraged GIs to avoid referring
to women as "broads" and thereby prevent the military from controlling their
thinking.[34]

Veterans writing for *The Bond*, the newspaper of the antiwar American Servicemen's Union, explained that sexism undermined GIs' marriages. They testified that during basic training, drill sergeants made them sing songs about
unfaithful women "to make us feel hostile to and distrustful of our wives or
girlfriends." Married GIs faced ridicule from sergeants, who encouraged them
to take their frustrations out on their wives, the men added. "The chain of command is simple," they wrote. "The CO [commanding officer] shits on the lifer
sergeants, they both shit on you, and you're supposed to go home and 'f——k the
shit' out of your wife or girlfriend." The connection between sex and violence
appeared in all sorts of places. "At the rifle range, we were told by the range
NCO [noncommissioned officer] to 'squeeze the trigger like you squeeze your
girl's t——s,'" the veterans explained.[35]

Although servicemen of various ranks used sexist language as part of their
inherited language and thought patterns, "anti-woman prejudice" was "a conscious policy of the high-ranking generals who run the military," the veterans
wrote. They argued that the armed forces pursued "a deliberate sexist policy,
that is, a policy of male superiority, to keep men and women divided. This policy
is designed to keep male GIs from uniting with their equally oppressed sisters,"
both military and civilian. Therefore, the vets called on GIs "to build a trust and
unity among brothers and sisters in the military and military dependents" and
not "play into the hands of the brass" by buying into its sexist ideology and com-

mitting "crimes against women."[36] The veterans argued that sexist language reflected the ideas that shaped US war policy toward Vietnam. Some GIs did not stop with the call to refuse to speak the language of military sexism. They implored fellow soldiers to rethink the ideology of male superiority and the gender roles on which it relied. A sailor wrote in *Dare to Struggle*, a GI antiwar newspaper published in San Diego, that the military brass used sexism to prevent men and women from joining in protest of military policy, thus keeping them subservient to military regulations. He argued that maltreatment of women was akin to the ways "lifers"—career military personnel—related to draftees or enlisted personnel who looked forward to the time when they were discharged. The only way to throw off the brass, then, was to "demand the liberation of women." Doing so would help defeat "the system that oppresses and robs us all of our humanity," the sailor concluded.[37]

An article in *Broken Arrow*, an antiwar newspaper published at Selfridge Air Base near Detroit, asked GIs why they would allow the military to control them into thinking that women were nothing more than sex objects. The author of the piece argued that "if the women are free to fight for liberation, we will all be a lot stronger. So we have to start thinking of our sisters as fellow human beings, the way *we* want to be treated."[38] Another article, entitled "Men and Women's Liberation," discussed what men gave up when they upheld gender roles that assigned them the role of financial provider while limiting women to that of homemakers. "Some men claim that they would enjoy staying home with the children, but their wives usually can't get jobs that pay as well as their husband's job." By adhering to mainstream gender roles, a man loses out on "the joys of having close relationships with his children. It is a sad society that alienates father and son." In addition to preventing healthy relationships from developing between fathers and children, warrior masculinity burdened men emotionally and physically. The article's author wrote that it was "unnatural" for a man not to cry, express fear, or feel pain. Suppressing such feelings was likely one of the main reasons men suffered "heart attacks, nervous disorders, and cases of high blood pressure."[39] The article implied that men who embraced the role of house husband or stay-at-home dad, far removed from the stoic warrior or organization man of popular culture, would have more emotionally fulfilling, less stressful lives.

A writer who identified himself as "a 22-year-old male" maintained that "Women's Lib is working for equal rights of the two sexes." He asked GIs to consider what their lives would be like if society gave men the inferior gender role. The author expressed empathy for women and, like the writers for other GI antiwar newspapers, connected sexism to a larger military program of repression. In addition to offering a general explanation of his opposition to mainstream gender roles, he discussed the issues military wives faced, including inadequate housing, poor medical services, and lack of jobs on or around bases. The author also gave a nod to enlisted women, acknowledging the harassment they faced from military men who did not want them around.[40]

An article in the December 1, 1969, issue of *Duck Power*, a GI antiwar newspaper published in San Diego, condemned the army's role in sustaining the sex trade in Vietnam. Entitled "The Army as PIMP," the article explained that the army's surgeon general in Vietnam advocated for brothels on military bases in hope of lowering the rate of venereal diseases among troops. Base commanders and medical personnel could control the Vietnamese women who worked at the brothels and ensure that they were free of disease. The article noted that "the good doctor doesn't seem concerned with the fate of the women subjected to this servitude." Protesting the degradation of Vietnamese women, the article also objected to the assumption that servicemen required prostitutes to satisfy their sexual desires.[41]

*The Bond* condemned the US military's decision in January of 1972 to allow prostitutes onto bases in Vietnam. Prior to the ruling, military personnel had to leave the base to find prostitutes or brothels, but the directive allowed "local national guests," including prostitutes, on base as long as they had a Vietnamese government-issued identification card. US officers told a reporter for the *New York Times* that "they supported the practice to keep peace within the increasingly disgruntled ranks" of American troops in Vietnam. Contending that the military command "have always used the oppression of women" to ensure the submission of troops, Private John Lewis, a reporter for antiwar newspaper *The Bond*, argued that "the brass's crimes show that they have used every low and disgusting tactic to try to keep every GI in a state of a dehumanized beast who is willing at any time to do the bidding of these sexist, racist, fascist monsters." Lewis reported that the US war in Vietnam forced more than 400,000 Vietnamese women into prostitution because the war destroyed farmland and thus pushed rural people into cities in search of work and as refugees. Calling South Vietnam a "colony" of the US with an economy run by the US military, Lewis maintained that many peasant women had no choice but to become prostitutes, the only job available to them in the military economy.[42] The article's headline read, "Legalized Prostitution—Brass's New Weapon against GIs and Vietnamese Women," suggesting that assumptions about servicemen's sexual desires were part of the larger US project in Vietnam, and that military authorities used those assumptions to control the behavior of troops.

Black GIs connected the degradation of women with the oppression of African Americans as a whole, and in antiwar newspapers they called for solidarity between black servicemen and servicewomen against military sexism and racism. John Wayne, whose personal politics aligned clearly with the conservative wing of the Republican party, was not the model of masculinity for all American men who served in Vietnam even though patriarchal attitudes were pervasive in alternative definitions of manhood. Leaders of the Black Panther Party articulated a version of manhood based on African Americans' achieving independence and control over their lives and communities. To them, manhood meant rejecting white social, political, economic, and cultural structures that had long been used to oppress blacks. Other African Americans saw manhood embodied in the boxer Muhammad Ali, who refused to report for army duty in 1965 after his petition for conscientious objector status was denied. In 1966, the Student Nonviolent Coordinating Committee, a leading organization in the black freedom struggles of the era, issued a statement in support of men who chose to avoid a war that the committee considered a racist endeavor of white imperialism against the Vietnamese.

Yet another form of masculinity was present in Hispanic communities. Through World War II, Mexican Americans had emphasized military service as an avenue for proving manhood and worthiness of citizenship. The desire to demonstrate loyalty and manhood fostered a "readiness to die" among young Chicanos that, according to George Mariscal, carried over to the Vietnam generation. But some young Chicanos built an antiwar movement around rejecting the imperialistic attitudes that John Wayne represented, identifying with Vietnamese resistance. This did not necessarily mean that they embraced the redefinition of gender roles, however, and paternalism and chauvinism affected definitions of manhood in every racial group. Regarding those men who became soldiers, either voluntarily or through conscription, Robert Jay Lifton wrote that, whatever an individual soldier's view of manhood, "a crucial factor was the super-masculinity promoted within the military."[43]

The GI antiwar newspaper *Demand for Freedom* told readers that "to use terms such as bitch, broad, chic [sic], hammer, or whore in recognizing our Black sisters is a failure to be Black . . . You don't even realize that in using these depressive terms, you are also speaking of your mother, wife, or daughter, because they too are Black sisters."[44] An article in *About Face*, an antiwar newspaper published by black GIs stationed in Heidelberg, Germany, invoked the honor of black women to discourage black men from getting involved with German women. The article equated black manhood with love for "the daughters of Africa."[45] While the celebration of black women sometimes objectified them, some black GIs demanded full equality for black women at home and on base.[46] Additionally, the writer of the article called for an extension of solidarity to all nonwhite women. Because Kadena Air Force Base, where *Demand for Freedom* was published, is located on Okinawa, the author called on black GIs to respect "our Okinawan sisters who have been forced by American capitalism and imperialism to engage in prostitution as a means of survival. Brothers, for the sake of the People's humanity and dedicated love and respect, recognize our black sisters and all Third World females."[47]

GI coffeehouses linked antiwar GIs to various civilian movements, including the growing women's movement. The Oleo Strut, near Fort Hood, Texas, opened a small health clinic, and its staff helped form the Killeen Women's Group, where members occasionally wrote articles about the women's liberation movement for the GI newspaper *Fatigue Press*. GI wives from Fort Hood worked with the Strut to plan rallies against the war for military families.[48] The cafes helped GIs view their struggle against the Vietnam War as part of a larger struggle against the oppression of mainstream American power symbolized by sexist expressions of masculinity. GI antiwar newspapers provided space for civilian women—usually GI wives—to vent about the war's impact on their lives and to criticize the military's gender ideology. Wives of GIs complained of poor housing on bases, lack of job opportunities in military towns, and the military's general disregard for families. They spoke about the impact the war had on military families, especially those of enlisted men, and showed how ideas from the women's movement intersected with antiwar sentiment in a critique of both war and sexism. The presence of women's articles in the antiwar papers demonstrates an openness to women's perspectives on the part of the papers' editors, who usually were soldiers or veterans. While some GIs no doubt skipped past those articles, others read them carefully and took to heart their opinions and grievances in ways that modified their thinking about gender and sexism.

Antiwar GIs and veterans—particularly those involved in the coffeehouse movement—considered women and the women's movement vital allies in the fight against the system that created both the Vietnam War and domestic social ills. Pete Zastrow, a veteran who served a one-year tour in Vietnam beginning in December 1968, said that women helped antiwar servicemen focus on "vital issues that, while they weren't direct veterans' issues, were issues that veterans damn well ought to be interested in—child care, the rights of women."[49] Mike McCain, a Vietnam veteran and member of Vietnam Veterans Against the War (VVAW), said of women in VVAW: "The women taught us boys a whole lot. They were mostly our girlfriends who ended up being some of the most valuable, the most dedicated, the most active, the most disciplined people in the organization."[50] Jeanne Friedman, a former civil rights activist and organizer of antiwar veterans, remembered that in VVAW, "women were doing a lot of the work. Women were paying attention to taking care of business."[51]

McCain and Friedman's comments are particularly interesting when considered in the context of the era's other social movements. One of the criticisms that has been levied against the civil rights, black power, and civilian antiwar movements is that women in those organizations often were relegated to clerical and other types of support jobs rather than leadership positions.[52] Based on McCain and Friedman's comments, it is unclear exactly what types of work women did in VVAW or whether they held positions of power; allowing women members did not necessarily imply that male veterans considered them equals. But given that the GI antiwar press repeatedly indicated that a redefinition of gender roles and a rejection of male chauvinism were required to liberate men from the warrior myth, it seems clear that at least some GIs and veterans approved of women taking active, and even leadership, roles in the movement. At the same time, it is not surprising that even amidst demands for change in the gender hierarchy, ambivalence about what such a transformation should look like remained.

As the Vietnam War began to wind down, some veterans offered public testimonies of violence and sexual assault against Vietnamese women, which they considered to be one of the grisly consequences of the military's gender ideology. From January 31 through February 2, 1972, Vietnam Veterans Against the War sponsored the Winter Soldier Investigation, a meeting in Detroit of approximately a hundred Vietnam veterans who testified about atrocities committed by US troops during the war. Several times during the event, the testimony turned to the rape and murder of Vietnamese women, and one panelist described how the Marine Infantry Training Regiment taught troops to scrutinize Vietnamese women more closely than men during interrogations. "They stress over and over that a woman has more places to hide things like maps or anything than a male," the veteran said.[53] His statement implied that Vietnamese women could be more dangerous than their male counterparts.

In addition to identifying enemies, treating Vietnamese women harshly also aimed to keep Vietnamese men from working against the Americans "because it makes a lasting impression on some guy—some 'zip'—that's watching his daughter worked over. So we have a better opportunity of keeping him in line by working her over," the veteran continued.[54] Another panelist, a marine corporal named Christopher Simpson, stated that sexual atrocities committed against Vietnamese women were "pretty usual over there." Instead of approaching a Vietnamese woman in the way of normal courtship, "they might stick a rifle in a woman's head and say, 'Take off your clothes,'" Simpson said. "That's the way it's done over there. 'Cause they're not treated as human beings over there, they're treated as dirt."[55] Linking violence against Vietnamese women to both sexism and a career in the military, Marine Sergeant Joe Bangert testified about the disembowelment of a Vietnamese woman that he observed: "I think the person involved was a freaked out sexist, if that's what you're trying to get at. I think maybe he had problems. He had to be—he was in the Army for 20 years."[56] In the Winter Soldier testimonies, Vietnam veterans exposed the dark side of the gender ideology at the root of the American presence in Vietnam.

## The Military in the Post–Vietnam War Era

The Vietnam War and its aftermath coincided with several events that together stimulated changes in gender roles and relations in the United States. The idea of extending equal rights to women echoed the beliefs of antiwar GIs who, along with feminist activists, argued for a gender liberation that would free both women and men from social constrictions.[57] The National Organization for Women (NOW) had pushed Congress to set an effective date for the integration of the service academies in 1975 after Congress authorized their integration. Speaking specifically about the integration of West Point, Betty Friedan, founder of NOW, asserted that rather than threatening masculinity, the admission of women brought "the possibility of a new model of what it is to be a man, a new kind of male hero in America, as men begin to share the care of the children and home with their wives, as women share the burdens and responsibilities of earning—even the hardships and dangers and glories of military careers."[58] Friedan added that attending West Point did not turn women into men; they maintained their femininity while proving their competence.[59] It was not women or femininity that needed to change, Friedan suggested, but men and masculinity that needed transforming, and that was happening as the military was opening more fully to women.

When the Equal Rights Amendment (ERA) was making its way through state legislatures, the issue of whether it would require women to be drafted into the military and serve in combat units caused conflict among feminists. The debate became especially heated in 1980, when President Jimmy Carter reinstated the Selective Service System in response to the Soviet invasion of Afghanistan and called for both men and women to register. Public debate and congressional hearings on the issue eventually led to the case of *Rostker v. Goldberg* in 1981, in which the US Supreme Court ruled that the draft exists primarily to fill combat positions, and since women are excluded from combat, it is legal to exclude women from selective service and the draft. In response to the *Rostker* ruling, NOW, along with the League of Women Voters and the National Federation of Business and Professional Women's Clubs, filed briefs with the Supreme Court arguing that drafting men but not women violated women's constitutional rights and privileges of citizenship. Military service, NOW reps argued, conveyed a right and an ability to lead.[60]

The outbreak of the first Gulf War in 1991 threw these issues into sharp relief. About 40,000 servicewomen served in Operation Desert Shield and Operation Desert Storm, and fifteen were killed: five in battle and the rest in noncombat incidents. "The Persian Gulf helped collapse the whole chivalrous notion that women could be kept out of danger in a war," said Representative Patricia Schroeder, a Colorado Democrat who was an advocate of rescinding all rules excluding women from combat. "We saw that the theater of operations had no strict combat zone, that Scud missiles were not gender-specific—they could hit both sexes and, unfortunately, did," Schroeder said.[61]

Captain Carol Barcalow, who served with the army in the war and was a member of West Point's class of 1980, said: "Until the Persian Gulf, the American people didn't understand the modern battlefield. Even in noncombat roles, women have been exposed to risk for some time." She continued: "As the military downsizes in the coming years, there will be a need to keep the best and the brightest, and women will need to be convinced they have the chance for future advancement. And that means combat arms cannot be closed to them."[62] Such change required that male officers think differently about female personnel, she said, and servicewomen's performance in the Persian Gulf was a start. "Many of the guys of my generation have had that experience, but the senior military ranks have never worked with women as peers," she said. "Someone 20 years my senior and a general still see women as a mother, wife, girlfriend or daughter. They know how to deal with guys but may not know what to do with women. It makes them uncomfortable."[63]

Opponents of the opening of combat positions to women blamed career servicewomen, who wanted the same advancement opportunities as their male counterparts, which meant having combat experience. Writing in the *National Review* in November 1991, Phyllis Schafly protégé Elaine Donnelly, founder of the Coalition for Military Readiness, which opposed the gender integration of the military, likened the expansion of military jobs to seeing men and women as interchangeable parts without physiological or psychological differences. Donnelly argued that the military was not primarily an institution to provide education, job training, and career advancement. It existed for national security purposes, and only an all-male military could protect American interests.[64] The Presidential Commission on the Admission of Women to the Armed Forces, of which Donnelly was a member, made this same argument in its recommendations in November 1992, concluding that women should not be allowed to serve in combat and should be limited further than that in terms of how they could serve. Commissioners referred to the case of *Craig v. Boren*, which determined that separate laws for men and women are unconstitutional unless there is a clear government interest to be served by such laws. Commissioners argued that the government interest in national security mandated a law limiting women's military service.[65]

When Elaine Donnelly criticized women in the military, she blamed feminists for the expansion of servicewomen's roles while at the same time noting that the Persian Gulf War was "universally abhorred by feminist ideologues."[66] That she saw feminists in both of these ways illustrated the complexity of feminists' attitudes toward war and the expansion of the military. In 1990, NOW passed a resolution supporting the opening of combat roles to women so that servicewomen could receive combat pay and combat-related opportunities for promotion. Designated combat zones and front lines no longer existed in late-twentieth-century warfare.[67] Yet NOW members also participated in a 1991 march for Middle East peace.[68] At the heart of the dispute were differing attitudes about the goal of feminism. For some feminists, the point was to achieve equality between women and men within the existing socioeconomic order, so that women would have access to the same opportunities for career and financial advancement as men. From this perspective, if women were excluded from any aspect of military service, they were excluded from full citizenship. But the Persian Gulf War also coincided with the rise of third-wave feminism, which was less concerned with equal opportunity to employment, education, and other civil liberties, the items that were central to the agenda of second-wave feminism.

Third-wave feminists emphasized race, sexuality, and cultural issues to understand the ways in which gender constructions were used to signify power. For them, the issue was not equal opportunity for women in the military but rather concerns about how the dominant conceptions of masculinity and femininity inform American demonstrations of power and force in the world. In February 1991, the feminist journal *off our backs* published articles by members of its editorial staff regarding the Persian Gulf War. Carol Anne Douglas wrote of a letter she received from a subscriber asking if journal issues could be sent to her in the Persian Gulf, where she was being deployed with her reserve unit. Douglas wondered "what it must be like to have a feminist and presumably internationalist consciousness and to be there." Would such a consciousness hurt the reader's chances at survival in the war?[69] For Douglas, feminism and military service in war were mutually exclusive.

## "You've Come a Long Way . . . Maybe"

Despite official measures to recruit women, military culture indicated that new policies did not necessarily stimulate changes in mindset. Although the services recognized the need to open their ranks to women in order to fill an all-volunteer force, military culture remained defined by gender difference, sexuality, and narrow ideas about appropriate roles for women in the armed forces. Combat remained the chief point of contention in debates about women's roles in the military. Lieutenant Colonel Richard Parker, chairman of the University of Michigan's Army Reserve Officers Training Program, acknowledged that women recruits could compete on the same level physically as men, but because of Americans' perceptions of soldiering as a man's field, neither women nor men could truly envision women in combat roles.

Regarding military culture, John Teahan, a psychology professor at Wayne State University, observed that "naturally the male inclination toward protectiveness is at work here; it's ingrained in our culture." Teahan went on to state that "male soldiers resent having to feel protective. It makes them feel more vulnerable because deep down they do not believe the women to be as competent. They fear women cannot back them up well on the battlefield, cannot qualify as a trustworthy member of the team."[70] Lieutenant Colonel Sherman Ragland, Walter Reed Army Medical Center's human resources officer, tried to explain the cultural imagery that was part of the dilemma: "A woman in most people's minds is symbolic of motherhood, so when you give a woman a gun, it's the same thing as giving your mother a gun and sending her off to fight." Peggy Paige, an instructor for the 8830th Military Police Brigade in Gaithersburg, Maryland, also drew on gendered imagery to explain her opposition to serving in combat: "Women are equal brain-wise, but not physically. I'm a delicate creature and I want to be treated that way."[71] Cultural changes in the way Americans viewed war and soldiering would have to come before legislation could successfully open combat to women.

In 1976, a *Washington Post* reporter interviewed cadets and officers at the US military academies, and they provided a variety of perspectives on the subject. Beth Lundquist, a midshipman at the US Naval Academy in Annapolis, wanted the opportunity to serve in combat because she believed it was a waste of time to go through the academy's rigorous training to take a desk job. Cheryl Spohnholtz, a fellow midshipman, also favored opening combat roles to women and said that her male counterparts resented women's exemption from them. Reginald Bassa and Todd Worthington, Air Force Academy cadets, complained that women got "all the bennies [benefits] but they're not doing the same as the guys. They spend all this money on training the girls and then send them to the adjutant corps." Lieutenant General Sidney Berry, the superintendent of West Point at the time, hoped women would not be assigned to combat units because he believed that "would tend to reduce the effectiveness of those combat units." Brigadier General Stanley Beck, the Air Force Academy's commandant of cadets, provided the most specific reason for wanting to keep combat roles closed to women. "The fact is the American people don't want women in combat, and I doubt that they will change," he said. "No country in the world wants women in combat. When you get right down to the heart of why not . . . one of the main factors is the effect of women being captured and becoming POWs. They would be subject to greater abuse than their male counterparts."[72]

Captain Douglas Murray, chairman of the Navy Reserve Officers Training Program at the University of Michigan, saw the debate over women in combat as part of a larger conversation about changing gender relations. "I'm of the generation that still holds chairs and opens doors," he said. "So my apprehensions are that men might do very foolish things in the name of gallantry. Like run into open fire to save her the risk." Murray went on to wonder what the demand for women in combat might mean about a transformation of gender relations in broader society. "Are these people a reflection of American womanhood? When will men stop opening doors? Where is this all headed?"[73]

Besides the combat issue, concerns arose that women in an integrated force would "lose their identity," or in other words, become masculine. As the services worked to increase the numbers of female personnel, they also enacted practices to maintain mainstream femininity. Reflecting on the Air Force Academy going coed, Colonel James P. McCarthy worried that women, who would be outnumbered about twenty-eight to one by men, would adopt "lower voices, athletic walks, and profane language" in order to blend in. "We want to graduate the most feminine women officers we can," McCarthy said.[74] Basic training for women marines at Parris Island, South Carolina, followed that of men's basic in style and substance, with drill instructors hurling orders and insults at women recruits and pushing them beyond their physical limits. Yet after physical training, women Marines spent the most time in a course called "image development." In the classroom where the course was held, desks turned into vanity tables, and recruits learned techniques for applying makeup, including shades of lipstick that did not clash with the red braid on the Marine cap.[75] The reality of having a coed force was acceptable as long as the image of difference between men and women, representing mainstream gender roles, remained intact.

This was due largely to concerns about sexuality, which were not new to the post-Vietnam era but which took on increased significance as women were integrated into the regular forces. Some men viewed their female counterparts as either "hopeless nymphomaniacs" or "a hopeless loser or a lesbian." Detailing some of these attitudes, *Family: The Magazine of Army/Navy/Air Force Times* published an article entitled "You've Come a Long Way . . . Maybe," a play on the slogan of Virginia Slims cigarettes. The article acknowledged the advances women in the military had made, including an expected increase in the number of women in the armed services due to heightened recruitment efforts, the removal of the upper limit on the percentage of women allowed to make up the forces, the ending of salary caps for women, and equalization of retirement regulations. By the time of the article's publication in 1972, the armed forces had seen five women generals. Hester Turner, onetime chair of the Defense Advisory Committee on Women in the Services, observed, "The women now in military service are beginning to fade that image of a benchwarmer and are becoming full and active members of the Armed Forces team."[76] But individual attitudes suggested a less-than-friendly opinion of servicewomen. Air Force Captain John Prince complained that too many members of the Women's Air Force "fit into the truck driver mold." An army captain argued that "the proximity of women to men in combat would cause problems. People don't react normally under combat. Sex is one of the outlets in a stress situation, and people have personality changes sometimes in combat."[77] Even after Vietnam, sexuality was central to some servicemen's views both of women's roles and of the military itself.

### Conclusion

Studying the military and its institutional decision making can illuminate broader social, cultural, and political attitudes in American history. The Vietnam War and its aftermath coincided with several events that together stimulated changes in gender roles and relations in the United States. The idea of extending equal rights to women echoed the beliefs of antiwar GIs who, along with feminist activists, argued for a gender liberation that would free both women and men from social constrictions. GI and veteran resistance to the warrior persona at times allied with struggles against racism and sexism on the home front. After 1975, the US military's decisions regarding the status of servicewomen opened up windows on Americans' beliefs about gender roles, real and imagined links between gender and military power, and divisions among women's rights activists about what stance feminists should take on military service. While the late 1960s and 1970s are remembered as a period of transformation in women's roles and rights, they were also a time, because of the Vietnam War, when masculinity and men's social roles were held up for scrutiny and change. This had an impact on the US armed services, which could no longer rely on old connections between manhood, citizenship, and military service to fill their ranks after the Vietnam War. Yet even in this time of change, the ideas which undergirded military masculinity were not easy to transform.

NOTES

1. Bob Christman, "Do Women Threaten West Point's 'Manly Environment?,'" *St. Louis Post-Dispatch*, May 23, 1975.

2. Gid Pool, "West Point Six Months after Feminine Invasion—The Walls Still Stand!!," *Pentagram News*, December 16, 1976.

3. Kristy N. Kamarck, "Women in Combat: Issues for Congress," Congressional Research Service, December 3, 2015, 5.

4. Victoria Sherrow, *Women in the Military* (New York: Chelsea House Publishers, 2007), 31. See also D'Ann Campbell, *Women at War with America: Private Lives in a Patriotic Era* (Cambridge, MA: Harvard University Press, 1984); Campbell, "Women in Combat: The World War II Experience in the United States, Great Britain, Germany, and the Soviet Union," *The Journal of Military History* 57, no. 2 (April 1993): 301–323.

5. Kimberly Jensen, *Mobilizing Minerva: American Women in the First World War* (Champaign: University of Illinois Press, 2008).

6. Leisa Meyer, *Creating GI Jane: Sexuality and Power in the Women's Army Corps during World War II* (New York: Columbia University Press, 1998).

7. Heather Marie Stur, *Beyond Combat: Women and Gender in the Vietnam War Era* (New York: Cambridge University Press, 2011); Beth Bailey, *America's Army: Making the All-Volunteer Force* (Cambridge, MA: Belknap Press, 2010).

8. Jeanne Holm, *Women in the Military: An Unfinished Revolution* (Novato, CA: Presidio Press, 1982), 260–288; Beth Bailey, *America's Army*, 133, 135.

9. Cynthia Enloe, *Does Khaki Become You? The Militarization of Women's Lives* (London: Pluto Press, 1983), 136–137.

10. For a detailed examination of Cold War gender imagery and US foreign relations, see Heather Marie Stur, *Beyond Combat: Women and Gender in the Vietnam War Era* (New York: Cambridge University Press, 2011).

11. Robert Jay Lifton, *Home from the War: Learning from Vietnam Veterans* (Boston: Beacon Press, 1992), 23–31.

12. Michael Kimmel, *Manhood in America: A Cultural History* (New York: Free Press, 1996), 252.

13. Ronald L. Davis, *Duke: The Life and Image of John Wayne* (Norman: University of Oklahoma Press, 1998); Kimmel, *Manhood in America*; Jerry Lembcke, *The Spitting Image: Myth, Memory, and the Legacy of Vietnam* (New York: New York University Press, 2000).

14. Tom Engelhardt, *The End of Victory Culture: Cold War America and the Disillusioning of a Generation* (New York: Basic Books, 1995), 71–72.

15. Enloe, *Does Khaki Become You?*, xxix.

16. Richard Slotkin provides a detailed analysis of the frontier idea in US history, including the policies related to the Vietnam War. See Slotkin, *Gunfighter Nation: The Myth of the Frontier in Twentieth Century America* (Norman: University of Oklahoma Press, 1998).

17. Robert D. Dean, *Imperial Brotherhood: Gender and the Making of Cold War Foreign Policy* (Amherst: University of Massachusetts Press, 2001), 169.

18. Donald Mrozek, "The Cult and Ritual of Toughness in Cold War America," in *Rituals and Ceremonies in Popular Culture*, edited by Ray B. Browne (Bowling Green, OH: Bowling Green University Popular Press, 1980), 183.

19. Ibid.

20. Jacqueline Lawson, "'She's a Pretty Woman . . . for a Gook': The Misogyny of the Vietnam War," in *Fourteen Landing Zones: Approaches to Vietnam War Literature*, edited by Philip K. Jason (Iowa City: University of Iowa Press, 1991); Emily Rosenberg, "Foreign Affairs after World War II: Connecting Sexual and International Politics," *Diplomatic History* (Winter 1994): 59.

21. Susan Jeffords, *The Remasculinization of America: Gender and the Vietnam War* (Bloomington: Indiana University Press, 1989), 117.

22. Kimmel, *Manhood in America*, 269.

23. Lloyd C. Gardner, *Pay Any Price: Lyndon Johnson and the Wars for Vietnam* (Chicago: Ivan R. Dee, 1995); see also Thi Dieu Nguyen, *The Mekong River and the Struggle for Indochina: Water, War, and Peace* (Westport, CT: Praeger Publishers, 1999), 87.

24. Enloe, *Does Khaki Become You?*, 35.

25. Christian Appy, *Working-Class War: American Combat Soldiers and Vietnam* (Chapel Hill: University of North Carolina Press, 1993), 101–102.

26. Toshio Whelchel, *From Pearl Harbor to Saigon: Japanese American Soldiers and the Vietnam War* (London: Verso, 1999), 13.

27. "GIs and Asian Women: The Army's Deadly Game," *Fatigue Press*, May 1971, 7. Wisconsin Historical Society.

28. Lifton, *Home from the War,* 30–31.

29. David Cortright, *Soldiers in Revolt: GI Resistance During the Vietnam War* (Chicago: Haymarket Books, 2005[1975]), 98–99.

30. Melvin Small, *Give Peace a Chance: Exploring the Vietnam Antiwar Movement* (Syracuse, NY: Syracuse University Press, 1992), 98.

31. Richard Moser, *The New Winter Soldiers: GI and Veteran Dissent during the Vietnam Era* (New Brunswick, NJ: Rutgers University Press, 1996), 132.

32. "Letters to the Ally," Clark Smith Papers, Box 2, Folder 6, Wisconsin Historical Society.

33. "GI Town Part I," *Fatigue Press*, August 1971, 7, Wisconsin Historical Society.

34. "Gooks and Broads," *Fatigue Press*, Issue 11 (Date missing), Wisconsin Historical Society.

35. "Anti-Woman Propaganda: How the Brass and Their Flunkies Use It against Us," *The Bond*, December 24, 1971, 2, Wisconsin Historical Society.

36. Ibid.

37. "Thoughts on Being Human," *Dare to Struggle* 1, Issue 9 (Date missing), 6, Wisconsin Historical Society.

38. "Freeks [sic] and Our Sisters," *Broken Arrow*, February 28, 1971, 5, Wisconsin Historical Society.

39. "Men and Women's Liberation," *Broken Arrow*, February 28, 1971, 6, Wisconsin Historical Society.

40. "The 'Fair Force' Fights Back!" *Broken Arrow*, November 17, 1970, 4, Wisconsin Historical Society.

41. "The Army as PIMP," *Duck Power*, December 1, 1969, 3, Wisconsin Historical Society.

42. John Lewis, "Legalized Prostitution: Brass's New Weapon against GIs and Vietnamese Women," *The Bond*, January 27, 1972, 4, Wisconsin Historical Society.

43. Curtis J. Austin, *Up against the Wall: Violence in the Making and Unmaking of the Black Panther Party* (Fayetteville: University of Arkansas Press, 2006), 78–79; James Westheider, *Fighting on Two Fronts: African Americans and the Vietnam War* (New York: New York University Press, 1997), 18, 27, 143; Lorena Oropeza, *Raza Si! Guerra No! Chicano Protest and Patriotism during the Vietnam War Era* (Berkeley: University of California Press, 2005), 111–126; George Mariscal, *Aztlan and Viet Nam: Chicano and Chicana Experiences of the War* (Berkeley: University of California Press, 1999), 203–212; Lifton, *Home from the War,* 239.

44. "Liberation for Our Black Brothers and Sisters," *Demand for Freedom*, November 16, 1970, 14, Wisconsin Historical Society.

45. Ibid.

46. Ibid.

47. Ibid.

48. "Strike Back Campaign," *Fatigue Press*, Issue 25 (Date missing), 7, Wisconsin Historical Society.

49. Richard Stacewicz, *Winter Soldiers: An Oral History of the Vietnam Veterans against the War* (Woodbridge, CT: Twayne Publishers, 1997), 364.

50. Ibid.

51. Ibid.

52. Sara Evans, *Personal Politics: The Roots of Women's Liberation in the Civil Rights Movement and the New Left* (New York: Vintage, 1980).

53. "Veterans' Testimony on Vietnam—Need for Investigation," *Congressional Record*, April 6, 1971, E2831.

54. Ibid.

55. Ibid.

56. Ibid.

57. Jeanne Holm, *Women in the Military*; Beth Bailey, *America's Army*.

58. Betty Friedan, *The Second Stage* (New York: Abacus, 1983), 171.

59. Friedan, *The Second Stage*, 189.

60. Linda Greenhouse, "Women Join Battle on All-Male Draft," *New York Times*, March 22, 1981. www.nytimes.com/1981/03/22/us/women-join-battle-on-all-male-draft .html.

61. Jon Nordheimer, "Women's Role in Combat: The War Resumes," *New York Times*, May 26, 1991. www.nytimes.com/books/97/06/15/reviews/military-gulf.html.

62. Ibid.

63. Ibid.

64. Elaine Donnelly, "What Did You Do in the Gulf, Mommy?," *National Review*, November 18, 1991, 44.

65. James D. Milko, "Beyond the Persian Gulf Crisis: Expanding the Role of Servicewomen in the United States Military," *The American University Law Review* 41 (1992): 1329.

66. Donnelly, "What Did You Do in the Gulf, Mommy?," 41.

67. Amanda Terkel, "Ban on Women in Combat Is Discriminatory, High-Level Military Panel States," *Huffington Post*, May 25, 2011. www.huffingtonpost.com/2011/01 /14/women-military-commission-combat_n_809241.html.

68. National Organization for Women, "Highlights." http://now.org/about/history /highlights.

69. Carol Anne Douglas, "Commentary: The Persian Gulf," *off our backs*, February 1991, 2.

70. Emily Fisher, "Women Mastering Combat, But Men Lag in Acceptance," *Philadelphia Inquirer*, November 25, 1976.

71. "Women: Moving Up," *Soldiers*, August 1975, 12–14.

72. Phil McCombs, "Women Cadets See Combat Roles as Key to Equality," *Washington Post*, December 23, 1976.

73. Fisher, "Women Mastering Combat."

74. "Air Force Academy, Going Coed, Ponders Pockets and Calories," *Wall Street Journal*, February 18, 1976, 1–2.

75. "Leathernecks with Lipstick," *Washington Post*, March 7, 1976.

76. Margaret Eastman, "The Woman in Uniform: How Liberated Can She Be?," *Family: The Magazine of Army/Navy/Air Force Times*, March 15, 1972, 7. Record Group 319, Box 94, Folder 792, National Archives Records Administration, College Park, MD.

77. Ibid., 8.

# 8

# Mobilizing Marriage and Motherhood

Military Families and Family Planning since World War II

KARA DIXON VUIC

As the military integrated women into its forces in the years after World War II, family and reproductive matters became part of military policy. The regulation of women's sexuality, pregnancy, and motherhood illustrated the military's view of women as part of the forces and concerns about how women in the forces might challenge traditional gender roles. That the military changed its reproductive policies over time reveals the impact of civilian world politics on the armed services. From *Roe v. Wade* to lower-profile cases, home front transformations in sexual and gender regulation affected how the military assigned benefits and classified mothers. This chapter explores the military's attempts to create its desired female force while also responding to changes in domestic sexual and gender norms.[1]

When Marine Sergeant Jocelyn Proano received deployment orders to Iraq in 2005, her daughter was little more than one year old. Although reluctant to leave her child, Proano found that the "mommy mentality" left her the instant she boarded the bus for training. Still, she called home every day to check on the little girl and cried the first time she said "Mama" over the telephone. Balancing motherhood and military service proved difficult, but even after a six-month separation from her family, Proano remained committed to her assignment and extended her tour so that she would not have to leave her unit.[2]

A half century earlier, military regulations did not allow women even to consider the tough choices that thousands of women like Proano faced during the Iraq War. During World War II, most Americans believed motherhood and military service were mutually exclusive. Even many servicewomen considered the two incompatible and expressed the contradiction in a witty marching cadence.

"If you're nervous in the service/and you don't know what to do," the women sang, "have a baby, have a baby."[3]

In the decades following World War II, the American military integrated women, removed restrictions on the ranks and positions they could achieve, and depended on their service to greater degrees. This evolution of women's military roles occurred alongside, and was possible in part because of, concurrent changes in policies that allowed women both to exercise and to limit reproduction. The more the military relied on women's service, the more commanders realized they would have to allow women to combine service and family, just as they would have to provide women with the means to limit reproduction if they wished to maintain a consistent force. In these ways, the evolution of the military's family planning policies mirrors its leaders' changing perspectives on the meaning of women's martial service and, particularly, enduring fears about how women's service might transgress normative gender roles. In all eras, the military's policies on reproductive matters have marked the state's efforts to regulate the sexual lives of women in uniform and thus to create the kind of female force it desired.

The military liberalized marriage and family planning policies at times when it most needed women. This is not to say that the military designed its family planning policies strictly to meet its personnel needs. At all times, more wives and daughters of servicemen have benefited from increased reproductive choices than have servicewomen. Additionally, officials have always made decisions in the context of changing social and cultural mores, women's demands for greater freedom, and the recommendations of medical personnel, never strictly based on any service's need for women. And yet one cannot ignore that liberalized policies came at times when the military most needed women in uniform.

Even as the military's family planning policies grew out of needs particular to the forces, they did not develop in a vacuum. Rather, they have reflected and shaped broader national debates about reproduction and its political meanings. Military officials and servicewomen debated motherhood, birth control, and abortion while the country as a whole experienced the postwar baby boom, the sexual revolution, and increasing political activism over abortion in the wake of the 1973 *Roe v. Wade* decision.[4] Increasingly, women who donned military uniforms brought with them expectations that they should enjoy the same freedoms to combine career and family that their male colleagues had traditionally taken for granted. Their demands combined with military need to produce tangible changes and placed the American armed forces at the center of transformative debates about the meanings of motherhood, reproductive rights, and women's military service.

## Sexual Respectability in World War II

In the months that preceded American entry into World War II, military commanders knew that they would need the services of women. The army and navy had both enlisted women in prior wars, and they both maintained a small permanent force of female nurses. But as the armed services considered utilizing women as soldiers and looked to enlist them in unprecedented numbers, they confronted a skeptical American public that believed women's martial service would undo the very fabric of domestic gender norms. Even if women could adapt to the "masculine" qualities presumed necessary for soldiering in a wartime emergency, many Americans feared the lifestyle would undermine American families and womanhood. Some even worried that allowing married women to serve would have detrimental effects on the national birthrate. Representative Clare Hoffman of Michigan voiced this notion perhaps most bluntly when he challenged the creation of the Women's Army Auxiliary Corps. "Who then will maintain the home fires?" he asked Congress. "Who will rear and nurture the children?"[5]

To overcome public reluctance and even opposition to the notion of female soldiering, the services began a multifaceted campaign to craft a respectable image of the women's corps.[6] They commissioned community and academic leaders to direct the women's branches, recruited heavily on college campuses, redesigned uniforms to appear more feminine and attractive, and developed a sophisticated recruiting campaign that defined women's service as patriotic and indispensable. The army also adopted regulations to create a corps of women who exhibited the qualities of middle-class womanhood. Although policies permitted the dismissal of women for any action that commanders believed brought disrepute to the corps, leaders used them specifically to impose stricter behavioral and sexual expectations on women than were demanded of male soldiers.[7] This meant, for example, that when a female soldier was discovered in a hotel room with a male soldier, she was punished and he was not. Under the Uniform Code of Military Justice, male soldiers had to commit a criminal offense to be dishonorably discharged. "Promiscuous" female soldiers, Women's Army Corps (WAC) Director Oveta Culp Hobby explained, could be "immediately discharged in the interest of unit spirit and welfare."[8] Warning that the public would judge the entire corps by the disreputable actions of one errant woman, Hobby insisted that each servicewoman behave as a "gentlewoman" and an ideal representative of the sexual respectability Hobby believed essential to the corps' survival and public acceptance.[9]

Once the women's corps became a full-fledged part of the army in 1943, however, officials planned to hold women to the same behavior standards as men, a move that would have loosened Hobby's grip on the moral standards of her corps.[10] While Hobby wanted her soldiers to be recognized as equals to the men with whom they served, in the wake of persistent rumors about servicewomen's sexuality, she vehemently resisted any policy that did not hold women to higher moral standards than men.[11] Public concerns about women's military service had reached a crescendo earlier that year in a slander campaign that alleged, alternately, that female soldiers served as prostitutes for male soldiers and that lesbianism ran rampant among the corps. Rumors that the army was providing prophylactics to women (as it did to men) only complicated matters further.[12] Seeking to counter allegations that she feared would undermine recruiting efforts and possibly the corps itself, Hobby concentrated her efforts on portraying servicewomen as sexually respectable, even at the cost of denying them access to information about sex and prophylaxis.

Hobby insisted, for example, that training officers not broach the subject of homosexuality for fear that an open discussion might make trainees "too curious" and cause the public to associate the corps with lesbianism.[13] Similarly, when the (unfortunately titled) Director of Venereal Disease developed plans to provide women with a sexual hygiene program similar to the one designed for men, WAC and Army Nurse Corps (ANC) leaders adamantly resisted. On recommendation from the National Research Council, medical officers had proposed to provide women with thorough information on sexuality and venereal disease and to distribute prophylactics via slot machines in the women's latrines, because everyone assumed that the women would be too embarrassed to ask for them in public. The pragmatic program, however, met great resistance from women's corps leaders, who instead adopted a "moral and idealistic" approach to sexuality that emphasized the "spiritual and permanent rewards of clean behavior."[14] Women received no real discussion of sexuality, no frank discussion of disease, no practical instruction in prophylaxis. In fact, in 1944, the War Department specifically prohibited military officials from giving women information on how to protect themselves from acquiring venereal disease and forbade them from issuing women prophylactic devices.[15]

But while the military stringently regulated female soldiers' sexuality, it also knew that it needed unprecedented numbers of women to enlist and therefore could not impose entirely Victorian notions of female chastity. In fact, the women's branches reversed prior trends by allowing married women to serve in uniform. This policy bolstered government claims that women's service was both necessary and respectable, and it confirmed the image of servicewomen as upstanding, certainly not the sexual deviants that many detractors claimed. While the female soldiering corps allowed women to marry from their origin— just as male soldiers were permitted to marry—the army and navy nursing corps had excluded wives since their founding in the early twentieth century and had dishonorably discharged women who married. The pressing needs of the war, however, forced the army and navy to change their policies and allow nurses to marry and remain on duty, though not in the same theater as their spouse. Female soldiers—unlike nurses—faced no restrictions on serving alongside their spouse and generally enjoyed the same opportunity to combine service and marriage that their male counterparts did.[16]

But while the military expanded its definitions of women's service by allowing wives to serve, it upheld notions of their service as temporary and incompatible with women's familial responsibilities. Any woman who became pregnant faced an immediate discharge, while women who found themselves responsible for the care of another person were often granted discharges regardless of their outstanding military commitment.[17] Following the practice of the ANC, the army initially discharged pregnant women honorably if married and dishonorably if single.[18] As with similar policies that permitted the women's corps to dismiss those whose behavior did not measure up to the corps' ideals, distinct discharge policies for pregnancy imposed a set of sexual morals and consequences upon the women that were not imposed on men who fathered children, married or not. Once the women's auxiliary corps integrated into the army, however, it had to follow standard regulations regarding discharge policies. Thus, "however moral and righteous of motive" Hobby believed the discharge distinction to be, after July 1943, women could only be dishonorably discharged from the service for violating military or civil law.[19] Because pregnancy—even out of wedlock—was no crime, all women who became pregnant were thereafter honorably discharged on the grounds that they were "no longer physically fit for duty."[20] The other services followed suit.[21]

Although rates of pregnancy among servicewomen remained much lower than among civilian women, and although policy called for women to be immediately discharged upon discovery of a pregnancy, some women did give birth while on duty.[22] If a woman stationed overseas was discovered to be pregnant at a late stage when travel was impractical, the military retained her on duty until the child was born and then discharged her for having a dependent.[23] Such occurrences proved disconcerting at best for military officials who "had to worry over miscarriages and being held responsible for miscarriages."[24] When officials managed to discharge a woman before she delivered, she received no maternal care in military hospitals. Although soldiers' wives could receive maternity care in military hospitals, servicewomen were no longer eligible for such care after they were discharged. As veterans, they could receive treatment at Veterans Administration hospitals, but because pregnancy was not a "defect, disease, or disability," they provided no maternity services.[25] As WAC Director Hobby scoffed, "alcoholism and bad tonsils could be cared for, but not a pregnant and often indignant former WAC."[26] Women who found themselves discharged from the military and without medical care relied on social services and the Red Cross for assistance, an imperfect solution at best. Only in late May 1945 did the army and navy begin to provide maternity care to former servicewomen at military hospitals.[27]

WAC histories maintain that, like the pregnancy rate among female soldiers, "the known abortion rate was extremely low."[28] Although specific data on the numbers of women who sought or had abortions during World War II has not survived, if indeed it was tracked at all, in early 1944, the WAC director learned of "four or five" women who had been dishonorably discharged for having had an abortion.[29] Constantly on vigil about women's sexuality and their perceived morals, Hobby explored the possibility of a policy that would allow the corps to dishonorably discharge women discovered to have had an illegal abortion.[30] Strictly speaking, the proposal was unnecessary. The army was free to discharge a woman it found undesirable for any reason merely by charging that she had committed conduct unbecoming a member of the corps.[31] Generally, the other services discharged women who had had abortions on grounds that they had committed conduct prejudicial to the service or for failing to report a pregnancy. Moreover, because most laws made abortion a crime committed by a physician, not the woman herself, and because the corps had little way of proving that a woman had an abortion in any case, it could not issue dishonorable discharges for abortion.[32]

At the same time, even an honorable discharge for abortion, warned Margaret D. Craighill, the army surgeon general's consultant for women's health and welfare, might "over-emphasize the magnitude of the problem" or "lead to bad publicity."[33] Craighill suggested that women who had abortions should be retained in the corps. "The fact of an abortion, in itself," she opined, "does not necessarily mean that she has an undesirable character, or that she will be a bad influence in the Army."[34] Other medical officers warned that "a person under sufficient social pressure to submit to this extreme measure would not be deterred by the risk of being discharged" and that an explicit policy might lead many to conceal their pregnancy or the complications of an abortion to prevent being detected and discharged.[35] Navy officials similarly hoped to keep such information out of public hands. In 1945, navy lawyers determined that commanding and medical officers bore no legal requirement to inform state authorities that illegal abortions had been performed, even though state laws might require such disclosure. Noting that state laws could not regulate the performance of naval duties, the assistant chief of naval personnel ordered that "under no circumstances are the names of Naval personnel, who may have had abortions . . . to be disclosed to the civil authorities."[36]

Ultimately, the military never found a way to dishonorably discharge women who had had abortions without drawing unwanted attention to matters of sexuality. Instead, it relied on a series of haphazardly enforced regulations that directed unit commanders to dishonorably discharge a woman they could prove had an illegal abortion, a difficult proposition at best. Dishonorable or honorable, discharges were enforced sporadically and always officially rendered because the woman had engaged in conduct unbecoming a member of the corps, not specifically because she had illegally terminated a pregnancy.[37]

### Cold War Wives and Mothers

As the military demobilized at the end of World War II, it prepared to dismantle the women's units that had been authorized as temporary measures for the wartime emergency. The near-immediate onset of the Cold War and President Harry Truman's institution of a peacetime draft, however, caused Congress and the military to reauthorize women's corps, this time on a permanent basis. The 1947 Army-Navy Nurse Act made the nursing corps regular services, while the Women's Armed Services Integration Act of 1948 established all women's corps as permanent parts of the army, navy, air force, and marine corps.[38] This integration of women occurred at a time of public focus on the nuclear family as a critical part of national defense and a time of much consternation over the ways in which deviant sexuality threatened the Cold War gender order.[39] Such concerns framed the ways the military responded to women's increasing demands that they be allowed to marry, become mothers, and remain in the service. Slowly but surely, officials removed restrictions that had forbidden women from combining career and family and thus embraced an image of domesticity that affirmed both women's conventional gender roles and their growing place in the military.

In the late 1940s and 1950s, the military both benefited from the service of married women and upheld prevailing ideas that women's marriage and careers were incompatible. It managed this seeming contradiction by permitting married women to serve on active duty and allowing them to request a discharge simply for being married, regardless of the prescribed terms of their enlistment.[40] The army and navy stipulated that married female nurses could serve only within the reserves, a less career-oriented and advantageous position.[41] These policies balanced ideological and personnel needs when the military needed relatively few women, but when the demand for women increased sharply during wartime, officials adapted the standing regulations. In June 1950, at the onset of the Korean War, the military temporarily reversed its policy of allowing married women to voluntarily leave the corps for fear that it would otherwise not have a sufficient number of women on duty.[42] A decade and a half later, the Vietnam War similarly pushed the ANC to broaden its ideas about married women serving on active duty. Although increasing numbers of married women served as nurses during the 1950s and 1960s, marriage remained the corps' greatest source of loss. When the army faced a desperate need for nurses in Vietnam, it relaxed its regulations by permitting married women to serve in the regular army and allowing student nurses to marry.[43] The number of married women increased in response to the relaxation of policies, and by October 1967, 24 percent of the corps' women was married.[44]

In addition to the pressing demands of wartime, the general social pattern of widespread and early marriage from the 1940s to the early 1960s transformed the military's family regulations. Many servicewomen utilized the voluntary discharge allowance and left the corps, resulting in a high turnover rate. Continually replacing such high numbers of women proved frustrating for the women's branches, and in 1964 Director of Women Marines Barbara Bishop recommended that married women who were stationed close to their husband not be allowed a marriage discharge but be required to fulfill their contracts. Although it meant a conscientious effort to assign spouses near each other, the other services adopted the plan and discontinued their tradition of allowing women to request a marriage discharge.[45]

The ANC, which assigned more women to the Vietnam War than any other service, assigned many married nurses to Vietnam with their spouses. The corps specified that it would not guarantee assignments to the same hospital or to nearby locations, nor did it promise couples housing quarters together even if they were assigned to the same location.[46] Still, couples requested that they be assigned to Vietnam together, and they adapted to varying housing situations. Several hospitals offered married billets—such as "Married Row" at the Twelfth Evacuation Hospital in Cu Chi—but married housing proved difficult to come by at smaller stations.[47] In 1968, Chief Nurse in Vietnam Jennie L. Caylor suggested that couples not be assigned to smaller surgical hospitals with smaller staffs and facilities. Otherwise, she noted that "there have been no more problems with [married women] than with other officers as a whole."[48] Three years later, her successor, Patricia T. Murphy, complained that "Married nurses with their husbands in Vietnam have created many problems . . . the married nurses required as much time and effort as 400 single nurses."[49] Such housing complications, along with complaints from civilian women that they could not visit their husbands stationed in Vietnam, dissuaded the WAC from assigning married women to Vietnam with their husbands.[50]

As the military slowly enabled married women's service, it reversed its long-standing discrimination against servicewomen's spouses. The 1948 Women's Armed Services Integration Act defined a servicewoman's husband as a dependent only if he relied on his wife for more than half of his income. This meant that many married servicewomen could not be assigned on-post housing, while their husbands were denied commissary and Post Exchange privileges as well as medical care.[51] Civilian advisory groups, such as the Defense Advisory Committee on Women in the Service and the Department of Defense Nursing Advisory Committee, warned that such discriminatory practices hampered the recruitment and retention of women, and in April 1971, the Department of Defense (DOD) announced it would extend the same benefits to servicewomen's husbands as it did to servicemen's wives. The department also sought congressional legislation allowing all servicewomen's husbands to be legally classified as dependents, regardless of their financial support.[52] With the matter stalled in Congress, a Supreme Court ruling finally secured equal spousal benefits. The court took up the question after Air Force physical therapist Sharron Frontiero filed a class action suit arguing that the denial of spousal benefits for her husband constituted sex discrimination. On May 14, 1973, the court ruled in *Frontiero v. Richardson* that the military could not deny spousal benefits based on sex.[53]

However much the military increasingly accommodated the needs of married women and their husbands, its policies on motherhood undermined women's ability to fully combine service and family and cost the various services a significant number of women.[54] The practice of discharging mothers stemmed from the 1948 Women's Armed Services Integration Act and an April 1951 executive order that, together, allowed the military to discharge any woman who became the parent, stepparent, or guardian of a child under the age of eighteen, or who became pregnant or gave birth to a child (even if she surrendered the child for adoption).[55] The military claimed these policies protected the welfare of the child, but as it did not also discharge single fathers who were their children's primary caregivers, the regulations revealed the military's gender expectations more than its concern for child welfare.[56]

These regulations perpetuated the idea that motherhood and career were incompatible, but they did not require the forces to dismiss mothers. Mothers and pregnant women who wished to remain in the military could request that they be allowed to remain on duty if they demonstrated that they could provide for their child without neglecting their military duties. Army officials insisted that mothers not "be given any special consideration in terms of not going out on field exercises or not doing this or that. They had to pull their share of the workload."[57] Throughout the 1950s, as women made up a small percentage of the forces, the military granted few waivers to remain. But when the army needed increasing numbers of medical staff for the Vietnam War in the mid-1960s, its nursing and medical specialist corps granted many.[58] One study estimated that 13 percent of women in the two corps had dependents in 1964.[59] Women stationed in Vietnam, however, were not considered for waivers but were immediately sent to the United States for discharge as soon as they were discovered to be pregnant.[60]

Increasingly, commanders like ANC Chief Anna Mae Hays called for the military to remove all restrictions on pregnant women and mothers. Although she rationalized the policies as rooted in changing social understandings of gender, Hays predicted that the corps would have to become "extremely liberal" about these matters. "We'd rather have a young Corps," she explained. "It may be a busy motherhood Corps but a young one."[61] Hays's prediction came true in 1970, a year that ushered in a tidal wave of change in the military's pregnancy and motherhood policies. As the women's movement gained speed, women called attention to the military's discriminatory policies toward mothers and demanded the same rights as men to combine family and career. Their willingness to sue over the matter frequently pushed the military to formalize policy changes under consideration, though each of the services responded individually. WAC Commander Elizabeth P. Hoisington, for example, believed mothers with young children had no place in the military and voiced harsh criticism of policies permitting them to remain on duty. Other services took a more proactive approach and debated more accommodating policies while women impatient with discriminatory practices took the matter to the courts.[62]

Lorraine R. Johnson served in the ANC Reserve for ten years before her son was born in 1968. When the corps automatically filed discharge papers for her, she requested a waiver and stated that in the event of her activation, her husband or mother would care for her son. When the corps denied Johnson's request, she filed for and won a temporary injunction granted by the US District Court for the Central District of California. Facing the prospect of a court ruling that might have overturned its waiver policy, the ANC allowed Johnson to remain in the corps.[63] A similar suit forced the navy to issue a waiver to Anna Flores. Even though Flores had miscarried her pregnancy, her commanding officer ordered her discharge. Reviving the moralistic language of the World War II era, he argued that allowing Flores to remain on duty "'would imply that unwed pregnancy is condoned and would eventually result in a dilution of the moral standards set for women in the Navy.'" Flores sued in US district court on grounds that the policy discriminated against women by punishing them but not men who fathered children out of wedlock. The American Civil Liberties Union took up Flores's case and pressed for the removal of all the military's sexually discriminatory policies. As in Johnson's case, before the courts could rule, the navy issued Flores a waiver and allowed her to remain on duty.[64]

Another case reached the US Supreme Court in 1971 and highlighted the ways the military's complicated policies on pregnancy presented pregnant single servicewomen with an unfortunate choice: either have an abortion and maintain their careers or continue the pregnancy and face discharge. When air force nurse Susan Struck became pregnant in Vietnam, the Air Force Nurse Corps returned her to the United States for discharge. She gave birth on December 3, 1970, and surrendered the infant for adoption. Air Force Nurse Corps policy, like that of the other services, held that a woman could remain in the corps if she terminated the pregnancy but that if she gave birth—even if she surrendered the child for adoption—she would be discharged.[65] Like Flores, Struck alleged that her discharge was discriminatory because men were not discharged for fathering children, but she lost in both district court and the US Court of Appeals for the Ninth Circuit.[66] Undeterred, Struck appealed again, and with the representation of the American Civil Liberties Union, she received a hearing before the US

Supreme Court. Arguing on Struck's behalf, Ruth Bader Ginsburg maintained that discharging women for pregnancy violated their right to equal protection under the law. Further, she argued that allowing women who had abortions, but not women who gave birth, to remain on duty forced Struck to choose between her religious opposition to abortion and her career. Fearing that the court would rule in Struck's favor, the air force permitted her to remain on duty before the court could rule on the case, effectively undermining the Supreme Court.[67]

The services issued new policies in the spring of 1971 that made waivers for pregnancy more common in an ill-fated attempt to ward off the widespread change that commanders feared would come in the wake of court rulings or the Equal Rights Amendment then pending before Congress. The services allowed mothers and some pregnant women to apply for waivers to discharges and granted the vast majority of requests. But without a court ruling or DOD policy to inform uniform practice, each service implemented changes in its own fashion. The air force, for example, began allowing women with children to enlist and ended discharges of women who miscarried or otherwise terminated a pregnancy.[68] The army began to allow married pregnant women to remain on duty but announced that single pregnant women would be discharged unless they terminated the pregnancy or surrendered the child for adoption. Married women could become mothers or terminate pregnancies and remain on duty, whereas single women—the vast majority of army women—faced a policy that required them, if pregnant, to either have an abortion or surrender the child if they wished to remain in the military. In late 1973, the army ceased distinguishing between wed and unwed pregnancies but continued to impose an array of regulations that, despite officials' hopes, did not prevent wholesale change.[69] The courts finally settled the matter in the 1976 Second Circuit Court ruling in *Crawford v. Cushman* that the discharge of a female marine for pregnancy violated her Fifth Amendment rights.[70]

## Military Families in the Wake of *Roe v. Wade*

As the armed forces liberalized their policies on motherhood and pregnancy, medical officers reconsidered related regulations on contraception and abortion. Until the mid-1960s, each of the services generally limited "surgical intervention" in a woman's reproductive capabilities, whether through abortion, sterilization, or contraceptives, to medically necessary cases.[71] As national debates about contraception and abortion heated up and the Supreme Court issued revolutionary decisions that transformed federal laws, military policies also came under scrutiny. The resulting debates and decisions pushed the military to the forefront of contentious debates about contraception, abortion, and federal politics and highlighted the sweeping influence of the feminist movement's concerted effort to increase contraceptive options for women.

The military initiated a discussion about its reproduction policies in February 1966, less than a year after the Supreme Court ruled in *Griswold v. Connecticut* that the Constitution guaranteed married couples the right to privacy in matters of reproduction.[72] Noting that the civilian medical community was pressing the service to perform elective sterilizations, the air force surgeon general requested that the Pentagon issue a uniform regulation on when such procedures were permissible.[73] Army policy, like that of the air force, allowed for sterilization or therapeutic abortion only when a review board determined the procedure to be medically indicated and thus followed the 1962 Model Penal Code recommended by the American Law Institute.[74] In most cases, physicians operated within the parameters of state limitations, but in 1966, the DOD ruled that state law held no jurisdiction over military medical practice, which meant that military physicians were free to perform abortions or sterilizations they deemed warranted regardless of state regulations that imposed harsher restrictions.[75] In the wake of the DOD ruling, army physicians, lawyers, and religious authorities reconsidered the army's policy and concluded that it "admirably served its purpose."[76] The chief of hospital chaplains, Father Joseph S. Chmielewski, voiced the loudest objection to any liberalization on the grounds that "therapeutic abortion can hardly be interpreted in any other manner except murder."[77] Although less strident, Army Surgeon General Leonard D. Heaton similarly recommended no change, warning that "any procedure undertaken purposely to interfere with pregnancy or to produce sterilization carries with it great ethical, moral and legal responsibilities to society."[78]

The DOD did not liberalize its policies on abortion or sterilization as a result of this policy review, but it did broaden the scope of its family planning services. Beginning in October 1966, the DOD made reproductive counseling, birth control devices, and the birth control pill available free of charge in military medical facilities. This new policy provided women much easier access to birth control information and devices, which they had previously had to purchase through civilian pharmacies.[79] Within nine months, women (most of them servicemen's wives) made more than 478,000 visits to military hospitals, nearly all of them for the purpose of obtaining the pill.[80] Acquiring family planning services was no doubt easier for women stationed in the United States than it was for women in

Vietnam, who remember very different ease of access to the pill. As the statements of three army nurses who were stationed together at the Seventy-First Evacuation Hospital in Pleiku demonstrate, whatever measures the army did or did not provide for women, it was not forthcoming about them. Sara J. McVicker could not remember any birth control options being available for nurses at the hospital, although she pointed out that a gynecologist worked at the nearby air base (where no women were stationed) and that nurses had to have permission to see him.[81] Her colleagues Sharon Stanley-Alden and Rose Mary Burke, however, both remembered that nurses could obtain birth control pills at the hospital.[82] These women's disparate memories reflect the opaque nature of the military's birth control policies as well as the widespread practice among physicians not to prescribe the pill to single women and thus to deny women the same sexual freedoms as men.[83]

Even as the DOD expanded the family planning services it provided women, it did not have a uniform policy on abortion. The services each performed only therapeutic abortions, but individual physicians and hospital commanders within each service determined for themselves exactly what constituted a medical necessity.[84] This varying situation frustrated the military's chief medical officer, Louis M. Rousselot, who wrote the Pentagon's first abortion policy and unwittingly launched a political firestorm in the Nixon White House. A World War II army surgeon and former director of surgery at New York's St. Vincent's Hospital, Rousselot became the assistant secretary of defense for health affairs in January 1968.[85] Rousselot was a political conservative and a practicing Roman Catholic. And yet, while church officials grew increasingly vocal in their opposition to birth control and abortion in the 1960s, Rousselot made medical decisions based on his understanding of best scientific and medical practices, not religious dogma. He did not favor a woman's right to choose, nor was he particularly versed in the wider political consequences that his medical policies might have. Instead, he recommended medical policies based on his belief about their safety, effectiveness, and necessity.[86]

Rousselot also valued standardized policies and disagreed with what he called "the local practice of medicine concept."[87] As he explained in his confirmation hearing, his charge as the military's chief medical officer was "to resolve technical and professional differences of opinion between the three services on very major affairs."[88] In response to a request from each of the military's surgeons general for a uniform abortion policy, Rousselot ordered in July 1970 that "pregnancies may be terminated in military medical facilities when medically indicated or for reasons involving mental health." Two physicians had to approve the procedure, and one could be a psychiatrist who testified to the woman's mental state. The policy imposed no time restriction and indicated that no personnel were required to assist in such procedures if doing so would be contrary to their religious, moral, or ethical beliefs.[89] In overseas medical facilities, abortions were to be carried out in accordance with the country's "pertinent mores, the applicable laws of the nations concerned and applicable status of forces agreements."[90] Although the policy again echoed the American Law Institute's Model Penal Code and the 1967 recommendation of the American Medical Association, it directly contradicted the laws of most states, which restricted abortion in all cases except to save the mother's life.[91] Secretary Rousselot's enforcement of a uniform policy also overrode the desire of the military's surgeons general, who preferred that state laws guide abortion practice.[92]

Military spokesmen insisted the policy was "not intended as a general abandonment of limitations upon the performance of abortions," nor was it designed to "make it easier for the wife of a serviceman to obtain an abortion."[93] Yet the policy did provide servicemen's wives—and servicewomen—more legal access to abortion than most civilian women enjoyed. By the end of 1970, only four states had more liberal laws, while thirteen permitted abortions under similar restrictions.[94] Consequently, the policy led to an increase in the number of abortions, though concrete data remain scattered. The Pentagon reported that the number of abortions performed in the air force increased from 44 in 1969 to 275 in 1970, most having occurred after the policy was instated.[95] After the 1973 *Roe v. Wade* decision further removed restrictions, the army reported even higher numbers of servicewomen who chose to terminate their pregnancies. According to a memorandum from the office of the assistant secretary of the army, of the 1,560 active-duty army women who became pregnant in 1974, 1,035 ended their pregnancy through an abortion.[96] Although the Pentagon conceded that it received some letters opposing the new policy, it maintained that the policy had "been well received."[97]

By all accounts, President Richard M. Nixon remained unaware of the DOD policy until December 1970, when his staff brought it to his attention. In a memo, advisor Patrick Buchanan characterized the policy as "permitting abortion very nearly on demand on military bases" and argued that the administration was "being lumped with the pro-abortion elements in the public mind."[98] Even if Buchanan's description of the policy and its reception was hyperbolic, the White House embraced the matter as a way to publically maneuver on the issue of abortion in anticipation of the upcoming presidential election. Noting that the Catholic church planned a campaign against abortion to begin on December 26, Buchanan recommended that Nixon rescind the DOD policy as a way to garner Catholic votes. A statement from Nixon outlining his personal opinion on abortion would "be morally correct," Buchanan assured, as well as "of some consequence and of assistance politically in the Catholic community."[99] The following month, White House Counsel John Dean agreed that the opposition of Americans in the "Nixon constituency" of the Midwest and South to abortion "makes it a political plus for the President to take a position opposing legalization of abortions."[100]

To capitalize on a public reversal of the DOD policy, though, Nixon needed to act quickly. When Buchanan learned that Congressmen Lawrence J. Hogan (R-MD) and John Schmitz (R-CA) planned to introduce legislation that would rescind the Pentagon order, he recommended that White House "ought to go mighty fast, lest it look like we bowed to political pressure."[101] Wanting to avoid appearing as if the White House was "responding to legislative initiative," Nixon's advisor for domestic affairs John Ehrlichman ordered Secretary of Defense Melvin Laird to "go forward with the policy change immediately."[102] Nearly three weeks later, in an Oval Office meeting with the president, Ehrlichman suggested that Laird was "ignoring" his directive. Nixon responded that he would personally write to the secretary that the "directive is to be changed and we're goddamn well not going to have it."[103]

To this, Laird responded. In a March 31 memorandum to each of the military branches, Laird noted that "although Service medical practice is not subject to regulation under State law," abortions must be conducted within their limits.[104] The White House quickly organized a public relations campaign that emphasized Nixon "intervened personally and directly."[105] Nixon explained his decision as motivated by a mix of political and personal belief. Abortion laws, he noted, had historically been determined by individual states, not the federal government, and that is where he believed the decision should remain. On a personal level, he assured voters, he believed in the "sanctity of human life" and considered abortion "an unacceptable form of population control."[106]

While Nixon justified his reversal in part as an attempt to return authority to the states, his new policy failed to limit abortions to those acceptable under state law. The new policy did significantly reduce the number of abortions performed—down to 363 in the three months following the new policy from 1,152 in the three months prior—but it did not prohibit women even in states with restrictive laws from having abortions. It simply made it more difficult.[107]

Because military personnel could travel for treatment to any facility with available space, women in states with restrictive policies (such as Louisiana, for example, where abortions were prohibited for any reason) could travel at military expense to a hospital in a state (such as New York) with liberal policies.[108] When Congressman Hogan complained that such allowances violated the spirit of Nixon's intention by allowing for federal funding of abortions regardless of state law, the White House defended the practice.[109]

Nixon's reversal of the DOD policy also had no direct effect on abortions performed in Vietnam because the commanders of overseas medical facilities determined their policies based on local custom and laws.[110] Even before the DOD issued its uniform policy, women had abortions performed in military hospitals. Julia Decker, chief nurse at the Thirty-Sixth Evacuation Hospital, remembered one of her nurses having an abortion performed by a gynecologist at an evacuation hospital in Long Binh.[111] Patricia Ryan, the chief nurse at the Ninety-Fifth Evacuation Hospital, recalled that though she personally did not agree with abortion, she mentioned it as an option to nurses who became pregnant.[112] In early 1971, the chief nurse in Vietnam directed that nurses seeking abortions should have the procedure performed in Vietnam before later noting without explanation that the policy was a problem.[113] Some women also traveled to Japan before the nurse corps ordered in May 1972 that abortions be performed at the US Army Hospital Saigon instead of at an army hospital in Okinawa.[114] Wherever the procedure was performed, women generally found that it caused little concern. "If I had gotten pregnant in the Army," nurse Hannah Wynne insisted, "I could've gone and had an abortion." Although the procedure "was hushed," she explained, "it was not a problem . . . It wasn't a big concern."[115]

The military continued to grapple with family planning policies as it adapted to evolving legal standards in the wake of the *Roe v. Wade* decision. In particular, during the mid- to late 1970s, the Pentagon insisted that military hospitals follow the dictates of the *Roe* decision even as individual states enacted restrictions designed to limit its effects.[116] Military officials also attempted to fight growing efforts to limit the use of federal funds for abortion. Representative Robert Dornan (R-CA) introduced the first congressional attempt to curb federal funding of abortions in the military as part of the 1979 defense appropriations bill. Describing the proposed limitation as "unduly restrictive," the Pentagon cautioned that a loss of funding would force military women to go outside the military medical system for abortions. Moreover, this limitation would prove "particularly burdensome," it explained, for women stationed outside the United States and in locations where they could not easily access safe or legal abortions.[117] In addition to matters of convenience, the Pentagon also argued that restricting funds would have an " 'adverse impact' " on the military.[118] The armed forces were struggling to adapt to the new all-volunteer system, and officials maintained that integrating women into a wider array of military specialties was crucial to that effort. In particular, they insisted that providing women with access to abortion was an important means of retention among the women it desperately needed. Not funding abortions, DOD officials warned, would create undue hardships "just at the time when the armed forces are trying to encourage more women to enter operational jobs with field units."[119] Despite these objections, Congress approved the limitation except in cases when the mother's life was endangered or when pregnancy resulted from rape or incest.[120]

Congress codified the restrictions in 1984, prohibiting the use of military medical facilities for abortions except in cases of maternal life endangerment, rape, or incest. Additionally, until 2013, US code prohibited women from using military medical insurance to pay for abortions unless their life was threatened by carrying the pregnancy to term. This limitation attracted public attention, as it forced women to pay to terminate pregnancies resulting from rape even as the rates of sexual assault on servicewomen were dramatically rising.[121] Women stationed outside the United States face additional hurdles, as they must travel off base to have an elective abortion. Those stationed in places where elective abortions are illegal, like Afghanistan, must request leave to return to the United States for the procedure at their own expense.[122]

In the years since the Vietnam War, as the armed forces ended selected service and instated an all-volunteer force, the services have each had to rely on women more than ever. The percentage of women has steadily increased in both the active duty and reserve forces to the current rates of 15.1 and 18.8 percent, respectively.[123] These women have fought for access to the service academies, to the highest echelons of the forces, and to an ever-expanding range of military occupations. They pressed the military both to accommodate their desires to combine career and family and to facilitate their access to family planning methods that would enable them to make reproductive choices. The policies brought on by their demands, evolving social and cultural mores, and the military's own pragmatic changes have gradually allowed servicewomen to be not only soldiers and sailors but also wives and mothers. Today, nearly half of active-duty women are married, and nearly 40 percent of them are mothers.[124]

Although the difficulties of combining career and family remain significant, especially for single mothers (and fathers) and for parents who deploy away from their families, military women today serve in a force that characterizes itself as not only family-friendly but as a family.[125] The family planning policies that the military adopted in the second half of the twentieth century brought real change for many women who in years prior would have enjoyed no options in their careers if they wanted to have families. As the military embraced wives and mothers, it also promoted a more palatable image of the armed services at home and abroad. Even more, in providing for the combination of women's careers and families, the military could suggest that its women were in fact continuing to perform the gendered roles of wives and mothers that they had long been expected to assume. As Margaret R. Higonnet and Patrice L.-R. Higonnet have written, "familial rhetoric can alter subtly to contain potential disruptions" to larger changes in the military's gendered nature.[126] And yet, at the same time, the military often placed itself on the side of progressive change in women's lives by adopting birth control policies that provided military women with more options than civilian women. As the military opens all specialties and positions to women, and as Congress continues to debate servicewomen's access to reproductive healthcare, the contentious history of the military's family planning policies is of timely importance.

NOTES

1. Research for this essay was funded by a research travel grant from the Gerald R. Ford Presidential Library Foundation and a faculty research fund award from Bridgewater College.

2. Quoted in Laura Browder and Sascha Pflaeging, *When Janey Comes Marching Home: Portraits of Women Combat Veterans* (Chapel Hill: University of North Carolina Press, 2010), 3, 104, 107.

3. Quoted in Carol Burke, "'If You're Nervous in the Service . . .': Training Songs of Female Soldiers in the '40s," in *Visions of War: World War II in Popular Literature and Culture*, edited by M. Paul Holsinger and Mary Anne Schofield (Bowling Green, OH: Bowling Green State University Popular Press, 1992), 132.

4. Roe v. Wade, 410 U.S. 113 (1973).

5. Quoted in Leisa D. Meyer, *Creating GI Jane: Sexuality and Power in the Women's Army Corps during World War II* (New York: Columbia University Press, 1996), 20, see also 24–25.

6. The services enlisted women in separate corps: the army's WAC, the navy's Women Accepted for Volunteer Emergency Service (WAVES), the coast guard's SPARS, and the marine corps (which refused to adopt a catchy acronym but insisted its women were simply marines).

7. Women's Army Auxiliary Corps Regulations, 1943, Paragraph 63f, Printed Matter Miscellaneous, 1943, Miscellany, Oveta Culp Hobby Papers, Manuscript Division, Library of Congress, Washington, DC (hereafter Hobby Papers).

The WAC refused to admit any woman with a criminal record or because of a history of venereal disease, neither of which necessarily disqualified men. The army surgeon general's office later determined that the WAC's venereal disease rate was about 18 percent of the men's, partly due to its exclusion policy. See Mattie E. Treadwell, *The Women's Army Corps*, The United States Army in World War II, Special Studies (Washington, DC: Office of the Chief of Military History, 1991), 619. www .history.Army.mil/books/wwii/wac/index.htm.

8. Oveta Culp Hobby to Joan Younger, March 25, 1952, 8, Interviews and Statements, 1944–1945, n.d., Miscellany, Hobby Papers.

9. Quoted in Treadwell, *The Women's Army Corps*, 499, 178–179.

10. In 1943, the Women's Army Auxiliary Corps, a unit that served with but not in the army, became the Women's Army Corps, a regular component of the army instead of an auxiliary unit.

11. Oveta Culp Hobby to Joan Younger, March 25, 1952, 3, Interviews and Statements, 1944–1945, n.d., Miscellany, Hobby Papers; Treadwell, *The Women's Army Corps*, 500.

12. Meyer, *Creating GI Jane*, 33–50; Ann Elizabeth Pfau, *Miss Yourlovin: GI, Gender, and Domesticity during World War II* (New York: Columbia University Press, 2008), chapter 2.

13. Allan Berube, *Coming Out under Fire: The History of Gay Men and Women in World War II* (New York: Free Press, 1990), 46–48, quotation on 47.

14. Oveta Culp Hobby to Joan Younger, March 25, 1952, 4, Interviews and Statements, 1944–1945, n.d., Miscellany, Hobby Papers; Meyer, *Creating GI Jane*, 104–107.

15. Treadwell, *The Women's Army Corps*, 615–620; Meyer, *Creating GI Jane*, 100–107; Jeanne Holm, *Women in the Military: An Unfinished Revolution* (Novato, CA: Presidio Press, 1992), 85.

16. Treadwell, *The Women's Army Corps*, 510–511; Oveta Culp Hobby to Joan Younger, March 25, 1952, 6, Interviews and Statements, 1944–1945, n.d., Miscellany, Hobby Papers; Holm, *Women in the Military*, 71–72; Cynthia Enloe, *Maneuvers: The International Politics of Militarizing Women's Lives* (Berkeley: University of California Press, 2000), 219; Susan H. Godson, *Serving Proudly: A History of Women in the US Navy* (Annapolis, MD: Naval Institute Press, 2001), 121–122, 142. Regulations at times prohibited women in the marine corps, navy, and coast guard from marrying within the service, though they could marry civilians or men in other branches.

17. Treadwell, *The Women's Army Corps*, 498.

18. The ANC preferred to keep pregnancy quiet during World War I and "'dealt very leniently'" with the forty-four pregnancies among nurses. Mary T. Sarnecky, *A History of the US Army Nurse Corps*, Studies in Health, Illness, and Caregiving (Philadelphia: University of Pennsylvania Press, 1999), 116.

19. Oveta Culp Hobby to Joan Younger, March 25, 1952, 6, Interviews and Statements, 1944–1945, n.d., Miscellany, Hobby Papers.

20. Women's Army Auxiliary Corps Regulations, 1943, Paragraph 63c, Printed Matter Miscellaneous, 1943, Miscellany, Hobby Papers. See also Meyer, *Creating GI*

*Jane*, 107–110; Bettie J. Morden, *The Women's Army Corps, 1945–1978*, Army Historical Series (Washington, DC: Center of Military History, 1990), 137–138.

21. Treadwell, *The Women's Army Corps*, 500–501; Sarnecky, *A History of the US Army Nurse Corps*, 181, 271–272.

22. See Treadwell, *The Women's Army Corps*, 176, 501–502, 580–581, 620–621, table 9 on 775; Sarnecky, *A History of the US Army Nurse Corps*, 271–272.

23. Treadwell, *The Women's Army Corps*, 501–502.

24. Oveta Culp Hobby to Joan Younger, March 25, 1952, 7, Interviews and Statements, 1944–1945, n.d., Miscellany, Hobby Papers.

25. Treadwell, *The Women's Army Corps*, 507.

26. Oveta Culp Hobby to Joan Younger, March 25, 1952, Answers to Questions, 7, Interviews and Statements, 1944–1945, n.d., Miscellany, Hobby Papers.

27. Treadwell, *The Women's Army Corps*, 508–509; Oveta Culp Hobby to Joan Younger, March 25, 1952, 7, Interviews and Statements, 1944–1945, n.d., Miscellany, Hobby Papers; Meyer, *Creating GI Jane*, 115–117.

Military hospitals provided care for the women, not VA hospitals, which, according to Treadwell's history, could not be convinced to provide maternity care. In 1976, VA hospitals still provided no routine maternity care. See John J. Corcoran to Bobbie Greene Kilberg, October 18, 1976, Abortion—General, Sarah C. Massengale Files, Gerald R. Ford Presidential Library, Ann Arbor, MI (hereafter Ford Library).

28. Oveta Culp Hobby to Joan Younger, March 25, 1952, 7, Interviews and Statements, 1944–1945, n.d., Miscellany, Hobby Papers.

29. Treadwell, *The Women's Army Corps*, 502.

30. "Inclosure I: Conversation with Colonel Hobby, 4 April 1944," Decimal 702, WAC General Correspondence 1942–1946, Record Group 165, Records of the War Department General and Special Staffs (hereafter RG 165), National Archives, College Park, Maryland (hereafter NACP); Holm, *Women in the Military*, 71–72.

31. Vera A. Mankinen, "Memorandum to the Director, WAC: Discharge because of Abortion," February 23, 1944, Decimal 702, WAC General Correspondence 1942–1946, RG 165, NACP.

32. "Memorandum for the Director, Policy of other services on determination of pregnancy discharges," March 25, 1944, Decimal 702, WAC General Correspondence 1942–1946, RG 165, NACP; Treadwell, *The Women's Army Corps*, 502–503; Meyer, *Creating GI Jane*, 110–112; Oveta Culp Hobby to Joan Younger, March 25, 1952, 7, Interviews and Statements, 1944–1945, n.d., Miscellany, Hobby Papers.

33. Margaret D. Craighill, Informal Memorandum to Colonel Hobby, April 6, 1944, Decimal 702, WAC General Correspondence 1942–1946, RG 165, NACP.

34. Margaret D. Craighill, Informal Memorandum to Colonel Hobby, April 6, 1944, Decimal 702, WAC General Correspondence 1942–1946, RG 165, NACP.

35. Margaret D. Craighill, Informal Memorandum to Colonel Hobby, April 6, 1944, Decimal 702, WAC General Correspondence 1942–1946, RG 165, NACP; Treadwell, *The Women's Army Corps*, 503.

36. W. M. Fechteler Memorandum to All Naval Activities in Continental United States, Women's Reserve Circular Letter No. 3-45, June 6, 1945, unnamed folder (approximately Decimal 701), WAC General Correspondence 1942–1946, RG 165, NACP.

37. Oveta Culp Hobby to Joan Younger, March 25, 1952, 7, Interviews and Statements, 1944–1945, n.d., Miscellany, Hobby Papers; Meyer, *Creating GI Jane*, 110–112; Treadwell, *The Women's Army Corps*, 503.

38. On the integration of the various women's services in the postwar period, see Holm, *Women in the Military*, chapters 9 and 10; Linda Witt, Judith Bellafaire, Britta Granrud, and Mary Jo Binker, *"A Defense Weapon Known to Be of Value": Servicewomen of the Korean War Era* (Hanover, NH: University Press of New England, 2005).

39. Works on this subject abound, including Elaine Tyler May, *Homeward Bound: American Families in the Cold War Era* (New York: Basic Books, 1988); Carolyn Herbst Lewis, *Prescription for Heterosexuality: Sexual Citizenship in the Cold War Era* (Chapel Hill: University of North Carolina Press, 2010); K. A. Cuordileone, *Manhood and American Political Culture in the Cold War* (New York: Routledge, 2005); David K. Johnson, *The Lavender Scare: The Cold War Persecution of Gays and Lesbians in the Federal Government* (Chicago: University of Chicago Press, 2004).

40. Holm, *Women in the Military*, 162–164; Morden, *The Women's Army Corps*, 137–140.

41. Sarnecky, *A History of the US Army Nurse Corps*, 291–292. Debates about integrating men into the nursing corps highlighted the issue of marriage, as both proponents and opponents of men's entry assumed that they would be able to be married and continue their careers. But because married women could only serve in the reserves, men were initially integrated into the nurse corps only in the reserves. They were permitted to serve in the regular army in 1966. See Kara Dixon Vuic, *Officer, Nurse, Woman: The Army Nurse Corps in the Vietnam War* (Baltimore, MD: Johns Hopkins University Press, 2010), 50–52.

42. Holm, *Women in the Military*, 156; Godson, *Serving Proudly*, 182.

43. "Fact Sheet," 341 Recruitment (1966), Army Nurse Corps Archives, Office of Medical History, Army Medical Department Center of History and Heritage, Fort Sam Houston, TX (hereafter ANCA); Carolyn M. Feller and Constance J. Moore, *Highlights in the History of the Army Nurse Corps* (Washington, DC: US Army Center of Military History, 1995), 38; United States Army Nurse Corps, *Education Opportunities for Students in the Field of Nursing* (Washington, DC: Government Printing Office, 1962), 2; Army Regulation No. 601-19, "Personnel Procurement: Army Student Nurse, Dietitian, and Occupational Therapist Programs," October 7, 1965, "ANC Education," General Subject Files, 1960–1969, Records of the Office of the Surgeon General (Army) Record Group 112 (hereafter RG 112), NACP.

44. Sarnecky, *A History of the US Army Nurse Corps*, 351; "Minutes of the Meeting, Department of Defense Nursing Advisory Committee," October 30, 1967, 2, 314.7-History-Vietnam-DOD Nursing Advisory Committee Documentation, ANCA.

45. Holm, *Women in the Military*, 289–290; Morden, *The Women's Army Corps*, 304. A 1971 study of army nurses' reasons for leaving the corps after their initial commitment found that far more married than unmarried nurses left the corps, citing a desire to be with their spouse. See Glennadee A. Nichols, "Young Nurses' Reasons for Joining, Remaining in, and Leaving the Army," *Military Medicine* 136, no. 9 (September 1971): 720–721.

46. Corinne Smith, "Nurses Follow Husbands to War," news clipping, 341 Recruiting-Buildup-Press, ANCA; Generic letter, n.d., "Army Nursing Corps-Arrivals,"

General Subject Files, 1960–1969, RG 112, NACP. See also "Fact Book," May 24, 1971, 314.7-History-Vietnam-Fact Sheet Status-ANC in Vietnam, ANCA.

47. Helene Carroll, interview by Mary Jo Kastleman, May 23, 1992, 5, ANC Oral Histories, ANCA.

48. "Personnel," in Jennie L. Caylor, "End of Tour Report," 314.7-History-Vietnam-Deployment Issues, ANCA.

49. Patricia T. Murphy, "End of Tour Report," January 15, 1971, 3, 314.7-History-Vietnam-End of Tour Report-Murphy, Patricia 1971, ANCA. In a speech after her tour, she specified that married couples stationed together in Vietnam drew a housing allowance from the army, while individuals stationed without their spouses did not. See Patricia Murphy, "Role of the Nurse in Vietnam," n.d. [late 1970 or early 1971], 18, ANC Oral Histories, ANCA.

50. Morden, *The Women's Army Corps*, 252.

51. Public Law 80-625, June 12, 1948. See also "Memorandum for Deputy Chief of Staff for Personnel," n.d. [after September 1970], 341 Recruitment (1970–1978), ANCA; Holm, *Women in the Military*, 289–291.

52. "Minutes of the Meeting, Department of Defense Nursing Advisory Committee," October 30, 1967, 2, 314.7-History-Vietnam-DOD Nursing Advisory Committee Documentation, ANCA; Office of the Surgeon General, "Recent Regulation Changes Affecting ANC Officers," April 27, 1971, "ANC Procurement," General Subject Files, 1960–1969, RG 112, NACP.

53. Ruth Bader Ginsberg argued the case on behalf of Frontiero for the American Civil Liberties Union. Frontiero v. Richardson, 411 U.S. 677 (1973); Holm, *Women in the Military*, 290–291.

54. In fiscal year 1963, for example, the ANC lost 3.3 percent of the corps due to pregnancy and parenthood, a number that rose to 4.9 percent in fiscal year 1966. See "ANC-Losses-FY 1963" and "ANC-Losses-FY 1966," both in "Army Nurse Corps—Gains and Losses," General Subject Files, 1960–1969, RG 112, NACP; Hal B. Jennings, Jr., *A Decade of Progress: The United States Army Medical Department, 1959–1969* (Washington, DC: Government Printing Office, 1971), 95.

55. Women's Armed Services Integration Act of 1948 (Public Law 80-625), 62 Stat. 356; Executive Order 10240, *Code of Federal Regulations*, title 3, sec. 749 (1949–1953). See also Holm, *Women in the Military*, 124–126, 292; Morden, *The Women's Army Corps*, 140.

56. The lone voice of dissent appears to be the chief of the navy's Bureau of Medicine and Surgery, who in 1949 recommended that women be allowed to serve and have a family. Pregnancy, he noted, is "'a normal biological phenomenon in women in the military age group.'" See Holm, *Women in the Military*, 291.

57. Cynthia A. Gurney, *33 Years of Army Nursing: An Interview with Brigadier General Lillian Dunlap* (Washington, DC: United States Army Nurse Corps, 2001), 278.

58. Holm, *Women in the Military*, 292; Feller and Moore, *Highlights in the History of the Army Nurse Corps*, 37; Anna Mae Hays, interview by Amelia Jane Carson, February 23, 1983, Project 83-10, US Army Military History Institute, Carlisle Barracks, PA (hereafter USAMHI), 141–142; Gurney, *33 Years of Army Nursing*, 278.

59. "Info Given to Lt. Col. John J. Sullivan DCSPER, Personnel Service Division," August 7, 1964, "Housing (BOQ, Enlisted Women) 901-07, 1963," Nurses' Quarters' BOQ's, furnishings, housing, 1946–1976, The Army Nurse Corps Papers, USAMHI.

60. Barbara E. Lane, "End of Tour Report," May 30, 1972, 314.7 History, Vietnam, End of Tour Report, 1972, ANCA.

61. "DOD Nursing Advisory Committee Meeting" transcript, October 5, 1970, 52–53, 314.7-History-Vietnam-DOD Nursing Advisory Committee Documentation, ANCA.

62. Morden, *The Women's Army Corps*, 232–240; Holm, *Women in the Military*, 294–295.

63. "Army Discriminates, Says Nurse-Mother," *American Journal of Nursing* 70, no. 11 (November 1970): 2283–2284; "If You're Pregnant (a Predicament in Army-ese) You May Not Have to Leave the Corps," *American Journal of Nursing* 71, no. 1 (July 1971): 1311; "Woman Officer Halts Discharge from Reserve," *The Birmingham News*, October 7, [1970], news clipping, "ANC Pregnancy Law," General Subject Files, 1960–1969, RG 112, NACP. See also Holm, *Women in the Military*, 297.

64. James T. Wooten, "Enlisted Woman, 23, Sues Navy over Sexual Rights," *New York Times*, August 26, 1970; "Military Women Making Waves over Sexist Rules," *Washington Daily News*, October 3, 1970, ANC Pregnancy Law, Military Historians Files 1960–1969, General Subject Files 1960–1969, RG 112, NACP; Holm, *Women in the Military*, 298; Judith Hicks Stiehm, *Arms and the Enlisted Woman*, 116.

65. WAC historian Betty Morden notes that the army similarly discharged women for becoming pregnant—even if the pregnancy ended in a miscarriage—because her pregnancy "proved she did not meet the moral standards necessary for military service." See Morden, *The Women's Army Corps*, 139.

66. "Court Backs Air Force's Ouster of an Unwed Pregnant Officer," *New York Times*, November 16, 1971.

67. Struck v. Secretary of Defense, 460 F.2d 1372 (9th Cir. 1971), vacated and remanded to consider the issue of mootness, 409 U.S. 1071 (1972); "Pregnancy Discharges in the Military: The Air Force Experience," *Harvard Law Review* 86, no. 3 (1973): 568–594; "Air Force Drops Effort to Oust Woman Captain," *New York Times*, December 2, 1972, 31; "Air Force Captain, Unwed, Has Baby," *New York Times*, December 4, 1970, 16; Fred P. Graham, "It Would Help If It Happened to a Man," *New York Times*, October 29, 1972; Fred P. Graham, "Justices to Weigh Pregnancy Issue," *New York Times*, October 25, 1972; "Excerpts from Senate Hearing on the Ginsburg Nomination," *New York Times*, July 22, 1993, A14; Ruth Bader Ginsberg, "A Postscript to *Struck* by Stereotype," *Duke Law Journal* 59 no. 799 (2010): 799–800.

For a discussion of other cases in which military women sued over the questions of pregnancy and motherhood, see Holm, *Women in the Military*, 296–303; Mary Ann Kuhn, "Military Women Making Waves over Sexist Rules," *Washington Daily News*, October 5, 1970, news clipping "ANC Pregnancy Law," General Subject Files, 1960–1969, RG 112, NACP; George C. Wilson, "Pentagon Shifts on Pregnancy," *Washington Post*, July 8, 1975.

68. Holm, *Women in the Military*, 297–300.

69. "The Army Decides Its Married Women Can Have Children," *New York Times*, April 21, 1971, 11; "Army Mothers," *New York Times*, April 25, 1971, E3; "If You're Pregnant (a Predicament in Army-ese)," 1311; Office of the Surgeon General, "Recent Regulation Changes Affecting ANC Officers," April 27, 1971, ANC Procurement, General Subject Files, 1960–1969, RG 112, NACP; Feller and Moore, *Highlights in the History of the Army Nurse Corps*, 43; Morden, *The Women's Army Corps*, 302–310.

70. Crawford v. Cushman, 531 F. 2d 1114 (CA2 1976); Holm, *Women in the Military*, 297–303.

71. George F. Conrad, SGO Administrative Letter, October 21, 1953, Sterilization (Sexual) Procedures, Historian Subject Files 1960–1969, General Subject Files 1960–1969, RG 112, NACP. Hull and Hoffer note that in 1962, forty-two states restricted abortion to save the life of the mother. See N. E. H. Hull and Peter Charles Hoffer, Roe v. Wade: *The Abortion Rights Controversy in American History* (Lawrence: University Press of Kansas, 2001), 98.

72. Griswold v. Connecticut, 381 U.S. 479, 85 S. Ct. 1678, 14 L. Ed. 2d 510, 1965 U.S.

73. R. L. Bohannon to Deputy Assistant Secretary of Defense (Health and Medical), February 21, 1966, Military Historians File 1960–1969, Sterilization (Sexual) Procedures, General Subject Files 1960–1969, RG 112, NACP.

74. American Law Institute Abortion Policy, 1962, in *Before* Roe v. Wade: *Voices That Shaped the Abortion Debate before the Supreme Court's Ruling*, edited by Linda Greenhouse and Reva Siegel (New York: Kaplan, 2010), 24–25.

75. Edward H. Vogel, Jr., to Col. McCabe, March 2, 1966, Military Historians File 1960–1969, Sterilization (Sexual) Procedures, General Subject Files 1960–1969, RG 112, NACP; Kryder E. Van Buskirk to Col. Rideout, March 11, 1966, Military Historians File 1960–1969, Sterilization (Sexual) Procedures, General Subject Files 1960–1969, RG 112, NACP; Marshall E. McCabe to Col. Chmielewski, March 4, 1966, Military Historians File 1960–1969, Sterilization (Sexual) Procedures, General Subject Files 1960–1969, RG 112, NACP.

76. Edward A. Zimmermann to Col. Van Buskirk, March 10, 1966, Military Historians File 1960–1969, Sterilization (Sexual) Procedures, General Subject Files 1960–1969, RG 112, NACP.

77. Joseph S. Chmielewski to Col. Zimmerman, March 7, 1966, Military Historians File 1960–1969, Sterilization (Sexual) Procedures, General Subject Files 1960–1969, RG 112, NACP.

78. Leonard D. Heaton to Deputy Assistant Secretary of Defense (Health and Medical), March 29, 1966, Military Historians File 1960–1969, Sterilization (Sexual) Procedures, General Subject Files 1960–1969, RG 112, NACP.

79. "Policy Clarified on Sterilization," *New York Times*, November 17, 1966; DA Message 794724, Policy Guidelines on Family Planning Services, December 1966, 401-02 Abortions (Birth Control, Sterilization, Family Planning), Legal Opinions and Precedents, 1942–1969, RG 112, NACP; "Military Eases Its Rules on Birth Control Pills," *New York Times*, January 10, 1967; Critchlow, *Intended Consequences*, 53, 78, 86.

The army surgeon general expressly noted that such liberalization of access to birth control did not alter guidelines for therapeutic abortion. See DA Message 791644,

Family Planning Services for Military Families, November 23, 1966, 401-02 Abortions (Birth Control, Sterilization, Family Planning), Legal Opinions and Precedents, 1942–1969, RG 112, NACP.

80. Critchlow, *Intended Consequences*, 86.

81. Sara J. McVicker, questionnaire by author, July 3, 2004, 9. In possession of the author.

82. Sharon Lea Stanley Alden, questionnaire by author, April 29, 2004, 9. In possession of the author. Rose Mary Burke, questionnaire by author, May 1, 2004, 9. In possession of the author.

83. The Supreme Court ruled in 1972 that physicians' refusal to prescribe birth control pills to unmarried women was unconstitutional. Eisenstadt v. Baird, 405 U.S. 438 (1972). For more on women and the pill, see Elizabeth Siegel Watkins, *On the Pill: A Social History of Oral Contraceptives, 1950–1970* (Baltimore: Johns Hopkins University Press, 1998); Beth Bailey, *Sex in the Heartland* (Cambridge, MA: Harvard University Press, 1999), chapter 4.

84. Fact Sheet, August 10, 1970, Abortions / Family Planning, Background Materials for "The WAC, 1945–1978," RG 319 Records of the Army Staff (hereafter RG 319), NACP; David F. Burrelli, "Abortion Services and Military Medical Facilities," *Congressional Research Service Report for Congress*, January 13, 2011, 3.

85. Rousselot became the assistant secretary of defense for health and environment in 1970 after the DOD reorganized and expanded its health care staff. To continue in the new position, Rousselot was formally nominated by President Nixon and approved by Congress. See "Nomination of Dr. Louis M. Rousselot to be Assistant Secretary of Defense (Health and Environment)," Hearing before the Committee on Armed Services, US Senate, 91st Cong., 2nd session, July 9, 1970 (Washington, DC: Government Printing Office, 1970).

86. Peter Rousselot, interviewed by author December 5, 2011. Recording in author's possession. "Louis Rousselot, Surgeon, 70, Dies," *New York Times*, March 29, 1974; Theodore Drapanas, "A Tribute to Louis M. Rousselot, M.D.," *Surgery* 77, no. 2 (1975): 165–166.

87. Louis M. Rousselot, Memorandum for the Surgeons General of the Military Departments, May 20, 1970, Abortions / Family Planning, Background Materials for "The WAC, 1945–1978," RG 319, NACP.

88. "Nomination of Dr. Louis M. Rousselot to be Assistant Secretary of Defense (Health and Environment)," Hearing before the Committee on Armed Services, US Senate, 91st Cong., 2nd session, July 9, 1970 (Washington, DC: Government Printing Office, 1970), 6.

89. Louis M. Rousselot, Memorandum for the Surgeons General of the Military Departments, July 16, 1970, Abortions / Family Planning, Background Materials for "The WAC, 1945–1978," RG 319, NACP; "Fact Sheet: Abortions in Military Hospitals," January 18, 1971, EX WE 3 Family Planning, January 1, 1971–April 30, 1971, White House Central Files, Nixon Archive; "Military Hospitals Approve Abortions," *Washington Post*, August 18, 1970; "Abortions Provided at Military Bases," *New York Times*, August 18, 1970.

90.  George J. Hays, Memorandum for the Assistant Secretaries of the Military Departments (M&RA), September 11, 1970, Abortions / Family Planning, Background Materials for "The WAC, 1945–1978," RG 319, NACP.

Rousselot provided the surgeons general with information on the legal precedent for military hospitals to operate without regard to state law, citing, among other examples, that military physicians practiced medicine in states where they were not licensed. Louis M. Rousselot, Memorandum for the Surgeons General of the Military Departments, May 22, 1970, Abortions / Family Planning, Background Materials for "The WAC, 1945–1978," RG 319, NACP.

91.  The military's new policy stopped short of embracing the American Medical Association's recommendations of the previous month, which called for abortion to be treated as a private decision between patient and physician. See American Law Institute Abortion Policy, 1962, American Medical Association Policy Statement, 1967, and American Medical Association Policy Statement, 1970, all in Greenhouse and Siegel, eds., *Before* Roe v. Wade, 24–29.

92.  Memorandum for the Assistant Secretary of Defense (Health and Environment), Directives Concerning Sterilization and Abortion, July 22, 1970, Abortions / Family Planning, Background Materials for "The WAC, 1945–1978," RG 319, NACP; Louis M. Rousselot, Memorandum for the Surgeons General of the Military Departments, July 31, 1970, Abortions / Family Planning, Background Materials for "The WAC, 1945–1978," RG 319, NACP.

Six days after Rousselot announced the new policy, the surgeons general wrote to say they had agreed that sterilization and abortion policies should be performed in accordance with state laws. Rousselot held his ground and reiterated that because state laws did not apply to military medical practice, procedures would be done irrespective of state law. Army officials feared that acting outside state law might open the Army Medical Department to state criminal charges and recommended that the DOD reconsider its decision to override state law. Although they admitted that charges against military officials would be "probably unsustainable," they reasoned that such charges could "raise serious questions among the public about the ethics of Army medicine." The DOD denied their request. See Summary Sheet: Family Planning Service, September 24, 1970, Abortions / Family Planning, Background Materials for "The WAC, 1945–1978," RG 319, NACP; Memorandum for Assistant Secretary of Defense (Health and Environment), Family Planning Service, Abortions / Family Planning, Background Materials for "The WAC, 1945–1978," RG 319, NACP; Summary Sheet, Family Planning Service, December 13, 1970, Abortions / Family Planning, Background Materials for "The WAC, 1945–1978," RG 319, NACP.

93.  "DOD Letter to Congressman," n.d., 3, EX WE 3 Family Planning, January 1, 1971–April 30, 1971, White House Central Files, Nixon Archive; "Nixon Orders End to Eased Abortions in Armed Services," *New York Times*, April 3, 1971.

94.  "Legal Considerations for Abortion Policy," November 1, 1970, EX WE 3 Family Planning, January 1, 1971–April 30, 1971, White House Central Files, Nixon Archive. Information on state abortion laws in late 1970 comes from Ruth Roemer, "Abortion

Law Reform and Repeal: Legislative and Judicial Developments," in Greenhouse and Siegel, eds., *Before* Roe v. Wade, 121–122.

95. "President Overturns Pentagon Abortion Rule," *Washington Post*, April 3, 1971; "President Opposes Unlimited Abortion," *New York Times*, April 4, 1971.

96. Clayton N. Gompf memorandum for Mr. Brotzman, April 23, 1975, Discharge/ Waivers-Pregnancy, Parenthood, Dependents, 1974–1978, Background Materials for "The WAC, 1945–1978", RG 319, NACP.

97. "Fact Sheet: Abortions in Military Hospitals," January 18, 1971, EX WE 3 Family Planning, January 1, 1971–April 30, 1971, White House Central Files, Nixon Archive.

98. Patrick J. Buchanan to the President, December 17, 1970, EX WE 3 Family Planning, January 1, 1971–April 30, 1971, White House Central Files, Nixon Archive.

99. Patrick J. Buchanan to the President, December 17, 1970, and Patrick J. Buchanan to John Ehrlichman, December 22, 1970, EX WE 3 Family Planning, January 1, 1971–April 30, 1971, White House Central Files, Nixon Archive.

100. John Dean to Ken Cole, Pat Buchanan, Henry Cashen, Don Hughes, January 15, 1971, EX WE 3 Family Planning, January 1, 1971–April 30, 1971, White House Central Files, Nixon Archive.

101. Patrick J. Buchanan to Ken Cole, February 10, 1971, EX WE 3 Family Planning, January 1, 1971–April 30, 1971, White House Central Files, Nixon Archive.

102. John D. Ehrlichman to Secretary Melvin Laird, March 4, 1971, EX WE 3 Family Planning, January 1, 1971–April 30, 1971, White House Central Files, Nixon Archive.

103. Oval Office, Conversation Number 472-11, March 23, 1971, White House Tapes. www.nixontapes.org/chron1.html. Daily Diary, March 23, 1981. www.nixontapes.org /pdd/1971-03-01_31.pdf.

Rousselot resigned from his position three months later. He explained in letters to friends that he was "asked to submit his resignation" for the "ostensible" reason of his unwillingness to divest his personal security portfolio, a move that might have appeared to be a conflict of interest with his appointed position in the DOD. He surmised, however, that his leaving the DOD was "part of a rather widespread shift in presidentially appointed positions" in which "appointees are chosen for the political impact on their State of origin" in anticipation of the 1972 election. See "Top Medical Officer at Defense Resigns," *Washington Post*, June 23, 1971; Louis M. Rousselot to William Metcalf, May 14, 1971, Correspondence: Me-Mu; Louis M. Rousselot to John Bunyan, June 28, 1971, and Louis M. Rousselot to Judge and Mrs. Adrian P. Burke, July 13, 1971, both in Correspondence: Bun-But, all in Louis M. Rousselot Papers MSC 357, History of Medicine Division, National Library of Medicine, Bethesda, MD.

104. Memorandum for the Secretaries of the Military Departments, March 31, 1971, EX WE 3 Family Planning, January 1, 1971–April 30, 1971, White House Central Files, Nixon Archive; Melvin P. Laird, Memorandum for the President, March 31, 1971, EX WE 3 Family Planning, January 1, 1971–April 30, 1971, White House Central Files, Nixon Archive.

105. Pat Buchanan to H. R. Haldeman, John Ehrlichman, and Ron Ziegler, April 2, 1971, EX WE 3 Family Planning, January 1, 1971–April 30, 1971, White House Central Files, Nixon Archive.

106. Richard M. Nixon, "Statement about Policy on Abortions at Military Base Hospitals in the United States," in *Public Papers of the Presidents of the United States: Richard M. Nixon, 1969–1974*, vol. 3 (Washington, DC: Office of the Federal Register, 1972), 500.

On Nixon's position on abortion generally, see Donald T. Chritchlow, *Intended Consequences: Birth Control, Abortion, and the Federal Government in Modern America* (New York: Oxford University Press), chapter 5; Dean J. Kotlowski, *Nixon's Civil Rights: Politics, Principle, and Policy* (Cambridge, MA: Harvard University Press, 2001), 250–252.

107. "Abortions Drop, Military Says," *Washington Post*, October 16, 1971.

108. "Abortion Rules Tied to States," *Army Times*, April 1971, news clipping, Abortions / Family Planning, Background Materials for "The WAC, 1945–1978," RG 319, NACP; "President Overturns Pentagon Abortion Rule," *Washington Post*, April 3, 1971; "President Opposes Unlimited Abortion," *New York Times*, April 4, 1971.

109. Lawrence J. Hogan to The President, August 31, 1971, EX WE 3 Family Planning, January 1, 1971–April 30, 1971, White House Central Files, Nixon Archive; Richard K. Cook to Larry [Hogan], September 23, 1971, EX WE 3 Family Planning, January 1, 1971–April 30, 1971, White House Central Files, Nixon Archive.

110. Unclassified Message 071931Z, April 1971, "Policy for Family Planning Program," Abortions / Family Planning, Background Materials for "The WAC, 1945–1978," RG 319, NACP; "President Overturns Pentagon Abortion Rule," *Washington Post*, April 3, 1971; "President Opposes Unlimited Abortion," *New York Times*, April 4, 1971.

111. Julia Decker, interview by Connie Slewitzke, May 24, 1992, transcript, 8, ANC Oral Histories, ANCA.

112. Patricia Ryan, interview by Mary Sarnecky, May 22, 1992, transcript, 8, ANC Oral Histories, ANCA.

113. Patricia T. Murphy, "End of Tour Report," January 15, 1971, 6–7, 314.7 History, Vietnam, End of Tour Report, Murphy, Patricia 1971, ANCA.

114. Barbara E. Lane, "End of Tour Report," May 30, 1972, 314.7 History, Vietnam, End of Tour Report, 1972, ANCA. On abortions in Japan, see Bernadette Palya Miller, questionnaire by author, March 29, 2004, 9, in possession of author, and Mary Reynolds Powell, *A World of Hurt: Between Innocence and Arrogance in Vietnam* (Chesterland, OH: Greenleaf Enterprises, 2000), 139–140.

115. Hannah Wynne, interview by author, May 28, 2004, San Antonio, TX. Tape recording and transcript, 25–27, The Vietnam Archive, Texas Tech University.

116. Unclassified Message, Subject: Interim Change to AR 40–3 (Change 2), November 1975, 701–01 Pregnancy, Background Materials for "The WAC, 1945–1978", RG 319, NACP; Unclassified communication, Subject: Interim Change to AR 40–3, Abortion—Defense Department Policy, Sarah C. Massengale Files, Ford Library.

117. Tom Philpott, "DoD Walks Thin Line on Abortions," *Army Times*, October 2, 1978, Abortions / Family Planning, Background Materials for "The WAC, 1945–1978," RG 319, NACP.

The 1976 Hyde Amendment, which prohibited the use of Medicaid and other federal funds for abortions unless the mother's life was endangered, did not affect the military's abortion policies. See "Military Effect Minimal in New Abortion Ruling," *Army*

*Times*, October 25, 1976, news clipping, Abortions / Family Planning, Background Materials for "The WAC, 1945–1978," RG 319, NACP.

118. Philpott, "DoD Walks Thin Line on Abortions."

119. "Army-Funded Abortions Out, Congress Says," *Army*, November 1978, news clipping, Abortions / Family Planning, Background Materials for "The WAC, 1945–1978," RG 319, NACP. On women and the all-volunteer force, see Beth Bailey, *America's Army* (Cambridge, MA: Harvard University Press, 2009).

120. David F. Burrelli, "Abortion Services and Military Medical Facilities," *CRS Report for Congress*, January 13, 2011, 4.

121. 10 USC 1093. In January 2013, the National Defense Authorization Act included a provision that ended a longstanding ban preventing victims of rape or incest from using their military medical insurance to pay for abortions. See "Shaheen Amendment Signed into Law" press release, January 3, 2013. www.shaheen.senate.gov//news/press/release/?id=014ebb9a-85fc-4bf8-8894-7c5df8d863c4.

122. Several congressional representatives have introduced legislation in recent years that would revise these limitations. For a recent example of this effort, see Diana Reese, "Rep. Slaughter Introduces Bill to Allow Abortions for Service Women at Military Hospitals," *Washington Post*, March 24, 2013. www.washingtonpost.com/blogs/she-the-people/wp/2013/03/25/rep-slaughter-introduces-bill-to-allow-abortions-for-service-women-at-military-hospitals.

For works on the recent effects of military abortion policies, see Amy E. Crawford, "Under Siege: Freedom of Choice and the Statutory Ban on Abortions on Military Bases," *University of Chicago Law Review* 71, no. 4 (Autumn 2004): 1549–1582; Kate Grindlay, Susan Yanow, Kinga Jelinska, Rebecca Gomperts, and Daniel Grossman, "Abortion Restrictions in the U.S. Military: Voices from Women Deployed Overseas," *Women's Health Issues* 21, no. 4 (2011): 259–264; Kathryn L. Ponder and Melissa Nothnagle, "Damage Control: Unintended Pregnancy in the United States Military," *Journal of Law, Medicine, and Ethics* 38, no. 2 (Summer 2010): 386–395.

123. Office of the Deputy Assistant Secretary of Defense (Military Community and Family Policy), *2014 Demographics: Profile of the Military Community*, 18, 66. http://download.militaryonesource.mil/12038/MOS/Reports/2014-Demographics-Report.pdf.

124. Office of the Deputy Assistant Secretary of Defense (Military Community and Family Policy), *2014 Demographics*, 45; Eileen Patten and Kim Parker, "Women in the US Military: Growing Share, Distinctive Profile," *Pew Social and Demographic Trends*, December 22, 2011. www.pewsocialtrends.org/files/2011/12/women-in-the-military.pdf. Petula Dvorak, "For Some Military Moms, a Long-Distance Juggle," *Washington Post*, May 7, 2011. See also Browder and Pflaeging, *When Janey Comes Marching Home*, especially 95–112.

125. Particularly relevant for the topics considered here, military women continue to face difficulties in accessing contraceptives (especially when deployed), and postpartum leaves—though generous when compared to many civilian US employers' policies—still require mothers to participate in field and training exercises that make child care and lactation especially difficult. See Janet C. Jacobson and Jeffrey T. Jensen, "A Policy of Discrimination: Reproductive Health Care in the Military," *Women's Health Issues* 21, no. 4 (2011): 255–258; Anne L. Naclerio, "Medical Issues for Women Warriors

on Deployment," Cara J. Krulewitch, "Reproductive Health," Amy Canuso, "Human Sexuality and Women in the Area of Operations," and Amy Canuso, "Mothers in War," all in *Women at War*, edited by Elspeth Cameron Ritchie and Anne L. Naclerio (New York: Oxford University Press, 2015).

On the military's efforts to cast itself as family-friendly, see Jennifer Mittlestadt, *The Rise of the Military Welfare State* (Cambridge, MA: Harvard University Press, 2015), especially chapter 5.

126.  Margaret R. Higonnet and Patrice L.-R. Higonnet, "The Double Helix," in *Behind the Lines: Gender and the Two World Wars*, edited by Margaret Randolph Higonnet et al. (New Haven, CT: Yale University Press, 1987), 45.

# 9

## The Dream That Dare Not Speak Its Name

Legacies of the Civil Rights Movement and the Fight
for Gay Military Service

STEVE ESTES

In 2010, the Pentagon concluded in its study of the ban on lesbians and gays
in the armed forces that, because the military had successfully integrated
African Americans and women, it could integrate gay service members as well.
In spite of a shared history of discrimination, Steve Estes shows this comparison has a long and troubled history. Gay rights activists used the comparison
in lawsuits in the 1970s and 1980s and in the fight to end the ban on gay
service members in the 1990s, and in each case they lost. Congress and the
courts deferred to the judgment of military authorities, who claimed that
lesbians and gays impaired military efficiency. That argument was so powerful
that the repeal of the Don't Ask, Don't Tell policy came only after gay rights
activists switched to emphasizing how the ban on gay service members hurt
military efficiency. From this story, it is clear there are many obstacles to
forging civil rights coalitions based on arguments about a shared history.

The young, black GI had faced discrimination before joining the military,
and he had hoped that the army would be different. It was supposed to be
a meritocracy. Promotions would be based on performance, not prejudice. He
found that this was mostly true. Still, he had to act differently in order to advance through the ranks; he had to perform in more ways than one. Everyone
could tell that he was different, but he had to prove to them that he was not. It
worked. Colin Powell became the first African American chairman of the Joint
Chiefs of Staff and eventually the first black secretary of state.

As chairman of the Joint Chiefs in the early 1990s, Powell had to advise Presidents George H. W. Bush and Bill Clinton on the issue of gays in the military.
Gay activists and their liberal allies began asking Powell in 1992 to reevaluate

the ban on gay military service, a policy that stretched back to the early twentieth century if not the founding of the republic.[1] "Are we to some extent here dealing with a prejudice that a majority has against a group of people?" Massachusetts Congressman Barney Frank asked Powell, leaving the type of prejudice and the "group of people" intentionally vague. Always politically savvy, Powell side-stepped the question, voicing the official policy rationale that lifting the ban on gays and lesbians would be "prejudicial to good order and discipline." Frank pointed out that even Secretary of Defense Dick Cheney acknowledged that gays and lesbians already served. Powell allowed that was true, but primarily because "they kept, so called, in the closet."[2]

While Barney Frank had only implied a connection between racial discrimination and homophobia, Colorado Congresswoman Pat Schroeder explicitly connected the two in a testy letter to Powell. She noted that the military had used the same arguments in the 1940s to forestall racial integration that Powell was using in the 1990s to defend the gay ban. "Your reasoning would have kept you in the mess hall a few decades ago," Schroeder wrote. Powell replied angrily: "I need no reminders concerning the history of African Americans in defense of their nation . . . I am part of that history."

For the chairman of the Joint Chiefs, the analogy between racism and homophobia just did not work. "Skin color is a benign, nonbehavioral characteristic," Powell argued. "Sexual orientation is perhaps the most profound of human behavioral characteristics. Comparison of the two is a convenient but invalid argument." With that, Powell crushed the dreams of liberals who had hoped that a pioneering black general might have sympathy for gay and lesbian troops.[3]

Connections between black civil rights and gay rights have long been fraught with tension. Whether the issue is military service or marriage, liberals have often tried to use the racial analogy to advance gay rights along paths pioneered by black civil rights activists. As historian George Chauncey explained, "The gay movement, like every other postwar movement for minority rights and social justice, was profoundly influenced by the powerful model of the black civil rights movement." Yet Chauncey acknowledged that the relationship between the gay rights movement and the struggle for black equality had always been "complex." Shedding the euphemism, Henry Louis Gates observed in the early 1990s that "even some of those sympathetic to gay rights, are unhappy with the models of oppression and victimhood which they take to be enshrined in the civil rights discourse that many gay advocates have adopted." Writing after the passage of Don't Ask, Don't Tell, scholar Alycee Lane criticized gay activists for their "problematic analyses of similarities between black and gay experiences in the military." She believed that "the way the issue of race was debated throughout this battle contributed to the failure to overturn the ban." Both Gates and Lane opposed the ban, but they recognized frustration in the black community over the cooptation of black civil rights history by gay activists. Other scholars compared historical racism and homophobia in the military as well as analyzing more general commonalities in the black civil rights and gay movements. "Whether or not race is precisely parallel to sexual orientation," David Ari Bianco argued, "military racism and military homophobia are strikingly similar." Thaddeus Russell noted that both the civil rights and gay liberation movements "have demanded that in order to gain acceptance as full citizens, their constituents adopt the cultural norms of what they believe to be the idealized American citizen—productivity, selflessness, responsibility, sexual restraint." Civil rights scholars have long called this the politics of respectability. Though respectability was not a hallmark of the early gay liberation movement, which emerged from the counterculture, it was certainly a component of the movement for openly gay military service. As Stevens noted, "advocates for the acceptance of homosexuals in the military have taken pains to refute the notion that gays and lesbians are driven by desire and have portrayed them instead as patriotic, rational, and chaste." In other words, though they were fighting unique forms of discrimination within different historical contexts, both black and gay movement activists wanted their respective minority groups to assimilate as much as possible into mainstream (white, middle-class, heteronormative) American society to win full civil rights.[4]

This chapter sketches out the ways that gay activists and allies attempted to draw the analogy between black civil rights—particularly the racial integration of the US military—and gay rights to challenge the ban on openly gay military service from the 1970s through the 2000s. This chapter begins by looking at the role the racial analogy played in the cases of two gay servicemen—one white and one black—who challenged the ban during the 1970s and 1980s. Although federal judges found validity in the argument that the military ban on sexual minorities was similar to earlier racial discrimination in the armed forces, court rulings in this era were too narrow to influence general military policy. I address briefly the ways that gender influenced this struggle, particularly the heavy impact of the gay ban on suspected lesbians, but a full account of the relationship between gender and sexuality in military policy is beyond the scope of this chapter. Moving into the 1990s and 2000s, this essay examines debates about the Don't Ask, Don't Tell policy, revealing that gay rights activists came to rely more on arguments about military efficiency than comparisons to the historical treatment of African Americans. Activists ultimately had more success when they talked about gay rights as civil rights in a general sense, instead of explicitly drawing the analogy between the black civil rights movement and gay liberation or between racism and homophobia. In fact, I argue this was one of the main lessons that gay activists took from the original battle that produced Don't Ask, Don't Tell. Starting in the mid-1990s, the racial analogy became a subtle backdrop to calls for gay civil rights. The post-9/11 campaign to lift the ban further buried this analogy, emphasizing the practical needs of war in the Middle East as reasons for military policy reform. In short, gay rights advocates shifted from a civil rights discourse to a military discourse. They continued this strategy even after the first black president invoked the racial analogy to call for repeal of Don't Ask, Don't Tell. It was ultimately nonracial claims to civil rights and arguments about military necessity that ended the ban. Today, the racial analogy continues to underlie many of the arguments for gay rights. If civil rights and gay rights activists are to build future progressive coalitions, it behooves us to consider the historical obstacles to such alliances.

Behind the official ban on open gay and lesbian military service lies a policy that has been continually reconsidered and revised. The passage of Don't Ask, Don't Tell in 1993 was simply the most public stage of this evolution. Elsewhere, I have called it a new paint job on an old closet door.[5] However, the military closet was never as closed as the term "ban" would suggest. Military leaders have long known that gay men and lesbians served in the armed forces. Men and women within the military, the courts, and the federal government have debated the ban since World War II, and public challenges began in the 1970s.[6]

## Making the Racial Analogy (1975–1992)

The years during and immediately after the Vietnam War were an early high tide for gay liberation, before the ebb that came with the AIDS epidemic and the conservative backlash to the social movements of the 1960s and 1970s. On the heels of the African American civil rights struggle and the women's movement, it appeared that gay rights might also be acknowledged. As gay and lesbian troops understood, honorable and open service in the military could serve as a foundation for other civil rights. These men and women began to speak out. One of the first to do so was an air force sergeant named Leonard Matlovich.

Matlovich was steeped in the military tradition, and he made an excellent airman. He was the son of a soldier. He volunteered for the air force and served three tours of duty in Vietnam. As he explained years later, "I had to prove that I was just as masculine as the next man. I felt Vietnam would do this for me."[7] During his first tour in 1966, Matlovich received his first of two air force commendation medals for bravery. In the face of a mortar attack, he went out to positions on his base's perimeter to improve the defenses and check for casualties among his comrades. He eventually won a Bronze Star and a Purple Heart.

Matlovich was inspired to challenge the ban on gay service because of his epiphany about racism in the military and in American society at large. When Matlovich returned to the States in the early 1970s, he became an instructor in a new program set up by the air force to improve race relations. Though Matlovich was born in the South and grew up as a self-avowed racist, he served with and befriended black troops in Vietnam. He was greatly moved by the civil rights movement and Martin Luther King, Jr. Tech Sergeant Matlovitch was consistently awarded the highest marks when up for promotion, and his 1974 evaluation in the race relations program praised him for being "dedicated, sincere, and responsible" and an "absolutely superior NCO in every respect." That was before Matlovich told the air force that he was gay.

"What does this mean?" the airman's superior officer asked when handed the letter announcing the sergeant's intention to challenge the ban on gays in the military in 1975. "It means *Brown v. Board of Education*," Matlovich told the African American captain. By comparing his legal challenge to the *Brown* case, Matlovich drew a direct parallel between black and gay struggles for equality. *Matlovich v. Secretary of the Air Force* landed the young airman on the cover of *Time* magazine and at the forefront of the movement for gay rights.[8]

When his case made it to the US district court in Washington, DC, in 1976, Matlovich's lawyers argued that the air force policy was a denial of their client's privacy and liberty, that it was arbitrary and capricious, and finally, that it was a denial of due process and equal protection—the same arguments used to win civil rights cases for African Americans. Judge Gerhard A. Gesell acknowledged the power of these arguments: "No one . . . who has studied the civil rights movement and the striving of blacks for opportunity will ever fail to recognize that the Armed Forces, more than any branch of government and far ahead of the private sector in this country, led to erasing the stigma of race discrimination . . . Here, another opportunity is presented." But it would not be presented by the court. While Judge Gesell strongly urged the air force to reconsider its ban on gays, he deferred to Pentagon decision makers. After five years of fighting, Matlovich accepted a settlement and an honorable discharge in 1980.[9]

As a result of the Matlovich case and other legal challenges by gay and lesbian service personnel, the federal government clarified and hardened its opposition to gays in the armed forces by arguing that the ban was a military necessity. Before the members of Jimmy Carter's administration left office early in 1981, they began to revise the wording of the ban. The new policy began bluntly: "Homosexuality is incompatible with military service." Though the new policy was a slight improvement over the old in that it offered an honorable discharge to most gays drummed out of the military, it codified the reasons why homosexuals (regardless of whether or not they broke the law against sodomy) should be banned from service. The Department of Defense explained that the primary reasons for retaining the ban were to "maintain discipline, good order, and morale," to "prevent breaches of security," and to ensure the successful recruitment and retention of heterosexual soldiers. As many activists and scholars pointed out, this rationale was similar to the defense of racial segregation in the armed forces during the 1940s, when federal officials feared that integration "would produce situations destructive to morale and detrimental to the preparations of national defense."[10]

Despite the new policy, gays and lesbians continued to serve their country, and a courageous cadre of activists followed in Matlovich's footsteps to challenge the ban in court. Vernon Berg, Miriam Ben-Shalom, Perry Watkins, Dusty Pruitt, Joe Steffan, Grethe Cammermeyer, Keith Meinhold, Zoe Dunning, and a handful of other active-duty servicemen and women risked their careers to defend their principles. In the wake of the feminist movement, lesbian service personnel and gay activists showed that women bore a disproportionate burden of homosexual discharges. In the 1980s, for instance, 25 percent of those discharged for homosexuality were women, though only one in ten members of the US armed forces was female, a discrepancy that would continue in the 1990s. Yet arguments about the relationship between sexism and homophobia found even less sympathy than the racial analogy. Although a few of the women and men who challenged the ban in this era won individual victories, none of their cases overturned the ban, and the courts refused to address the larger question of whether it was constitutional to ban gays and lesbians from military service.[11]

As a black man who had been openly gay when he was drafted into the army during the Vietnam War, Perry Watkins's challenge to the ban all but required judges to address the relationship between race and sexuality in military policy. Because many straight men claimed to be homosexual to avoid the draft during Vietnam, no one batted an eye during the psychiatric examination when Perry Watkins admitted that he was a gay man who had oral and anal sex. Watkins, who had studied ballet and tried out for the cheerleading squad, had been openly gay since junior high school. He was a young man at peace with himself, despite the intense social pressure against such a proud gay identity in the mid-1960s. Inducted into the US Army in 1967, Perry Watkins never tried to hide his sexual orientation. In fact, he became something of a minor celebrity for his drag shows as "Simone" in enlisted men's clubs. Superior officers consistently praised Watkins's job performance and even officially commended him for entertaining the troops as "Simone." After serving on various posts in the United States, Germany, and South Korea, Watkins was finally discharged from the army in 1981 based on his explicit acknowledgement of his homosexuality in the late 1960s. Watkins then sued to keep his job.[12]

In 1988 a three-judge panel from the Ninth Circuit Court of Appeals delivered an astonishing judgment in Watkins's case that explicitly linked gay rights to black civil rights, comparing military discrimination against homosexuals to its past discrimination against African Americans. Judge William Norris held for the first time that homosexuals were a "suspect class"—a minority group that deserved special legal protection from discrimination. "Discrimination faced by homosexuals in our society is plainly no less pernicious or intense than the discrimination faced by other groups," he wrote. Drawing the direct parallel to racial discrimination in the armed forces, Norris continued, "For much of our history, the military's fear of racial tension kept black soldiers separated from whites. Today it is unthinkable that the judiciary would defer to the Army's prior 'professional' judgment that black and white soldiers had to be segregated to avoid interracial tensions." But that is exactly what previous decisions had done in upholding the military ban of homosexual personnel. Judge Norris came to a different conclusion, holding that "the Army's regulations violate the constitutional guarantee of equal protection of the laws because they discriminate against persons of homosexual orientation." Whether it was because he was black *and* homosexual or simply because the panel of judges from San Francisco's liberal Ninth Circuit wanted to make a statement about gay rights, Watkins had won, in part, by claiming that gays deserved civil rights just as African Americans did.[13]

This victory proved short-lived; the court continued to defer to the Department of Defense and its claim that gays were bad for military efficiency. When the full Ninth Circuit heard the case on appeal, the majority refused to address the larger questions of the constitutionality of the military's gay ban. They did, however, order the army to reinstate Watkins, because he had never lied about his sexual orientation. In 1990 the Supreme Court refused to hear the military's appeal, prompting the journalist Randy Shilts to dub the Watkins decision "a historical turning point in that the nation's highest court had for the first time ordered the armed forces to accept an openly gay soldier."[14]

As important as the Watkins precedent may have been, Watkins himself all but disappeared from the looming debate about gay military service at the very same time that the racial analogy was eclipsed by arguments about military efficiency. In the early 1990s, scholar Alycee Lane argues, gay rights advocates chose white male veterans as spokespeople to drive home the point that gay service personnel were just "like everybody else." Keith Meinhold, a white seaman who came out to challenge the gay ban in 1992, became the public face and voice of activists' efforts. Watkins felt betrayed by gay rights leaders, who did not ask him to "lend his voice" to the struggle against the ban in this era. Race had receded so much from the debate by the early 2000s that one historian wrote about Watkins's "intriguing challenge" to the ban without even mentioning that the army sergeant was African American or that race had played a part in his case. Although the Watkins decision and other rulings in the 1980s and 1990s offered evidence that the courts might recognize gay civil rights as they had black civil rights in the 1940s and 1950s, the debate about military policy shifted to the political arena and from civil rights rhetoric to military discourse.[15]

In September 1992, presidential candidate Bill Clinton was asked whether homosexuals should be allowed to serve. "Yes," he replied. "I support the repeal of the ban on gays and lesbians serving in the United States Armed Forces."[16] Two months later, Clinton was elected president. He entered office in 1993, believing that after a meeting with the Joint Chiefs of Staff, he would lift the ban on gay service with an executive order, much the same way that Harry Truman had desegregated the armed forces.

But Clinton faced surprisingly stiff resistance from the Joint Chiefs, from Congress, and, most importantly, from a change in the way the gay ban was framed. Clinton's first meeting with the Joint Chiefs went badly, with unanimous resistance to lifting the ban, despite the president's argument that the military could have saved $500 million in the previous ten years if it hadn't investigated and discharged 17,000 gay service personnel. The Chiefs, including their chairman, General Colin Powell, were unmoved. Powell argued once again that lifting the ban would be "prejudicial to good order and discipline." In other words, military necessity trumped civil rights concerns. When Powell's opposition became public knowledge, the liberal press immediately drew the racial analogy to chastise him. From the *Atlanta Constitution* to the *Philadelphia In-quirer,* newspapers pointed to the irony that Powell "of all people" should be the one "enforcing bigotry." But few pundits were more frank in this critique than Abe Rosenthal of the *New York Times.* Powell, Rosenthal argued, owed his posi-tion to the courageous actions of President Harry Truman, who went against popular sentiment (and the advice of his own generals) to order racial integration of the military in 1948. "Because he is the chief of chiefs, because he is black and does not have to be told about discrimination, and because he commands respect throughout the nation," Rosenthal argued that Powell had a unique opportunity to do the right thing by gay service personnel. Directly addressing Powell's ear-lier argument that skin color was a "benign characteristic" but that sexuality in the military was "far more complicated," Rosenthal snapped: "Sure, sex can get complicated. But skin color was not all that 'benign' a characteristic when it meant the difference between freedom and slavery, and when even after military integration, blacks could only ride southern buses in the back." The column did not change Powell's mind, but it clearly stung. The general paraphrased much of Rosenthal's essay in his autobiography, rebutting it with the assertion that com-paring gays' service in the military to civil rights struggles was simply a political strategy, one that should never outweigh military necessity.[17]

Despite the fact that Powell had disputed the validity of the racial analogy, it remained a central strategy of the activists pushing to lift the ban in 1993. An ad-hoc group of activists and Washington insiders called the Campaign for Mili-tary Service (CMS) organized the anti-ban witnesses for congressional hear-ings on gays in the military that year. According to Alan Berube, an independent historian who advised CMS, the strategy was "to get these powerful men to take antigay discrimination as seriously as they supposedly took racial discrimina-tion, so they would lift the military ban on homosexuals as they had eliminated official policies requiring racial segregation." In selecting witnesses, CMS chose white (mostly male) gay veterans in the hopes that by "mirroring" the racial and gender makeup of the congressional committees they would elicit more support. Yet the opponents of lifting the ban called African American ministers and vet-erans to shoot down the racial analogy in congressional hearings. Highly critical of the CMS approach, Berube suggested that the group get a black, gay veteran like Perry Watkins to testify. CMS rejected that idea, setting up what Berube described as "a racialized dramatic conflict that reinforced the twin myths that gay is white and African Americans are anti-gay." In other words, CMS's strategy played directly into the hands of their opponents, creating congressional hear-

ings that pitted middle-class, white, male homosexuals against socially conservative black Christians, the kind of men who had led in the original civil rights
movement and could speak with authority on the racial analogy.[18]

In 1993 the racial analogy was as hotly debated as the issue of the ban itself.
Was homophobia a form of discrimination akin to racial bigotry? Was this debate
really about civil rights or sexual morality? Ron Dellums, an African American
veteran of the marine corps and the Democratic chairman of the House Armed
Services Committee from California, saw this as a civil rights issue. Other black
veterans disagreed. The "homosexual lifestyle has never been embraced as a
value within the black community," one navy veteran testified. Lieutenant General Calvin Waller, retired from the US Army, scoffed at the racial analogy. "I
had no choice regarding my race when I was delivered from my mother's womb,"
he said. "To compare my service in America's Armed Forces with the integration
of avowed homosexuals is personally offensive to me." Like Dellums, other members of the Congressional Black Caucus—some of whom represented urban dis-
tricts with both black and gay constituencies—argued that this *was* a civil rights
issue, but many black religious leaders balked at the comparison. "Gays are not
subject to water hoses or police dogs, denied access to lunch counters or prevented
from voting," one minister argued. "Most gays are perceived as well educated, socially mobile, and financially comfortable." In other words, a stereotype existed
that all gays were white, male, and middle-class. The leading black scholar of the
day, Henry Louis Gates, gave voice to both sides in his 1993 article on the topic.
Ultimately, however, Gates believed that it was fair to compare the two movements, reminding readers about the important role played by gay, black activists
like Bayard Rustin in the original civil rights movement and the difficult social
position of black gays and lesbians, who were often invisible in the 1993 debate.
Journalist Roger Wilkins agreed, writing, "If any people should understand another group's desire, drive, and thirst for full citizenship, it should be us."[19]

Though it was not a popular opinion within the military in 1993, there was at
least one vocal, black proponent of lifting the ban from the rank and file. He was
not nearly as well-known or as powerful as Powell, but Vince Patton would also
achieve an African American first, becoming the first black master chief of the
US Coast Guard. Over the course of his thirty-year career in the coast guard, Patton served in almost every capacity, from radioman to recruiter and drug enforcement officer to peacekeeper. At every post and at every stage of his career, he
made it his mission to fight discrimination and foster appreciation for diversity.
One of his biggest heroes, in fact, was Leonard Matlovich, who had not only

served honorably in Vietnam but also spoken up and challenged discrimination. In 1993 Patton was assigned to research the parallels between Truman's executive order desegregating the armed forces and Clinton's proposal to lift the ban on gays in the military as part of a presidential commission to study the issue. "We did a briefing with then Chairman General Powell," Patton later recalled, "and I didn't keep my mouth shut as I was instructed to do . . . I thought it was a healthy dialogue between myself and General Powell and a couple of other people about the executive order. I felt that the executive order was all that the President needed, and I related to President Truman doing it." But Powell remained steadfast in his opposition to lifting the ban, continuing to argue that it would hurt order and morale. More importantly, Powell believed that Congress was going to intervene to defend the ban. Patton resigned from the commission in protest. He felt that other members also opposed the ban but that they were too afraid to risk their careers by speaking up. Although Patton was the only one to take such a stand on the committee, his actions and later activism to lift the ban suggested that some African Americans and gay allies saw the campaigns for minority rights as intertwined.[20]

President Clinton agreed with Patton's position in principle, but the consummate politician was swayed by congressional opposition, the resistance of the Joint Chiefs, and, most importantly, opinion polls showing that about 48 percent of the American public opposed lifting the ban versus 42 percent who were in favor of the president's position.[21] Charles Moskos, a white sociologist from Northwestern University and the intellectual architect of Don't Ask, Don't Tell, argued vociferously against the racial analogy in his scholarship and counsel to the president. Moskos, who had been a staunch supporter of fully implementing Truman's executive order when he served in the 1950s, believed that it was "misleading" to compare racial integration to "the proposed acceptance of overt homosexuality." The sociologist argued that such a comparison "trivializes the black experience. The black struggle, [as] an enslaved people, is quite different, I think from the gay/lesbian analogy." A March on Washington coordinated by gay rights activists and veterans groups in the spring of 1993 sought to persuade the president and the American people that there was a connection between civil rights and gay rights. The march demanded an end to many types of discrimination including racism, sexism, and homophobia as well as an end to the ban on gay military service. Clinton was unmoved. The young president, who had never served in the armed forces himself, deferred to experts like Moskos, the Joint Chiefs, and ultimately Congress. Together, they crafted a legislative compromise that would come to be known as "Don't Ask, Don't Tell." The Department of Defense would no longer ask recruits about their sexuality, but if they were caught committing a homosexual act or if they admitted to being homosexual, gay and lesbian service personnel would be immediately discharged. "It's not a perfect solution," Clinton admitted at the time—he later termed it a political "loss"—but Don't Ask, Don't Tell became law in 1993. More significantly, it was a defeat for the racial analogy that activists had hoped would gain equality for gays in the military.[22]

### Unmaking the Racial Analogy (1993–2010)

The activist groups that emerged from the fight to lift the ban shifted their message and tactics to focus on military effectiveness after the passage of Don't Ask, Don't Tell. Organizations like American Veterans for Equal Rights (AVER), Human Rights Campaign (HRC), and Servicemembers Legal Defense Network (SLDN) continued to couch the campaign against Don't Ask, Don't Tell in terms of civil rights or human rights, but these groups began to pursue other strategies to repeal Don't Ask, Don't Tell as well. Activists still talked about civil rights, but they did so in a more general or race-neutral context of free speech. Mostly, activist groups began to focus on proving that the military necessity argument for excluding gay service personnel was wrong. SLDN, for instance, had been modeled on the NAACP Legal Defense Fund and Lambda Legal. Like these other legal activist groups, SLDN did more than simply counsel service personnel who were investigated because of their sexuality or assist legal challenges to the ban. SLDN tallied and analyzed homosexual discharges in the years after the passage of Don't Ask, Don't Tell to show the continuing cost of enforcement both on individuals and the military. The annual number of discharges for homosexuality dropped by about half after the passage of Don't Ask, Don't Tell to just over 600 service members in 1994. That number crept back up to more than 1,200 a year by 2001. Drawing connections between sexism and homophobia, SLDN also pointed out that a disproportionate number of those discharged every year continued to be women. The year after Don't Ask, Don't Tell was implemented, more than 25 percent of gay discharges were suspected lesbians even though only 12 percent of military personnel were women. Activist groups and scholars noted that the new policy came at financial cost as well. Training, investigating, discharging, and replacing gay and lesbian troops cost over $350 million in the fifteen years after the passage of the new policy.[23]

The other strategy that activist groups pursued during the Don't Ask, Don't Tell era was to change public attitudes by documenting the stories of heroic gay and lesbian veterans. Black civil rights organizations and African American newspapers had used a similar strategy during World War II with heroes like Dorie Miller, who had manned a deck gun during the attack on Pearl Harbor despite the fact that the navy assigned him to be a messman because of his race. The example of heroic service by Miller and other African Americans in World War II helped inspire Truman's executive order just a few years later.[24] As civilian attitudes toward homosexuality became more tolerant in the 1990s and 2000s, gay and lesbian veterans felt freer to come out after they left the military. This not only increased the visibility and public awareness of gay veterans but also made people reconsider whether gays were incapable of military service. SLDN, HRC, and AVER teamed up to chronicle the stories of gay and lesbian veterans based on oral history interviews in a 2004 publication called "Documenting Courage." The editors hoped that the veterans' stories would "resonate in the hearts of all Americans" because their service proved "that patriotism knows no boundaries of sexual orientation or gender identity." Though the editors did not mention race or civil rights in the preface, the second page of the publication was taken up entirely by a picture of an older, distinguished African American veteran with an American flag. "Americans long ago desegregated our military," explained retired Army Major General Vance Coleman on the following page. "The time has come to end another vestige of inequality in our country—the ban on military service by gay, lesbian, and bisexual Americans." Coleman, a straight, black veteran, concluded, "I would be proud to serve alongside these patriotic GLBT veterans." The racial analogy was too powerful to let go of entirely, but the predominantly white leadership of veterans groups decided that it was important to have this argument come from an African American veteran—even (or especially) one who was not gay. None of the stories that followed were from gay African Americans, and more importantly, none explicitly referenced the racial analogy.[25]

Instead, "Documenting Courage" included the stories of people like Rebecca Kanis, a white West Point graduate who commanded two special operations units before resigning her command in protest of Don't Ask, Don't Tell in 2000. "This policy takes away the most basic freedom we are supposed to enjoy as Americans," Kanis explained, "the right to free speech." She concluded, "It makes no sense to me that the same people whose duty includes supporting and defending the Constitution are subject to such a blatant violation of their civil rights." This publication exemplified the new discourses being used to fight the ban. It was explicitly not about documenting difference but about drawing similarities.

These were patriotic Americans. They were not "gay Americans" but Americans who happened to be gay.[26]

The wars in Afghanistan and Iraq tested a new generation of American patriots, and as with all previous American wars, some of them were gay. SLDN was quick to point out the apparent hypocrisy of reduced enforcement of Don't Ask, Don't Tell during wartime. After the invasions of Afghanistan and Iraq, gay discharges dropped immediately as manpower needs from these wars skyrocketed. A few years into the War on Terror, the number of gay discharges had declined to between 600 and 750 a year, levels not seen since a decade earlier in the first year after the passage of Don't Ask, Don't Tell. In addition to making the argument that this selective enforcement was hypocritical, activist organizations trumpeted the fact that the military was kicking out gay and lesbian personnel with essential skills, such as translators specializing in Arabic, Farsi, and other languages absolutely critical to the war effort. In short, the campaign to end Don't Ask, Don't Tell subsumed questions of civil rights beneath questions about military effectiveness and efficiency.[27]

The speaking tour of gay marine corps veteran Eric Alva was an example of this new strategy. "I am appalled at the involuntary separation of thousands of skilled service members during a time of war," the third-generation marine testified before Congress in 2008. He argued the policy threatened "our country's military readiness for no good reason." Alva had lost a leg to a land mine in the Iraqi desert in 2003, earning the "dubious honor," he explained, of becoming the first American wounded in the Iraq War. Given his hard-won Purple Heart, prosthetic leg, close-cropped hair, and chiseled good looks, it would have been hard for anyone to ignore Alva's story. His testimony before Congress was just one stop on a national speaking tour for the Human Rights Campaign. Whenever he spoke, Alva introduced himself as "a former Marine and patriotic American." He did not talk much, if at all, about his Latino heritage. He did not talk about how his grandfather and father, who fought in World War II and Vietnam, respectively, may have experienced discrimination not because of their sexuality but because of the color of their skin. Yes, Don't Ask, Don't Tell was discriminatory, Alva seemed to be saying. Yes, it hurt individual Americans. But it hurt America and the American military even more.[28]

As gay activists backed away from the racial analogy and shifted to "race-neutral" claims for civil rights and arguments for military effectiveness, the racial aspects of civil rights took center stage once again with the election of President Barack Obama. Obama made a campaign promise to lead an effort to repeal

Don't Ask, Don't Tell. Secretary of Defense Robert Gates and Chairman of the Joint Chiefs Admiral Michael Mullen publicly supported lifting the ban. Even Colin Powell eventually softened his opposition to gays in the military, acknowledging that "attitudes and circumstances" had changed dramatically since the passage of Don't Ask, Don't Tell. Though there was growing support for the repeal in the Pentagon, the president moved carefully, prioritizing other issues. Obama finally addressed the question of gays in the military in a speech to an HRC dinner in 2009. Acknowledging the frustration of gay activists who had hoped to see the ban lifted early in his presidency, Obama linked the gay rights struggle to the civil rights movement with an allusion to Dr. Martin Luther King's "Letter from a Birmingham Jail." "It's not for me to tell you to be patient any more than it was for others to counsel patience to African Americans petitioning for equal rights half a century ago," Obama said. The president then explicitly placed the gay rights movement in the broader context of American civil rights struggles. "That's the story of the movement for fairness and equality, and not just for those who are gay," Obama observed, "but for all those in our history who have been denied the rights and responsibilities of citizenship." Though he explicitly drew the racial analogy and compared the gay rights movement to the African American struggle for equality, Obama rested his primary argument for ending Don't Ask, Don't Tell on military effectiveness. "We cannot afford to cut from our ranks people with the critical skills we need to fight," he concluded. "We should be celebrating their willingness to show such courage and selflessness on behalf of fellow citizens, especially when we are fighting two wars."[29]

The campaign against Don't Ask, Don't Tell got another shot in the arm when the Department of Defense released its own study of how repealing the ban on gay service might affect the military in 2010. The 257-page document based on historical research and extensive surveys with active-duty military personnel concluded that "the risk of repeal of Don't Ask, Don't Tell to overall military effectiveness is low." Much of the report was dedicated to proving that openly gay military service would not hurt unit cohesion. Surveys suggested that only around 30 percent of military personnel feared that the repeal would hinder military missions. Nearly 70 percent of troops responded that they had already served with gay comrades, and 92 percent of them believed that the presence of gay soldiers had no negative effect on unit cohesion. Perhaps most surprisingly, given that gay rights activists had downplayed the racial analogy, the report explicitly addressed it. "Though there are fundamental differences between matters of race, gender, and sexual orientation," the report's authors cautiously noted, "we believe the US military's prior experiences with racial and gender integration are relevant." The report pointed out that many military leaders after World War II had opposed racial integration, "making strikingly similar predictions of the negative impact of unit cohesion." Yet racial integration was nearly complete by the end of the Korean War, and by the twenty-first century, the military could boast that it was "probably the most racially diverse and integrated institution in the country." If the military could successfully integrate African Americans and women, the report argued, it could adapt to openly gay service members as well, incorporating "within its ranks the diversity that is reflective of American society at large."[30]

Despite support from Obama and the Department of Defense, Congress moved at a glacial pace in reconsidering Don't Ask, Don't Tell. Bills like the "Military Readiness Enhancement Act" proposed throughout the first decade of the 2000s picked up few cosponsors and seemed dead on arrival at the steps of the capitol. Another legislative strategy by congressional opponents of the ban was attaching the repeal of Don't Ask, Don't Tell to a larger military appropriations bill that would be difficult to oppose during a time of war. Senate Republicans, led by navy veteran John McCain from Arizona, shot down the last of such amendment proposals in the fall of 2010. With a lame duck Democratic congress on the way out and conservative Republicans tallying big victories in the elections that year, it looked as if Don't Ask, Don't Tell was safe for the foreseeable future. As one retired army colonel wrote in an op-ed for *USA Today* in early December 2010, patience was a virtue when reconsidering such an important military policy. "Proponents of allowing homosexuals to serve openly have sought to frame the debate as a matter of civil rights," the veteran wrote. "The civil rights claim itself is debatable. More important, serious consideration must be extended to questions of military effectiveness."[31]

Within weeks of that op-ed, however, Congress took up the issue again, this time as a standalone bill simply to repeal Don't Ask, Don't Tell. When the House of Representatives passed the measure, gay activists weighed their words carefully and kept their focus on military efficiency. "The only thing that matters on the battlefield is the ability to do the job," the president of HRC said. "Momentum is solidly on the side of ending 'Don't Ask, Don't Tell.' Now it is up to the Senate to consign this failed and discriminatory law to the dustbin of history." When the bill reached the Senate for debate, Senator John McCain warned that repeal of Don't Ask, Don't Tell would come "at great cost" and it would "probably . . . harm the battle effectiveness" of the American military. But McCain was on the losing side of the debate this time as a handful of his fellow Republicans joined the Democrats in the Senate to lift the ban. Signing the repeal of Don't Ask, Don't Tell into law, President Obama observed: "Our people sacrifice a lot for this country, including their lives. None of them should have to sacrifice their integrity as well." Gay rights activists had successfully refuted the argument that gay troops hurt military efficiency.[32]

Newspapers across the country hailed the repeal of Don't Ask, Don't Tell as a civil rights victory, yet the battle over the legacies of the black civil rights movement and gay rights movement was far from over.[33] For some commentators, this remained a problematic analogy. Even the family of Martin Luther King, Jr., was divided on the issue. King's widow, Coretta Scott King, was a staunch advocate for gay rights until her death, as were some of their children, but King's niece was quoted as saying that her uncle "did not take a bullet" for gay rights. Writing for *Newsweek* just as Congress was repealing Don't Ask, Don't Tell, Eve Conant titled her article on the racial analogy "Uncivil Rights?" "Gay activists are taking their cue from Rosa Parks and Martin Luther King," she observed, "but are their struggles the same?" This remained a valid question, but the premise that spurred the query was incorrect, because few gay rights activists were making the racial analogy by 2010.[34]

### Conclusion

Activists pushing for the repeal of Don't Ask, Don't Tell downplayed and sometimes entirely avoided connections between the black freedom struggle and the gay rights movement after this analogy proved so controversial in the 1993 effort to lift the ban on gay military service. Don't Ask, Don't Tell ushered in two silences in this regard. Gays in the military could not speak openly about their sexual orientation, and gay activists were just as careful about deploying the racial analogy. Legacies of the black civil rights movement have been contested for many reasons. African Americans watched women, immigrant groups, the disabled, the elderly, and gays and lesbians gain rights using some of the same tactics and arguments as black activists even as African Americans continued to face discrimination and limited economic opportunities. The analogy between black civil rights and gay rights particularly bothered African Americans whose faith led them to view homosexual acts as sinful and immoral. Conservatives of all races used the problematic nature of this analogy to turn back gay rights campaigns both because it offended African Americans and also because it fit with a conservative view of the civil rights movement as history—a glorious chapter in our nation's past in which racial discrimination was definitively overcome. Using race-neutral claims to civil rights or "citizenship rights," gay activists seeking to lift the military ban after 1993 largely avoided this trap. Straight allies, particularly black allies like Barack Obama, drew a connection between the two movements, but they did so with the power of racial authenticity—as proxies for gay rights groups. As Alan Berube and others have pointed out, the real problem with the racial analogy was that it whitened the gay movement and straightened the civil rights struggle in such a way that the two seemed mutually exclusive when both were actually diverse, sometimes overlapping movements for rights. In an ideal world, the various struggles for minority rights would reinforce one another, not vie for authenticity and advancement. Expansion of citizenship rights for various groups of Americans need not be a zero-sum game. But in the real world, coalitions of minority rights groups have never been seamless. Thus, for better or worse, the legacy of the black civil rights movement for the campaign to end Don't Ask, Don't Tell became the dream that dared not speak its name.

NOTES

1. For historical studies of gays and lesbians in the military, see Allan Berube, *Coming Out under Fire* (New York: Free Press, 1990); Randy Shilts, *Conduct Unbecoming: Lesbians and Gays in the US Military, Vietnam to the Persian Gulf* (New York: St. Martin's Press, 1993); and Nathaniel Frank, *Unfriendly Fire: How the Gay Ban Undermines the Military and Weakens America* (New York: Thomas Dunne Books, 2009). Shilts and Frank suggest that the first man literally drummed out of the American military for having sex with another man was an officer in the Continental Army, though as Frank points out, scholars are reluctant to ascribe homosexual identities to men and women with same-sex attractions before the late nineteenth century. Technically, this officer was not discharged for being gay but for committing sodomy.

2. Colin Powell with Joseph E. Persico, *My American Journey* (New York: Ballantine Books, 1996), 532–533.

3. Frank, *Unfriendly Fire*, 62–63.

4. George Chauncey, *Why Marriage? The History Shaping Today's Debate over Gay Equality* (New York: Basic Books, 2004), 3, 23–24; Henry Louis Gates, Jr., "Backlash? African Americans Object to Gay Rights–Civil Rights Analogy," *The New Yorker*, May 17, 1993; Alycee J. Lane, "Black Bodies / Gay Bodies: The Politics of Race in the Gay/Military Debate," *Callaloo* 17, no. 4 (1994): 1074–1088; David Ari Bianco, "Echoes of Prejudice: The Debates over Race and Sexuality in the Armed Forces," in *Gay Rights, Military Wrongs: Political Perspectives on Lesbians and Gays in the Military*, edited by Craig A. Rimmerman (London: Routledge, 1996), 47-70; and Thaddeus Russell, "The Color of Discipline: Civil Rights and Black Sexuality," *American Quarterly* 60, no. 1

(March 2008): 101–128. For more on the evolving relationship between the civil rights establishment and gay rights movement, see Keith Boykin, "Your Blues Ain't Like Mine: Blacks and Gay Marriage," *The Crisis*, January–February 2004, 23–25.

5. Steve Estes, *Ask & Tell: Gay and Lesbian Veterans Speak Out* (Chapel Hill: University of North Carolina Press, 2007).

6. For criticism of Don't Ask, Don't Tell, see Aaron Belkin and Geoffrey Bateman, *Don't Ask, Don't Tell: Debating the Gay Ban in the Military* (Boulder, CO: Lynne Rienner, 2003), and Frank, *Unfriendly Fire*. For support of the ban, see Melissa Wells-Petry, *Exclusion: Homosexuals and the Right to Serve* (New York: Regnery Gateway, 1993).

7. Matlovich interview in Mary Ann Humphrey, *My Country, My Right to Serve* (New York: HarperCollins, 1990), 151. Leonard Matlovich Birth Certificate Folder 75, Box 2; Recommendation for AF Commendation Medal (February 1966) Folder 6, Box 3. Leonard Matlovich Papers owned by the Gay Lesbian Bisexual Transgender (GLBT) Historical Society, housed at the San Francisco Public Library.

8. Sergeant Performance Report (June 14, 1973 to June 13, 1974), Box 2, Matlovich Papers; Andrew Kokind, "The Boys in the Barracks," *The New Times*, August 8, 1975, 19–27; "Gays on the March," *Time*, September 8, 1975, 33–43; and Lesley Oelsner, "Homosexual Is Fighting Military Ouster," *New York Times*, May 25, 1975, 1, 24.

9. US District Court Opinion of the Honorable Gerhard A. Gesell, July 16, 1976, File 58, Box 2; Appellant Brief by David F. Addlestone, May 17, 1979, File 56, Box 2; and Gregory Gordon, UPI Wire Story on Matlovich, November 24, 1980, File 64, Box 2, Matlovich Papers.

10. Wilbur J. Scott and Sandra Carson Stanley, *Gays and Lesbians in the Military: Issues, Concerns, and Contrasts* (New York: Aldine de Gruyter, 1994), 19, 123, 221. Department of Defense Directive 1332.14, *Federal Register* 46, no. 19 (July 29, 1981): 9571–9578. For more on the limitations of the comparison between the discourse surrounding ban on gays and the racial segregation of the armed forces, see Alycee J. Lane, "Black Bodies / Gay Bodies: The Politics of Race in the Gay/Military Debate," *Callaloo* 17, no. 4 (1994): 1074–1088.

11. Estes, *Ask & Tell*, 130–151, 185–196; Frank, *Unfriendly Fire*, 10–12, 18–23. For more on the connection between sexuality and gender in the military, see Melissa S. Herbert, *Camouflage Isn't Only for Combat: Gender Sexuality, and Women in the Military* (New York: New York University Press, 2000).

12. For more on Watkins, see Shilts, *Conduct Unbecoming*, 60–65, 155–156, 395–398, and 729–730.

13. Sergeant Perry J. Watkins v. United States Army et al., 837 F.2d1428 (February 1988); Shilts, *Conduct Unbecoming*, 640–642, 729.

14. Shilts, *Conduct Unbecoming*, 640.

15. Lane, "Black Bodies / Gay Bodies," 1083–1084; Timothy Haggerty, "History Repeating Itself: A Historical Overview of Gay Men and Lesbians in the Military Before 'Don't Ask, Don't Tell,'" in *Don't Ask, Don't Tell: Debating the Gay Ban in the Military*, edited by Aaron Belkin and Geoffrey Bateman (Boulder, CO: Lynn Rienner, 2003), 37.

16. Susan Yoachum, "Clinton for the Record," *San Francisco Chronicle*, July 20, 1993.

17. Clinton gives the estimated cost of the ban and his personal take on this meeting in his memoirs. Bill Clinton, *My Life* (New York: Alfred A. Knopf, 2004). See also Eric

Schmitt, "Clinton Aides Seek Indirect Solution to Gay-Rights Rift," *New York Times*, January 13, 1993; and "Joint Chiefs Fighting Clinton Plan to Allow Homosexuals in Military," *New York Times*, January 23, 1993. Powell quotes from several editorials, including in the *Atlanta Constitution* and the *Philadelphia Inquirer*, in his memoir. Powell, *My American Journey*, 570–574; A. M. Rosenthal, "General Powell and the Gays," *New York Times*, January 26, 1993.

18. Alan Berube, "How Gay Stays White and What Kind of White It Stays," in *My Desire for History: Essays in Gay, Community, & Labor History*, by Alan Berube (Chapel Hill: University of North Carolina Press, 2011), 207–214.

19. Carolyn Lochhead, "Gays Denounced and Defended at Dellums' Lively Hearing," *San Francisco Chronicle*, May 5, 1993; and "Rep. Dellums Assails New Gay GI Policy," *San Francisco Chronicle*, July 22, 1993. For a full transcript of the House hearings, see "Policy Implications of Lifting the Ban on Homosexuals in the Military: Hearings Before the Committee on Armed Services, House of Representatives," 103rd Congress, First Session, May 4 and 5, 1993. Waller and the black minister are quoted in Gates, "Backlash?" Roger Wilkins is quoted in Lane, "Black Bodies / Gay Bodies," 1086. See also Garry L. Rolison and Thomas K. Kayama, "Defensive Discourses: Blacks and Gays in the US Military," in *Gays and Lesbians in the Military: Issues, Concerns, and Contrasts*, edited by Wilbur J. Scott and Sandra Carson Stanley (New York: Aldine de Gruyter, 1994): 121–133.

20. Vince Patton, interviewed by the author on April 23, 2004. Excerpts included in Estes, *Ask & Tell*, 203–209. A complete transcript of this interview can be found in the Vincent Patton Collection (AFC/2001/001/43230), Veterans History Project, American Folklife Center, Library of Congress.

21. Polling data reported in Eric Schmitt, "Pentagon Chief Warns Clinton on Gay Policy," *New York Times*, January 25, 1993; and "Public Views of Gays in the Military," *San Francisco Chronicle*, January 28, 1993. Clinton acknowledged his reliance on these polls. See Clinton, *My Life*, 485.

22. Susan Yoachum, "Clinton for the Record," *San Francisco Chronicle*, July 20, 1993; Moskos quoted in Frank, *Unfriendly Fire*, xv–xvii, 26–28; Clinton, *My Life*, 514. For much more detail on the Don't Ask, Don't Tell controversy and legislation, see Gary Lehring, *Officially Gay: The Political Construction of Sexuality* (Philadelphia: Temple University Press, 2003); Aaron Belkin and Geoffrey Bateman, *Don't Ask, Don't Tell: Debating the Military Ban* (Boulder, CO: Lynne Reiner Publishers, 2003); Janet E. Halley, *Don't: A Reader's Guide to the Military's Anti-gay Policy* (Durham, NC: Duke University Press, 1999); and Wells-Petry, *Exclusion*.

23. Servicemembers Legal Defense Network, *Conduct Unbecoming: The Eighth Annual Report on 'Don't Ask, Don't Tell'* (Washington, DC: Servicemembers Legal Defense Network, 2002), and Frank, *Unfriendly Fire*, 169. For more on the costs of Don't Ask, Don't Tell, see the Blue Ribbon Commission Report, *Financial Analysis of 'Don't Ask, Don't Tell': How Much Does the Gay Ban Cost?* (Santa Barbara, CA: The Palm Center, 2006).

24. "Torpedo Hit the *Arizona* First," *New York Times*, December 22, 1941; "Navy Cross for Dorrie Miller," *Pittsburgh Courier*, May 16, 1942; and Secretary of the Navy Public Relations Office to Walter White, March 5, 1942, NAACP Papers, Manuscript

Division, Library of Congress, Washington, DC. As a result of coverage and pressure from black newspapers and civil rights groups, Miller was ultimately awarded the Navy Cross. He returned to duty in the Pacific and perished in 1943.

25. C. Dixon Osbourne, Cheryl Jacques, and A. J. Rogue, *Documenting Courage: Gay, Lesbian, Bisexual, and Transgender Veterans Speak Out* (Washington, DC: Human Rights Campaign, 2004).

26. Ibid.

27. Nathaniel Frank, *Research Note on Pentagon Practice of Sending Known Gays and Lesbians to War* (Santa Barbara, CA: The Palm Center, July 2007), 1, 6–7; and Frank, *Unfriendly Fire*, 169, 215–236.

28. Eric Alva, "Don't Ask, Don't Tell: Telling My Story to Congress," *Huffington Post*, July 23, 2008.

29. Barack Obama, "It's Not for Me to Tell You to Be Patient," Remarks to Human Rights Campaign Dinner, Washington, DC, October 11, 2009, in *Vital Speeches of the Day* 75, no. 12 (December 2009): 543–545; Susan Cornwell, "General Powell Backs Obama Move on Gays in the Military," Reuters, February 3, 2010.

30. *Report of the Comprehensive Review of the Issues Associated with a Repeal of "Don't Ask, Don't Tell"* (Washington, DC: United States Department of Defense, November 30, 2010), 3, 7–8, 81–88.

31. Mark Thompson, "'Don't Ask' Repeal Hits the Skids," *Time*, November 11, 2010; David Bedey, "Don't Rush to Repeal," *USA Today*, December 1, 2010.

32. Jennifer Steinhauer, "House Votes to Repeal 'Don't Ask, Don't Tell,'" *New York Times*, December 16, 2010; Dana Milbank, "After McCain Flares Up, Senate's Cooler Heads Prevail," *Washington Post*, December 19, 2010; Barack Obama, "We Are Not a Nation That Says, 'Don't Ask, Don't Tell,'" December 22, 2010. www.whitehouse.gov /blog/2010/12/22/president-signs-repeal-dont-ask-dont-tell-out-many-we-are-one.

33. Oren Spiegler, "An Ugly Era Ends Don't Ask, Don't Tell," *Pittsburgh Post-Gazette*, December 26, 2010; Chris Michaud and Ali Aman, "Gays Look to Future after 'Don't Ask, Don't Tell Falls," *Chicago Tribune*, December 24, 2010; Pauline Jelinek, "'Don't Ask, Don't Tell' Officially Discharged," *Houston Chronicle*, December 23, 2010; Peter Nicholas, "'Don't Ask, Don't Tell' Repeal Signed by Obama," *Los Angeles Times*, December 23, 2010; and "For Gays in the Military, A Measure of Equality," *Denver Post*, December 21, 2010.

34. Eve Conant, "Uncivil Rights?," *Newsweek*, December 20, 2010.

# Conclusion

DOUGLAS WALTER BRISTOL, JR.,
*and* HEATHER MARIE STUR

O ne of the great ironies of American history since World War II is that the military, typically a conservative institution, has often been at the forefront of progressive action toward civil rights. The tension between these contradictory elements has produced a mixed record. On the one hand, the military is not only bound by tradition but also struggles to overcome a long history of discrimination. Additionally, even when military leadership has found pragmatic value in expanding access to the forces, it has had to respond to a public that has been resistant and even hostile to integration efforts that challenged deeply rooted ideas about military culture and American power. Yet on the other hand, the military's progress at integrating African Americans, Japanese Americans, women, and gays into its forces has been remarkable. In the 1940s, the 1970s, and the early 2000s, military integration policies were in many ways more progressive than similar efforts in the civilian world. Furthermore, social reform in the military has shaped public debate on controversial issues such as affirmative action, integration, marriage, reproductive rights, and sexual harassment. To examine these issues, this book has compared integration on the basis of race, gender, and sexuality since World War II. We hope that viewing these experiences through the lens of America's militarized past will lead readers to rethink the history of social movements in the United States.

It seems only fair to conclude by addressing some of the objections that have been raised to comparing the history of African Americans with the history of other groups struggling for civil rights. After reviewing alternative viewpoints, we make the case for the validity of drawing parallels between African Americans and other groups. First, we examine cases in which black men and women in the military invited comparisons with their white counterparts. Then, we extend our argument by showing that all three groups share a history of dissent. We finish by arguing that historical comparisons are useful for comprehending recent transformations of the US military.

Steve Estes has provided a starting point for this discussion with his analysis of the 1993 debate over ending the ban on gays in the military, which largely hinged on whether it was valid to make comparisons between African Americans and members of the LGBT community. Supporters of ending the ban thought that, because the groups shared a history of discrimination, it was logical to compare African Americans and gays. For example, Air Force Technical Sergeant Leonard Matlovich, who was awarded the Purple Heart and served three tours of duty in Vietnam, made the comparison in 1975 to justify his decision to challenge the ban on gays in the military. When a black captain asked Matlovich to explain his choice, Matlovich said, "It means *Brown v. Board of Education*."

However, in 1993, many prominent African Americans thought the history of enslavement and Jim Crow made their suffering greater and thus fundamentally different from the history of lesbians and gay men. For example, Vernon Jarret, a black columnist for the *Chicago Sun-Times*, wrote, "I consider [the black/gay comparison] offensively disrespectful of the recorded and unchronicled sufferings of millions of my people who were kidnapped, chained, shipped and sold like livestock." Although Jarret's statement is true to an extent because African American history is unique, it also has political implications. He was implying that gays are less worthy of protection by the federal government because they have not suffered as much as African Americans have suffered. By citing such remarks, conservative commentators were able to say the African American experience provides the standard for measuring whether groups deserve civil rights. By this reasoning, few groups were entitled to what they regarded as affirmative action or "special rights."[1]

Feminist scholar Alycee Lane offered a very different point of view in her analysis of the 1993 debate over gays in the military. According to Lane, the black/gay comparison hid as much as it revealed because of an unspoken premise: all blacks were straight and all gays were white. According to Lane, this was not accidental. She claimed that white, male gay rights activists deliberately erased race in order to emphasize their privileges as white men. Similarly, Lane claimed that black, straight leaders deliberately erased sexual orientation to emphasize their privileges as heterosexual men. To illustrate her point, she quoted

David Smith, the spokesperson for an organization fighting the gay ban, who claimed the history of the two groups was interchangeable. Smith noted that the same arguments against integration fifty years ago were being heard again in the debate over gays in the military. He went so far as to claim one could substitute the words "gay and lesbian" for the word "Negro" in the history of military discrimination. According to Lane, Smith omitted two key points. He had forgotten that GIs could be black and gay. He had also failed to grasp that racism shapes homophobia. Lane's point was that racial and sexual identities overlap each other.[2]

Lane's point seems academic without a specific example, but fortunately, two black GIs who appeared earlier in these pages, Jackie Robinson and Perry Watkins, allow us to compare the experiences of straight and gay black men in the military. In temperament, the two men were similar. They were disciplined and friendly, but neither would tolerate abuse. As Douglas Bristol has shown, Robinson challenged a white bus driver and got arrested by military police rather than accepting second-class treatment. Watkins also fought back, but his sexual orientation presented him with different challenges than Robinson faced. Six months after he was drafted in 1968, Watkins was by himself on a quiet Sunday afternoon in his deserted barracks. Suddenly, he heard the footsteps of five cooks, who lived on the floor above, rapidly coming downstairs. They surrounded him and demanded oral sex. When Watkins refused, they tried to force him. Watkins jumped over lockers and shoved bunk beds to defend himself, and eventually, the would-be rapists grew tired and left. Watkins reported the incident to his supervisor, angrily telling him that "it's your job to protect me!" However, rather than investigating Watkins' assailants, who were never charged, the army opened an investigation of Watkins for being a homosexual.[3] Because Watkins's sexuality was viewed as deviant, he was considered fair game for rape by his fellow GIs. Watkins' homosexuality made him more vulnerable to abuse than if he had been heterosexual, but racial discrimination shaped his military career as well.

The outcome of the army's investigation of Watkins shows how race influenced antigay discrimination in the military. To put Watkins's situation in context, one needs to be mindful of what Heather Stur and James Westheider have shown, namely that racial discrimination was rife in the military during the Vietnam War. As to why the army enlisted Perry Watkins even though he told the medical examiner at the induction center that he was gay, Watkins chalked it up to racism. Watkins reflected later that the white examiner probably assumed he would end up as cannon fodder. The army turned a blind eye to his sexual orientation again when he was investigated after reporting the attempted rape.

Army officials said there was "insufficient evidence" that Watkins had engaged in sodomy to conclude he was gay.[4] So, although he had admitted to being gay at the induction center and again when he reported the assault, the army refused to believe him and forced the black conscript to keep serving in the military during the Vietnam War.

Another example of how race shaped the way that army treated Watkins happened at Fort Dix. Watkins had struck up a friendship with a gay, white GI, and one day they were talking about local gay hangouts. When Watkins suggested they make plans to go out that weekend, his white friend said he could not because he was being discharged for being gay. Watkins asked him what had happened. His friend said he had just admitted being gay to his commanding officer, who immediately began his discharge paperwork. When Watkins did the exact same thing, he was told once again that he would have to prove he was gay before the army would discharge him.[5] Racism kept Watkins in the military while letting his white, gay friend out. Just as it is difficult to compare the experience of two black GIs, Robinson and Watkins, it is difficult to compare Watkins to other gay GIs who were white. Lane says the answer to these problems is to examine identity as the intersection of race, gender, and sexuality.

There are also less theoretical reasons for viewing African American history, specifically the black military experience, as distinct. One reason is that it is a very long history. In every war that the United States has fought since the American Revolution, African Americans have served in the US military. By contrast, historians have shown that the gay identity has only existed since the late nineteenth century and was not embraced by sizable numbers of people until after World War II. That is not to say there were no same-sex desires in the military. The US military policed sodomy as far back as the American Revolution, when George Washington had two men drummed out of the Continental Army for being caught in the act. For the purposes of this comparison, what matters is that large numbers of military personnel did not see themselves as gay until the emergence of the gay rights movement in the 1970s, so the gay military experience is much shorter than the black military experience. The history of women's military experience is also relatively short. Women did not serve in the military until World War II, and they could not have military careers until the passage of the Women's Armed Services Integration Act of 1948. Like gays, their numbers did not grow appreciably until the 1970s, when the military became an all-volunteer force.[6]

African Americans also differed from the other two groups because they lacked full citizenship. By contrast, women have enjoyed the right to vote since the suffragist movement secured the passage of the Nineteenth Amendment on August 18, 1920. Gay men and lesbians provide a less straightforward comparison. While they could vote, they were, and in half of the United States still are, without any legal protections from discrimination. The legal status of each group, however, looks different in the military context. With the creation of equal opportunity programs in the 1970s, African Americans had removed all legal barriers to their equality in the military just as women and gay men joined the ranks in sizable numbers. The lag between the groups is striking. While experiments were made with racially integrated units in 1945, the Pentagon did not announce an end to the ban on women in combat until 2013. Similarly, gay men and lesbians have only been allowed to serve openly since 2011. Hence full integration of women and gays is only just beginning, while racial integration has been officially complete for more than thirty years.

Perhaps because the struggle for racial equality in the military has gone on for so long, black GIs have a distinct tradition of resistance. As Douglas Bristol, Jr., and James M. McCaffrey show, Jim Crow shaped the way African Americans and Japanese Americans experienced World War II. Black soldiers in the South dealt with a reign of terror by fighting back against racial discrimination. They not only responded to violence with violence but also publicly rejected Jim Crow. Japanese American soldiers also rejected segregation, confronting racist bus drivers alongside black soldiers, but they experienced fewer confrontations and were treated better by military officials. Moreover, black women as well as black men resisted Jim Crow. When black Women's Army Corps (WAC) Private Beatrice Jackson cursed the whites aboard a Chattanooga bus in 1944 for wanting her to sit in the black section, she ended by warning them about "a coming revolution which would completely change the situation for the colored race." She was right, at least in the US armed forces, which integrated in the decade following World War II. By the Vietnam War, segregation was gone in the military, but James E. Westheider showed that militant African Americans continued to demand reform. Black soldiers and civil rights organizations complained of racial discrimination in assignments, military justice, off-base housing, and promotions. Westheider concludes that the failure to deal with institutional racism led to violent racial conflicts after the death of Martin Luther King, Jr., fueled in part by the emergence of the black power movement. To sum up, African Americans have served in the military longer and under harsher constraints than women and gays, and they have a tradition of resisting discrimination in the military. Before shifting to an examination of the parallels between these groups, it is important to consider one final difference in their experiences—the influence of gender roles and sexuality.

Gender roles profoundly shaped the lives of women and gays in the military. In the collective American psyche, war, the military, and masculine power have been closely tied together. For example, it proved difficult for many Americans to comprehend the creation of the Women's Army Corps in 1942, even though WACs were not assigned combat positions. Social critics and concerned citizens argued that women who joined the services were either lesbians or whores, both categories of women who allegedly saw the military as a space in which to express their sexual deviance.[7] The "lesbian or whore" dichotomy remained in place through the end of the Vietnam War and the draft, when the armed services stepped up their recruitment of women in order to meet personnel needs at a time when military service had lost credibility among men. Moreover, unlike straight black men and gay white men, who could claim manhood as a reason for access to the military, women, regardless of race or sexuality, were in a different category that did not fit in with the symbolic image of the US armed forces.

Even after women began military careers in 1948, critics of women in the military remained dissatisfied and vocal. In order to placate those who opposed women's service, the army took care to show the public that military women were proper "ladies." As Tanya L. Roth has demonstrated, recruitment materials published in the 1950s emphasized the femininity of the army uniform and called the woman who wore it a "brand-new beauty." They were "first ladies of the land," not to be confused with the tough combat soldier who was poised to defend the nation. Defense needs did not change the image of what American women ultimately were supposed to become—wives and mothers living the white, middle-class, suburban American Dream à la June Cleaver and Donna Reed, two perfect mothers on popular television shows during the 1950s.

Sexuality was the key to maintaining the status quo in gender norms. Army recruitment materials suggested that military service could help establish heterosexual relationships by offering a potential servicewoman a venue in which to meet her future husband. Roth explains how recruitment pamphlets showed men and women holding hands and traveling, all via the military. These images were crucial in the 1950s, when anti-gay rhetoric threatened to ruin lives and careers during the "lavender scare" of the McCarthy era. Not only did the military work to suppress both real and imagined gays and lesbians within the ranks, the armed services also promoted mainstream gender roles through their recruitment efforts.

The army's handling of reproductive rights and family issues highlights another way that sexuality led to women being treated differently in the military. Kara Vuic tells the story of Lorraine R. Johnson, a member of the Army Nurse Corps Reserve who was discharged after a decade of service when her son was born in 1968. From this case, it is evident that women in the military did not possess the same reproductive rights as their male counterparts. However, Johnson challenged her discharge in court, and the US District Court for the Central District Court of California ordered the ANC to allow her to remain enlisted. As other women personnel used the legal system to challenge the military's policy of discharging servicewomen who became pregnant, the services had to reevaluate their pregnancy, family, and reproductive policies to equalize the treatment of men and women. From these examples, it should be clear that we are not arguing, like gay rights activist David Smith, that the military histories of African Americans, women, and gays are interchangeable. There are significant differences between them that form part of the historical context for understanding diversity and social reform in the military. However, it is useful to compare the experiences of African Americans, women, and gays in spite of their differences.

After all, if individuals and groups were not different, there would be no need for civil rights movements. Feminist historian Joan Wallach Scott says that marginalized groups make claims for equality by overlooking differences between individuals in a specific context. Rather than trying to eliminate all differences between individuals, movements for social equality seek to abolish a particular set of differences, such as the ban on African Americans and women in combat or the ban on gays in the military. Scott frames the issue another way by asking, if all individuals or groups were identical, would they need to ask for equality?[8] We agree with Scott that it is reasonable to overlook differences in specific contexts, in this case the military service of African Americans, women, and gays, in order to clarify the big picture—the role that the military has played in advancing social equality since World War II.

Joan Scott also points out that emphasizing the differences between groups can promote inequality. She made this argument in response to the sex discrimination case that the Equal Employment Opportunity Commission brought against Sears, Roebuck, and Company in 1978. The decision in the case hinged on whether a lack of interest by female employees in commission sales jobs could be attributed to "fundamental differences" between men and women. In order for Sears to develop hiring policies for commission sales jobs that treated male and female employees equally, it would be necessary to ignore the fact that men and women had traditionally held different jobs in the past. Instead, the court exonerated Sears. Scott's assessment of the court's ruling was that "difference was redefined as simply the recognition of 'natural' difference." Scott made this observation to note the practical consequences of emphasizing difference, which she and other feminist scholars had done in their work. However, she also noted that the alternative—emphasizing sameness in a bid for equal treatment—is problematic as well. When women are placed into the general category of human beings, distinctive aspects of their lives, such as motherhood, are overlooked. Instead, Scott contends that the fundamental problem is pairing equality and difference as opposites.[9] Gender roles often seem so natural that we do not question them. As a result, Scott notes, it is easy to miss a flaw in the logic of the debate over women in the workplace: The opposite of equality is inequality, not difference. We hope this discussion of Scott's argument provides a context for understanding the specific comparisons we make below.

Let us start by looking at parallels that African Americans drew between themselves and whites in the military. Black women have a long history of having to work in jobs associated with men, which led many to challenge their femininity. Consequently, black women had more reason to fear being called lesbians and whores than white women. Tanya Roth documented one response of black women, which was to emphasize their similarity to white women in the military in order to claim respectability and femininity. Specifically, Roth describes *Ebony* magazine's feature about military service as a viable career option for black women. Like the recruitment materials featuring white women, the *Ebony* coverage portrayed military service as a path to the middle class, not a means of subverting dominant gender norms. *Ebony's* editors also took care to make the point that military service did not compromise black women's respectable femininity. Similarly, James Westheider provided an overview of the tradition of black men staking a claim to equality by serving as patriotically as white soldiers. He notes that the tradition of black men earning a reputation as "super soldiers" continues to this day. Other historians of Vietnam have argued that black GIs embraced the hypermasculinity of the warrior role traditionally associated with white men to put teeth into demands for black power.[10] These examples demonstrate that African Americans sometimes invited favorable comparisons to their white counterparts because it advanced their interests. They assimilated white, middle-class gender roles to overcome racial stereotypes.

Since white men and women in the military also sought new gender roles, this appears to be an important parallel between different groups serving in the military. But unlike African Americans, whites revolted against their inherited gender roles. Charissa Threat shows that male nurses asked if the "sex of the practitioner matter[ed]" in a bid to overturn a gendered division of labor within the military. Faced with conscription during World War II and the Cold War, male nurses reasoned they should be able to use their professional skills in the military. They ran up against the conventional wisdom that nurses were "caregivers," which was a feminine quality. Female nurses responded to this challenge to their monopoly by expressing their support for traditional gender roles. Although male nurses were mostly white and straight, they paid a price for challenging gender roles in the military—they were stereotyped as sexual deviants, of being "crooked" or unseemly men. As noted above, they shared this burden with their female counterparts, establishing a parallel between their histories. The irony is that men got to be nurses in the military because of traditional gender roles. After the news media relayed the horrifying story of the "Angel of Dien Bien Phu" in 1954, military leaders, concerned about exposing women to combat, accepted male nurses. It was the association of nursing with combat that changed it into a man's job. While the battle of the sexes in military nursing reinforced traditional gender roles, the forces of dissent against Vietnam generated a revolt against them.

Heather Marie Stur shows that, as the Vietnam War grew increasingly unpopular, both men and women in the military revolted against traditional gender roles. The Vietnam-era GI antiwar movement focused its attention in part on gender and the oppressive, dehumanizing nature of warrior masculinity that they had grown up with watching John Wayne movies. Servicemen and veterans wrote in antiwar newspapers that men, as well as women, needed to be liberated from the gender norms that had been forced upon them by the military, the media, and American society. But when women were integrated into the regular army in the late 1970s, media coverage revealed that military culture still perpetuated 1950s gender norms. When asked about women students entering the Air Force Academy, Colonel James P. McCarthy assured a reporter that the school would "graduate the most feminine officers we can." Another article quoted Air Force Captain John Prince lamenting that airwomen "fit into the truck driver mold." Just like during World War II, obsessions about servicewomen's femininity remained part of military culture even after policy shifts had opened more doors to women.

Perhaps the most significant parallel between African Americans, women, and gays is the role that military necessity played in integration. As far back as

World War II, the military's demands for manpower (and eventually woman-power) were so great that military authorities had to make accommodations for African American and Japanese American troops. Personnel needs also let African American volunteers fight in the Battle of the Bulge, let men enter the Nurse Corps during the Korean War, let Perry Watkins serve as an openly gay soldier in Vietnam, and let women fill the ranks of an all-volunteer military starting in the 1970s. Military necessity also barred African Americans, women, and gays from combat. The same argument was used each time: Letting this group serve in combat will reduce military efficiency by lowering morale and unit cohesion. And each time, it was impossible to disprove this argument without the opportunity to serve in combat with regular troops. That is why experiments with African American and Japanese American troops were so significant. Al-though they involved small numbers of soldiers, they gave social scientists the chance to document how integration changed the attitudes of white soldiers toward racial minorities. Showing that white soldiers had a positive view of black soldiers undermined the logic of the argument because unit cohesion is not a problem if people appreciate each other. Yet this example of how arguments about morale and unit cohesion can be wrong did not prevent military officials from us-ing the same argument against women and gays. Steve Estes showed that the op-posite was true because many rejected the validity of comparing African Ameri-cans and gays. In fact, so powerful is the force of military necessity that Don't Ask, Don't Tell was not overturned until gay rights activists switched their argu-ment to emphasize how the ban on openly gay soldiers hurt military efficiency.

To sum up, we have argued it is valid to compare the military experiences of African Americans, Japanese Americans, women, and gays because there are important parallels between them. The contributors to this book shed new light on how these groups are linked by issues of race, gender, and sexuality. All of them challenged their assigned gender roles to advance their interests as a group. While African Americans staked a claim to white, middle-class gender roles, white nurses and antiwar soldiers in Vietnam revolted against them. The outcomes of both efforts show that gender conventions were not easily overturned. Con-sidered alongside the black discontent that followed racial integration, it would seem that the US military, or the American society it represents, is slow to change. How is this comparison of the military experience of African Americans, women, and gays useful for understanding today's military? We argue that it fur-nishes a historical perspective for understanding the current experience of women and gays.

Straight women are not a legally marginalized group anymore, especially now that the Department of Defense has opened combat specialties to them. However, the struggle to get to this point runs parallel to the activism of African Americans and gays for access to the armed forces. Women have had to overcome stereotypes and suspicions about their motives for wanting to serve. They have had to challenge the gender and sexual ideologies that defined who should fight and who was in need of protection. Military authorities may have seen the integration of women into the services as a pragmatic way to address military necessity by recruiting women, but change at the ground level has proved difficult and slow. Resistance to women in the military took on the ugly forms of sexual assault and rape, illustrating the danger and violence women faced as they confronted status quo ideas about military service and power.

The Persian Gulf War was the first conflict in which a significant number of servicewomen in the gender-integrated military were deployed.[11] According to Veterans Administration statistics from the war, the risk of attack was highest during wartime deployments.[12] Army reports indicated that at least twenty-four servicewomen were victims of sexual crimes while deployed to the Persian Gulf. Assaults and rapes occurred in showers, during guard duty, inside military quarters, on an R-and-R cruise ship, and in a medical clinic. One victim was assaulted at knifepoint. Some servicewomen delayed reporting the assaults out of fear that their superiors would not believe them. Perpetrators were often higher-ranking, including one accused army captain, which may have contributed to victims' reluctance to file reports.[13]

The notion of an American servicewoman being taken prisoner, and the real or perceived potential for sexual assault against a woman prisoner of war (POW), also raised concerns about women in the military during Operation Desert Shield and Desert Storm. Two US servicewomen, Melissa Rathbun-Nealy, an army truck driver with the 233rd Transportation Company, and Major Rhonda Cornum, an army flight surgeon, were taken prisoner by Iraqi forces. They were the first American women POWs since World War II, when the Japanese had captured seventy-eight army and navy nurses in the Philippines and held them for three years. When both servicewomen revealed that they had been sexually assaulted during their captivity, opponents of women in combat and those calling for additional limits on women's military service made women POWs central to their arguments. Rathbun-Nealy and Cornum both accused the media and the Presidential Commission on the Assignment of Women in the Armed Forces of playing up the sexual assaults. They asserted that what they experienced was no worse than other forms of abuse male and female POWs received.[14] Critics accused commissioners of portraying women POWs, but not male prisoners, as victims in order to further the notion that women did not belong in combat or even in the military.[15]

Whether the root of the problem was the presence of women or the nature of military culture has not been resolved. The Tailhook scandal of 1991, in which navy and marine corps aviators sexually assaulted eighty-three women and seven men at the Tailhook Association's annual convention in Las Vegas, raised concerns among military authorities and civilians about a martial culture that enabled that type of behavior. Tailhook, a private organization composed of active and retired pilots, independent defense contractors, and others associated with the navy and marines, had been holding a yearly convention since 1956, and it became known for its debauchery. Its alcohol-fueled parties typically featured strippers, nudity, and sex acts of varying degrees of lewdness.[16] A few months after Tailhook 1991, a navy lieutenant named Paula Coughlin reported that she had been sexually assaulted at the convention, and her complaint launched an investigation that revealed the degree to which aggressive sexual behavior was part of the event. In the aftermath, Secretary of the Navy H. Lawrence Garrett III resigned, and naval officials issued a zero tolerance policy regarding sexual assault.[17]

A female navy commander linked the excesses of Tailhook 1991 to men's anger over the presence of servicewomen in the Persian Gulf War and the ongoing debates about women in combat: "This was the woman that was making you, you know, change your ways," she said. "This was the woman that was threatening your livelihood. This was the woman that wanted to take your spot in that combat aircraft."[18] Journalist and cultural critic Susan Faludi observed that those who were disciplined were charged with violations such as "indecent exposure" and "conduct unbecoming an officer," not sexual assault. It was a boys-will-be-boys slap on the wrist administered with a wink and an eye roll in the direction of feminists who had spoken out against the military culture that instigated the Tailhook assaults, Faludi argued. The message that the navy sent was that it would punish the accused for their immaturity, not for their sexually violent behavior.[19]

In a broader context, the Tailhook scandal coincided with Anita Hill's decision to reveal that Supreme Court nominee Clarence Thomas had sexually harassed her for years when she had worked for him in the US Department of Education and the Equal Employment Opportunity Commission. Taken together, Tailhook and Anita Hill's testimony illustrate the tension between the expansion of military and career opportunities for women and a deep-seated culture of separate spheres that crossed the military-civilian divide. Laws opening military jobs and civil employment opportunities to women could not force opponents of gender equality to change their minds. Women flying navy aircraft and working as lawyers in federal offices challenged conventional wisdom about what men and women do. They also confronted the assumption that sexual lasciviousness, in word and deed, was simply normal male behavior. Once women were in the picture as equals, the old sexual stereotypes on which everything from jokes to some heterosexual men's sense of themselves collapsed. In responding to the perceived threat of lost identity, some men attacked women rather than attack the culture that had so narrowly defined what it meant to be a man. The rise in reports of sexual assault on US university campuses in the early twenty-first century is another indication of the danger that exists in a culture where sexual prowess is an important measure of what it means to be a man.

During America's most recent wars, in Iraq and Afghanistan, disturbing reports about sexual assault and rape have surfaced.[20] According to a 2014 RAND Corporation study, sexual harassment and assault are commonplace in the experiences of servicewomen. More than twenty thousand women and men were assaulted in 2013, about 5 percent of active-duty women and 1 percent of active-duty men in a force of approximately 1.3 million active personnel. Many male victims reported that their attacker intended to humiliate or haze them. Among those who filed sexual assault complaints, 52 percent of women believed that their superiors or peers retaliated against them in terms of professional advancement or social stigmatization.[21] Knowledge of the extent of sexual assault in the twenty-first-century military has encouraged authorities to investigate its role in past eras. The Veterans Administration continues to seek testimony from servicewomen who were sexually assaulted and raped during World War II and the Vietnam War.[22] Historians have much more work to do to fill in the story about the role of sexual violence in these conflicts.

The US wars in Afghanistan and Iraq illustrate that resistance to women in the military can be counterproductive to security goals in addition to creating a dangerous environment for servicewomen. Female Engagement Teams (FETs) have been crucial components of the army's strategy in Afghanistan because of their ability to interact with Afghan women. Local culture prohibits Afghan women from interacting with men they are not related to, but US military advisers have viewed engagement with women as crucial to understanding specific village issues and broader Afghan culture. As army historian Michael Doidge points out in his research on an FET in Paktika province, women make up approximately half of Afghanistan's population, so interacting with them provides vital insights into civil-military relations, healthcare concerns, and educational needs, all of which are part of US military efforts to "win the hearts and minds" of Afghans.[23] In America's twenty-first-century wars, cultivating the support of the citizenry has been as important as traditional combat, and in that context, FETs were critical security forces.

As the United States continues to engage militarily in conservative parts of the world, especially Muslim regions, servicewomen will play a leading role. Military leadership appears to understand this security need, but as long as the culture on the ground remains rooted in old ideas about gender and the military, US servicewomen will continue to be subject to harm at the hands of their male comrades. It is ironic that the more opportunities open to women in the military, the more dangerous a place the military becomes for them. It remains to be seen how military culture on the ground will respond to the opening of combat specialties to women. Will American women taking up arms finally force a lasting change in the US military's gender identity, or will it result in an increase of assaults on servicewomen?

When Secretary of Defense Ashton B. Carter announced in December 2015 that combat arms would no longer be closed to women, he stated that servicewomen would "be allowed to drive tanks, fire mortars and lead infantry soldiers into combat. They'll be able to serve as Army Rangers and Green Berets, Navy SEALs, Marine Corps infantry, Air Force parajumpers and everything else that was previously open only to men."[24] Pentagon officials have stated that the branches of the service will not modify their standards or set quotas for women. Those in favor of allowing women to officially serve in combat hail the decision as a crucial step toward the full integration of women into the military and the removal of a barrier to career advancement.[25] Opponents cite studies indicating women's physical limitations and argue that women in combat will weaken unit cohesion. Some feminists argue that integrating women into the military fails to challenge a war-making system grounded in patriarchal ideas about power and domination.[26] Buttressing the various opinions in the debate are cultural beliefs about gender, citizenship, and security that are rooted in earlier concerns about women in the military.

The slow but steady history of women in the military suggests that the opening of all combat specialties to women would be the next step in a century's worth of progress toward gender equality in the US military. In summer 2015, several months before Carter's announcement about women and combat, the first two women graduated from the army's elite Ranger School.[27] But neither the Pentagon nor the president can force a change in Americans' beliefs about who can and should fight, and resistance to women serving in infantry jobs exists even though servicewomen have already seen direct combat in Iraq and Afghanistan. Before those conflicts, in the Vietnam War, female military nurses worked in hospitals that were routinely attacked, and WACs found themselves diving into bunkers with their male comrades to ride out mortar attacks. There were no front lines in Vietnam, Iraq, or Afghanistan.

At the heart of some critics' resistance to women in combat is conscription. Opponents worry that if the United States reinstates the draft, women will have to be subject to it because they can now serve in combat. The primary purpose of a draft is to fill infantry positions vacated when a soldier is killed or wounded. Congressman Duncan Hunter, a Republican from California and a marine corps veteran of the wars in Iraq and Afghanistan, put it this way: "If you're going to have women in infantry units, if a draft ever occurred, America needs to realize that its daughters and sisters would be included. The reason you draft people is because you have infantrymen dying."[28] More than questions about women's ability to carry sixty-plus pounds while maneuvering a weapon and running, the notion that the federal government could order daughters and sisters to the front lines is, to some critics, the most troubling consequence of opening combat positions to women. This mindset is deeply rooted in the ideas that men are to protect women, especially younger women who are or could be mothers, and that the home front and the battlefront are gendered, separate spheres to be controlled by women and men, respectively. If sons and brothers are drafted and subsequently killed in war, it is a tragic but necessary fulfillment of duty to the nation. If the same happens to daughters and sisters, it is a cause for outrage against the gender equality movement for upending the natural order of things.

That more male service members are now reporting sexual assaults may come as a surprise to some readers, but that is what a Pentagon study of sexual assault cases in 2012 revealed. Of the approximately twenty-six thousand reports of sexual attacks filed in 2012, 53 percent involved men assaulting other men. Some male victims of sexual assault in the military argue that the repeal of Don't Ask, Don't Tell (DADT) will make servicemen more willing to report sexual violence because they no longer have to worry that they will be accused of being gay and thus subject to discharge. The testimonies of servicemen who were raped while in the military indicate that the perpetrators typically identified themselves and their victims as heterosexual, and Pentagon analysts have concluded that male-on-male assaults tend to be more about humiliation than sexuality. However, during the years of DADT and earlier, if a serviceman reported that he was raped, he likely would have been deemed homosexual and discharged. With that threat out of the way, more men appear to be willing to come forward about being sexually assaulted in the military.[29]

Some, like Michael F. Matthews, a veteran of the US Air Force, kept his rape secret for thirty years, all the while battling depression and struggling to maintain personal relationships. He attempted suicide several times before finally opening up to a Department of Veterans Affairs social worker. Now, he speaks out about rape in the military and is the creator of *Justice Denied*, a documentary about male military sexual assault.[30] Although Pentagon prosecutors do not consider most male-on-male rapes to be linked to homosexuality, their prevalence illustrates that sex and dominance remain part of military culture. Congress and the Department of Defense are working to reshape the justice system for victims of sexual assault in the military, and victims and their advocates hope that the legal transformations will force cultural changes.

We can think in similar ways about whether the repeal of DADT will change the ways in which gay men and lesbians have been cast in military culture. Will allowing gay personnel to serve openly end concerns about sexuality by demystifying the notion of the gay and lesbian soldier? Or will gay servicemen and women face a period of heightened persecution? It is not yet clear how long it will take for military culture to fall in line with the legislation that opened the forces to openly gay personnel. In the case of the repeal of DADT, military policy is an example of progressive social change in advance of the larger American society. To make a broader point, it appears that popular support for civil rights leads the military to initiate reform. The same thing happened in the black military experience during World War II. Popular support for soldiers led to black GIs gaining access to integrated stores and recreational facilities on military bases, decades before African Americans would make the same gains in civilian life. In the same way, as Kara Vuic shows, changing views of reproductive rights on the home front led to changes in military life. The repeal of DADT follows this trend by heralding a trend toward greater legal protections for gay men and lesbians, as seen in the 2013 repeal of the Defense of Marriage Act. There are still critics who oppose such comparisons, and they raise interesting questions for the historian.

As Steve Estes pointed out, there is an irony to the repeal of DADT, namely that it was achieved only after gay rights activists stopped drawing parallels to the African American experience. They focused instead on military efficiency, arguing that it hurt the war effort in Afghanistan and Iraq to discharge gay service members who had critical skills such as translation. This new strategy also had the virtue of no longer demanding rights. Gay rights activists focused on explaining why it was in the national interest for gay Americans to serve in the military.

This strategy also had the unintended consequence of making it easier for prominent African Americans, such as Colin Powell and President Obama, to openly support ending the gay ban. Estes notes that not everyone joined the choir. Martin Luther King's niece, Eve Conant, asked readers of *Newsweek* magazine whether the struggles of gay activists were the same as her uncle's struggle, answering in the negative. Surprisingly, the chief advocate of drawing parallels between African Americans and gays was the Pentagon. According to the Pentagon's *Report of the Comprehensive Review of the Issues Associated with a Repeal of Don't Ask, Don't Tell* (November 30, 2010), there are strong parallels between the repeal of DADT and the integration of African Americans into the military. According to the *Comprehensive Review*, critics of ending the gay ban were raising the same concerns about the impact on unit cohesion and effectiveness that had been raised about desegregation in the 1940s. The *Comprehensive Review* concludes that, since these issues had turned out to be groundless, the repeal of DADT could also be implemented successfully.[31] But what does it mean that the Pentagon endorsed the notion that it is useful to compare the black military experience with gays? In all likelihood, the presence of openly gay men and lesbians in the military will have a bigger impact on public opinion than the rationale the Pentagon offered to justify its new policy. Is it possible that it is useful to make historical comparisons between African Americans and other groups seeking civil rights but unacceptable to make them in the political realm?

If drawing historical parallels is so controversial and problematic, you may ask, why do it? How is it useful? It helps us peer into the future of women and gays in the military, and there is value in seeing major changes in civilian life through a military lens. Since World War II, the emphasis on national security has touched nearly every facet of American life, shaping culture, politics, and the economy. It has transformed families and offered opportunities for upward mobility, both in military careers and via federal assistance such as the GI Bill. Progressive military policies have not always fostered cultural change, however, and the essays in this book have shown that African Americans, Japanese Americans, women, gays, and lesbians have had to battle stereotypes and resistance to their presence in the military. Although individual experiences differ, the common thread weaved through the stereotypes is a fear of the breakdown of the traditional image of American service personnel.

Americans have invested their beliefs in US power in the image of the white, heterosexual, male soldier. As black men have taken up arms, as gays and lesbians can now don the uniform openly, and as women begin to serve alongside men in combat units, Americans will have to continue rethinking their ideas not only about the military but also about race, gender, sexuality, and power. Perhaps it is telling that the Senate confirmed with little fanfare the nomination of Eric Fanning, who is openly gay, to be secretary of the army in 2016. Republican Senator Pat Roberts of Kansas had stalled the proceedings due to a dispute over plans to close the prison at Guantanamo Bay, but he and other senators on both sides of the aisle expressed support for Fanning. That an openly gay man became army secretary and nobody seemed to care suggests movement in the direction of mainstream acceptance of gays in the military. It remains to be seen how civilians and military personnel will respond to a show of affection between a gay couple in the enlisted ranks, where the traditional image of the American fighting man and all the image means about power and military strength is located.

In the twenty-first century, the War on Terror national security state has replaced the Cold War national security state, ensuring that American society will remain militarized for the foreseeable future. Therefore, servicemen and women have the potential to continue the activism their predecessors began some seventy years ago. By examining the struggles of African Americans, Japanese Americans, women, lesbians, and gay men in the military in one book, we highlight their collective impact on Americans society since World War II. The challenges these groups launched against the racial, gender, and sexual status quo transformed overarching ideas about power, citizenship, and America's role in the world. We hope that the lessons offered in these essays will provide a template for understanding how the military shapes American society and for guiding current and future military policies that have the potential to advance social changes in the civilian world.

## NOTES

1. Quoted in Lena Williams, "Blacks Reject Gay Rights Fight as Equal to Theirs," *New York Times*, June 28, 1993, A1, A12; Thomas Byrne Edsall and Mary D. Edsall, *Chain Reaction: The Impact of Race, Rights, and Taxes on American Politics* (New York: W. W. Norton, 1992); Jacquelyn Dowd Hall, "The Long Civil Rights Movement and the Political Uses of the Past," *Journal of American History* 91 (March 2005): 1233–1263; Matthew Lassiter, "Inventing Family Values," in *Rightward Bound: Making America Conservative in the 1970s*, edited by Bruce Schulman and Julian E. Zelizer (Cambridge, MA: Harvard University Press, 2008).

2. Alycee J. Lane, "Black Bodies / Gay Bodies: The Politics of Race in the Gay/ Military Battle," *Callaloo* 17 (Autumn 1994): 1074–1088.

3. Randy Shilts, *Conduct Unbecoming: Gays and Lesbians in the US Military* (New York: St. Martin's Press, 1993), 60–63, 83.

4. Ibid., 82.

5. Ibid., 63–64.

6. Bernard C. Nalty, *Strength for the Fight: A History of Black Americans in the Military* (New York: Free Press, 1986). On the Continental Army, see Jonathan Ned Katz, *Gay American History: Lesbians and Gay Men in the USA, A Documentary History*, rev. ed. (New York: Plume, 1992), 24; Allan Berube, *Coming Out Under Fire: The History of Gay Men and Women in World War II*, 20th anniversary ed. (Chapel Hill: University of North Carolina Press, 2010); John D'Emilio, *Sexual Politics, Sexual Communities: The Making of a Homosexual Minority in the United States, 1940–1970*, 2nd ed. (Chicago: University of Chicago Press, 1998). Technically, no openly gay people served as active-duty GIs until September 20, 2011, when the Don't Ask, Don't Tell policy was officially repealed. "Don't Ask, Don't Tell Repeal Act of 2010, Public Law No. 111–321, September 20, 2011: An Historic Day," Human Rights Campaign website. www.hrc.org/laws-and-legislation /federal-laws/dont-ask-dont-tell-repeal-act-of-2010?gclid=CMqPkdu _oLoCFUhk7AodsxEAXA.

7. Leisa Meyer, *Creating GI Jane: Sexuality and Power in the Women's Army Corps during World War II* (New York: Columbia University Press, 1998).

8. Joan Wallach Scott, "The Sears Case," in her *Gender and the Politics of History* (New York: Columbia University Press, 1988), chapter 8.

9. Ibid., 171.

10. Jacqueline Jones, *Labor of Love, Labor of Sorrow: Black Women, Work, and the Family, from Slavery to the Present* (New York: Basic Books, 2009); Herman Graham, *The Brothers' Vietnam War: Black Power, Manhood, and the Military Experience* (Gainesville: University Press of Florida, 2003); and Steve Estes, *"I Am a Man!": Race, Manhood, and the Civil Rights Movement* (Chapel Hill: University of North Carolina Press, 2005).

11. Approximately 40,000 US servicewomen served in the Middle East in Operation Desert Shield and Desert Storm, 1990–1991. A few women served in US military interventions in Grenada and Panama in the 1980s.

12. Kimberly Hefling, "Female Soldiers Raise Alarm on Sexual Assaults," Associated Press, July 21, 2008. www.nbcnews.com/id/25784465/ns/us_news-military/t/female -soldiers-raise-alarm-sexual-assaults/#.VybGc4RZH7Y.

13. "24 Army Women Assaulted, Raped during Gulf War," *Washington Post*, July 21, 1992. http://articles.sun-sentinel.com/1992-07-21/news/9202200757_1_army-records -rapes-or-assaults-army-sergeant.

14. Elaine Sciolino, "Female POW Is Abused, Kindling Debate," *New York Times*, June 29, 1992. www.nytimes.com/1992/06/29/us/female-pow-is-abused-kindling-debate .html?pagewanted=all.

15. Linda Bird Francke, "Women in the Gulf War," in *Women's America: Refocusing the Past*, edited by Linda Kerber and Jane Sherron De Hart (New York: Oxford University Press, 2010), 654.

16. "The Tailhook Association," PBS *Frontline*. www.pbs.org/wgbh/pages/frontline /shows/navy/tailhook/assoc.html.

17. Michael Winerip, "Revisiting the Military's Tailhook Scandal," *New York Times*, May 13, 2013. www.nytimes.com/2013/05/13/booming/revisiting-the-militarys-tailhook -scandal-video.html.

18. "The Tailhook Association," PBS *Frontline*.

19. Susan Faludi, "Going Wild?," *New York Times*, February 16, 1994. www.nytimes .com/1994/02/16/opinion/going-wild.html.

20. Eric Schmitt, "Rapes Reported by Servicewomen in the Persian Gulf and Elsewhere," *New York Times*, February 26, 2004. www.nytimes.com/2004/02/26 /national/26MILI.html.

21. Andrew R. Morral et al., *Sexual Assault and Sexual Harassment in the US Military*, vol. 2, *Estimates for Department of Defense Service Members from the 2014 RAND Military Workplace Study* (Santa Monica, CA: RAND Corporation, 2016).

22. Hefling, "Female Soldiers Raise Alarm on Sexual Assaults."

23. Michael J. Doidge, "Combat Multipliers: Tactical Female Engagement Teams in Paktika Province," in *Vanguard of Valor*, vol. 2, *Small Unit Actions in Afghanistan*, edited by Donald P. Wright (Fort Leavenworth, KS: Combat Studies Institute Press, 2012), 105–124.

24. Matthew Rosenberg and Dave Phillips, "All Combat Roles Now Open to Women, Defense Secretary Says," *New York Times*, December 3, 2015. http://nytimes .com/2015/12/04/us/politics/combat-military-women-ash-carter.html.

25. Jena McGregor, "Military Women in Combat: Why Making It Official Matters," *Washington Post*, May 25, 2012. www.washingtonpost.com/blogs/post-leadership/post /military-women-in-combat-why-making-it-official-matters/2012/05/25/gJQAOsRvpU _blog.html.

26. Noah Berlatsky, "The Feminist Objection to Women in Combat," *The Atlantic*, January 25, 2013. www.theatlantic.com/sexes/archive/2013/01/the-feminist-objection-to -women-in-combat/272505.

27. Gayle Tzemach Lemmon, "Women in Combat? They've Already Been Serving on the Front Lines, with Heroism," *Los Angeles Times*, December 4, 2015. www.latimes.com /opinion/op-ed/la-oe-1204-lemmon-women-combat-20151204-story.html.

28. Austin Wright, "Republicans Raise Alarm about Women in Combat: Their Subtle Warning; It Could Force All Young Women to Register for the Draft," *Politico*, December 3, 2015. www.politico.com/story/2015/12/pentagon-women-in-combat -republican-reaction-216412.

29. James Dao, "In Debate Over Military Sexual Assault, Men Are Overlooked Victims," *New York Times*, June 23, 2013. www.nytimes.com/2013/06/24/us/in-debate -over-military-sexual-assault-men-are-overlooked-victims.html.

30. Michael F. Matthews, "The Untold Story of Military Sexual Assault," *New York Times*, November 24, 2013. www.nytimes.com/2013/11/25/opinion/the-untold-story-of -military-sexual-assault.html.

31. Department of Defense, "Don't Ask Don't Tell report," chapter 8, 85. www .defense.gov/home/features/2010/0610_gatesdadt/DADTReport_FINAL _20101130(secure-hires).pdf.

# Contributors

*Beth Bailey* is a Foundation Distinguished Professor of History at the University of Kansas

*Douglas Walter Bristol, Jr.,* is an Associate Professor of History at the University of Southern Mississippi

*Steve Estes* is a Professor of History at Sonoma State University

*Isaac Hampton II* is a Command Historian in the US Army South at Fort Sam Houston, Texas

*James M. McCaffrey* is a retired Professor of History from the University of Houston-Downtown

*Tanya L. Roth* is an Instructor at the Mary Institute and St. Louis Country Day School, St. Louis, Missouri

*Heather Marie Stur* is an Associate Professor of History at the University of Southern Mississippi

*Charissa Threat* is an Assistant Professor of History at Spelman College

*Kara Dixon Vuic* is the Benjamin W. Schmidt Professor of War, Conflict, and Society at Texas Christian University

*James E. Westheider* is a Professor of History at the University of Cincinnati

# Index